529 & Other College Savings Plans For Dummies®

Cheat Sheet

Available College Savings Plans

Not all savings plans are created equal. What works best for your neighbor may not work for you. Below are some of the major differences in the college savings schemes discussed in this book.

Savings Vehicle	Tax Issues	Possible Contributors	Possible Uses	Taxed Individual (if Applicable)
529 plans	No tax paid on interest earned until distributions are made. Currently, distributions used for qualified educational expenses are tax-exempt.	No relationship or income-limitation test.	Any expenses you choose. However, distributions used to pay for nonqualified expenses are subject to income tax on the earnings portion, plus a 10% penalty.	Designated beneficiary.
Coverdell accounts	No tax paid on interest earned until distributions are made. Currently, distributions used for qualified educational expenses are tax-exempt.	No relationship test. Must satisfy income-limitation test.	Any expenses you choose. However, distributions used to pay for nonqualified expenses are subject to income tax on the earnings portion, plus a 10% penalty.	Designated beneficiary.
Series EE and Series II savings bonds	No tax paid on interest earned if redeemed bonds are used for qualified educational expenses.	Must satisfy relationship and income-limitation tests to qualify for tax-free treatment of interest upon redemption.	Any expenses you choose. However, only the portion used for qualified educational expenses is tax-free.	Bond owner.
Personal investment accounts	Tax paid yearly on income earned within the account. No additional tax assessed when you take distributions for any reason.	You contribute to your own account or may make gifts into someone else's.	All expenses.	Account owner.
Trust accounts	Tax paid yearly on income earned within the account. No additional tax assessed when you take distributions for any reason.	Trust grantor (the donor) only.	All expenses.	In years in which distributions are made, person receiving distribution. All other years, the trust pays tax.
Retirement accounts	Tax deferred until you take distributions. Early distributions may also be subject to an additional penalty.	Account owner only.	Any expenses. But, distributions used to pay for nonqualified expenses are subject to income tax on the earnings portion, plus 10% penalty.	Account owner.
Home equity	No tax owed if you refinance and use some or all of your equity to pay for college expenses. If you sell your house, you may be liable for a capital gains tax.	Anyone may buy you a house or make payments against an existing mortgage; generally, only the homeowner actually does.	All expenses.	Homeowner.

For Dummies: Bestselling Book Series for Beginners

529 & Other College Savings Plans For Dummies® — Cheat Sheet

Identifying Wasteful Spending

One of the first ways to start saving, or start saving more, is to cut out what I call wasteful spending. Nowhere in this book will you see me advocate cutting back on necessities — or even all of the fun "extras" — in your college-saving quest. But this stuff is far from necessary — and most of it isn't fun.

- **Checking-account minimum-balance penalty:** Get the balance up or switch banks.
- **Insufficient-funds penalty:** Quit with the bounced checks.
- **Credit-card interest:** Start paying down that balance.
- **Over-limit credit-card fees:** Don't push the limits.
- **Late-payment fees for credit cards, car loans, utilities, and so on:** Get that check in the mail a few days sooner or go with the automatic debit option that everyone is pushing these days.
- **Late charges on video rentals:** Suck it up, get in the car, and return the movies on time.
- **Health-club dues to a club you haven't attended for over a year:** Either get on the exercise bike or get on the phone and cancel your membership. If you're not using the gym, the only thing getting thinner is your bank balance.
- **Newspaper and magazine subscriptions that you just haven't gotten around to canceling:** Read or dial.
- **Hitting the coffee shop *every* morning:** Get up five minutes earlier, three times a week, make coffee at home, and save ten bucks.
- **Going out to lunch *every* day:** Embrace the brown bag a few times a week.

Section 529 and Coverdell Account Sunset Provisions

The existence of Section 529 plans and Coverdell Education Savings Accounts seems fairly set in stone, but many of the specific regulations governing them aren't. The following list describes some of the provisions set to revert to older law on January 1, 2011.

- Income on distributions that is currently tax-exempt will become taxable income to the designated beneficiary.
- Contributions to Coverdell accounts will revert to a maximum of $500 per year.
- Distributions used to pay primary and secondary school educational expenses will no longer be qualified under Coverdell rules.
- The list of available relatives of your current designated beneficiary will narrow, excluding first cousins, aunts, and uncles.
- You will no longer be able to contribute in any given year to both a Coverdell Education Savings Account and a Section 529 plan. You'll have to choose.
- You won't be able to superfund a Section 529 plan after December 31, 2010, without triggering a gift tax. On January 1, 2011, the law is set to return to a maximum annual contribution of no more than the current exclusion amount ($11,000) per donor per beneficiary.

For Dummies: Bestselling Book Series for Beginners

529 & Other College Savings Plans

FOR DUMMIES®

by Margaret A. Munro

WILEY

Wiley Publishing, Inc.

529 & Other College Savings Plans For Dummies®

Published by
Wiley Publishing, Inc.
111 River St.
Hoboken, NJ 07030-5774
www.wiley.com

For general information on our other products and services or to obtain technical support, please contact our Customer Care Department within the U.S. at 800-762-2974, outside the U.S. at 317-572-3993, or fax 317-572-4002.

Wiley also publishes its books in a variety of electronic formats. Some content that appears in print may not be available in electronic books.

Library of Congress Control Number: 2003115023

ISBN: 0-7645-3747-4

Manufactured in the United States of America

10 9 8 7 6 5 4 3 2 1

1O/QZ/RS/QT/IN

WILEY

About the Author

Margaret A. Munro, EA, (who answers to Peggy and is still trying to figure out why her parents named her Margaret) is a tax consultant/advisor/writer/lecturer with over 30 years of experience in various areas of finance and taxation. She is an enrolled agent, licensed by the federal government to represent clients in the areas of tax and tax-related issues. She currently operates a widely diverse private practice that specializes in the financial concerns of families with school-age children, a group that is near and dear to her heart.

In addition to counseling her clients with young families on the advisability of college savings plans, Peggy has great personal experience in the area of paying for college. She began receiving grants and loans in 1977, is currently helping to pay for her husband's education, and realizes that, without college savings, she won't finish paying her son's college loans until 2027, fifty years after she began accumulating her own college debt. In the process of writing this book, she has taken her own advice and begun to save regularly.

Peggy is a graduate of The Johns Hopkins University and has also attended University College Cork and the Pontifical Institute of Mediaeval Studies in Toronto. She lives with her husband, Colin; her son, Jacob; and the family dog, Angus Mor, in central Vermont, where she teaches at her son's religious school and volunteers at the local elementary school.

Dedication

To Colin, Jacob, and Angus Mor, who make sure I'm fed and watered during tax season and beyond. You deal with my episodes of stress and psychosis and love me in spite of them. You knew I could do this even when I didn't. Everything I achieve is sweeter to me because you're there to share it with me.

Author's Acknowledgments

It's hard to know where to begin when looking back at all the people who helped make this book happen. And I should start with Mrs. Benedetto in the 5th grade and Mr. Hancock, in the 11th, who taught me all about grammar and how to write so that it made sense.

While the ability to write is a necessary component of any book, an understanding of your subject matter is also key. I have been blessed to have many fine teachers and mentors who fostered this knowledge along the way: Sheldon Kaplow, who gave me my first job and taught me how to use a ten-key adding machine; Palmer Worthen, who threw me into the tax grinder and made sure I emerged relatively unscathed; and Marvin Sparrow, Monica Lewis, and all the other fine people at Goulston & Storrs, P.C., who honed my basic tax knowledge and taught me to look beyond the mere laws to how they affected people.

Obviously, this book would not exist without input from my extended family, my friends, and my clients (who, for obvious reasons, need to stay anonymous, but who know who they are), who have been coming to me for several years with questions about how, and how much, they should be saving for their children's educations. Our discussions over time have been largely responsible for my thinking about common misconceptions and the amount of misinformation that flies around every sort of financial topic.

And then there are all the people who worked with me on this book: Scott Mendel and Pam Mourouzis, who started the ball rolling; Norm Crampton, whose enthusiasm is contagious; Jennifer Connolly, Mike Baker, and Chrissy Guthrie, my project editors who did just enough hand holding; Tina Sims for her copy-editing expertise (I'm sure I've been a trial to her); and Dave Murray and Molly Yuska at The National Center for College Costs, for their technical expertise. This book stands as a testament to all of you, and I thank you.

Finally, to Jacob, who kept feeding me the names of all of his classmates when I couldn't think up yet another name for an example, and to Colin, who was (is) my practice *For Dummies* reader and who made sure he could understand what I was talking about before I shipped chapters off to my editors — I really couldn't have done this without you guys.

Publisher's Acknowledgments

We're proud of this book; please send us your comments through our Dummies online registration form located at www.dummies.com/register/.

Some of the people who helped bring this book to market include the following:

Acquisitions, Editorial, and Media Development

Project Editors: Mike Baker, Jennifer Connolly, Chrissy Guthrie

Acquisitions Editor: Norm Crampton

Senior Copy Editor: Tina Sims

Assistant Editor: Holly Gastineau-Grimes

Technical Editor: Molly Yuska

Editorial Managers: Christine Meloy Beck, Jennifer Ehrlich

Editorial Assistants: Melissa Bennett, Elizabeth Rea

Cartoons: Rich Tennant, www.the5thwave.com

Production

Project Coordinator: Courtney MacIntyre

Layout and Graphics: Andrea Dahl, Joyce Haughey, Clint Lahnen, Barry Offringa, Shae Lynn Wilson

Proofreaders: Laura Albert, TECHBOOKS Production Services

Indexer: TECHBOOKS Production Services

Special Help: Laura K. Miller, Chad Sievers

Publishing and Editorial for Consumer Dummies

Diane Graves Steele, Vice President and Publisher, Consumer Dummies

Joyce Pepple, Acquisitions Director, Consumer Dummies

Kristin A. Cocks, Product Development Director, Consumer Dummies

Michael Spring, Vice President and Publisher, Travel

Brice Gosnell, Associate Publisher, Travel

Kelly Regan, Editorial Director, Travel

Publishing for Technology Dummies

Andy Cummings, Vice President and Publisher, Dummies Technology/General User

Composition Services

Gerry Fahey, Vice President of Production Services

Debbie Stailey, Director of Composition Services

Contents at a Glance

Table of Contents

Introduction

*W*elcome to *529 & Other College Savings Plans For Dummies,* the practical reference for those who are thinking about and planning for college in the future for themselves or those nearest and dearest to them, and who want an explanation of all the options, pro and con, that can help them save for it.

College. Whether you've been there yourself or not, you've read all the information, looked at the charts and graphs, and you know that people who graduate from college land better jobs and earn better pay than those who don't. So, of course, because you want the very best for yourself and your family (you do — that's why you're reading this), you want everyone you know, including yourself, to have that opportunity.

That is, until you look at the price tag. You're already paying for food, housing, and clothing (not to mention phone, cable, insurance, and everything else under the sun, including dog grooming) and maybe even stashing a little bit into your retirement plan. And then you sneak a peek at the projected cost of college for the year in which your student expects to begin. And just as you never look at the least wrinkled car in a car crash, your eye automatically drifts to the highest number on that chart of projected college costs. And you begin to sweat.

There's no question: The cost of college continues to soar, even when the rest of the economy stagnates, and this reality is not likely to change any time soon. Fortunately, everyone, including you, the various governments (federal and state), and the colleges themselves, are in on this secret, so everyone can plan and plot, well in advance of that eventual first day of your child's freshman year, ways to get that child there, and ways to help you pay the bills when they happen. Consider this book to be your accomplice.

About This Book

The world of college savings plans is new, exciting, and changing daily (or so it seems — legislative leaders can't seem to resist continuously tweaking the laws). Which is another way of saying that it also can be complicated and confusing — to everyone including the professionals, the financial planners, the tax folks, and your local bank or brokerage.

In this one-size-fits-all world, the powers that be have recognized that all people don't save money the same way. Some save more, some save less, some can live with risk, and others can't tolerate any risk. Clearly, no two are alike, but you're all savers, either present or potential. Numerous options exist that make saving possible and desirable for everyone.

Piling savings option upon savings option has created opportunities for most people. But all the new options have also muddied the waters, because choosing between Plan A and Plan B can be downright difficult when they seem so similar. So many people may choose to opt out, admitting confusion and doing nothing, because it's all so confusing, and no one wants to screw up a choice that has so much riding on it.

And yet, it doesn't have to be that way. I'm here to tell you that it *is* possible to understand the costs associated with college, both right now and in the future, and then to find ways to pay for those costs, in the most advantageous manner for you, both from a personal point of view and from a tax perspective. And you can't focus on the personal and ignore the tax implications, nor can you do the reverse. Both are essential components, and the most successful savings program takes both elements into consideration.

That's where this book comes in. It's designed to explain the strategies that are out there to help you save, save, save. There's no doubt that the bill will be large; there's also no question that, with planning, strategy, and purpose, you can achieve your goal and provide the means that will allow you and your family all the benefits of a college education.

529 & Other College Savings Plans For Dummies is simply a way to find a reasonable solution to a seemingly unreasonable problem: saving for future college costs in the sanest, least stressful way possible for you. In keeping with the theme of stress reduction, you can use this book in a variety of ways:

- **As a reference:** It's all here: the ins, the outs, the do's, and the don'ts. The world of college savings is one of very specific rules, and they're here, in all their glory, and they're all explained.

- **As an advisor:** It's a case of the very good savings techniques, the merely okay savings techniques, and the truly ugly techniques (which you really want to avoid), and this book highlights them all. It's true that what works for you may not work for your neighbor, but every savings option involves risks, concerns, and just-plain crystal ball reading. This book explores all the ups and downs and ins and outs.

- **As a little light reading:** Amazingly enough, the topic of money can be mildly amusing, and college savings is no exception. Read this with an eye towards the absurd, and you won't go far wrong.

Parts of *529 & Other College Savings Plans For Dummies* are about very specific situations that you will, most likely, never come across. Still, this book would be lacking as a complete reference if I didn't include a lot of the minutiae in the text on the chance that someone, somewhere, may need to know what happens to a Section 529 plan in the event of a death of a plan owner, for example.

Also, as a caution, be aware that any projections in the book are just that: projections. I have no special hotline to the powers that determine rates of returns on investments, increases in tuition payments, inflation rates, tax rates, utility rates, or postage increases (which might be really useful). Increases and decreases may be greater or lesser over time — I have no way of really knowing. All the projections should provide you with is a picture of relationships between like numbers; don't read any more into my crystal ball projections than that.

Conventions Used in This Book

To help you navigate through this book, I use the following conventions:

- ✔ *Italic* is used for emphasis and to highlight new words or terms that are defined.
- ✔ **Boldfaced** text is used to indicate keywords in bulleted lists or the action part of numbered steps.
- ✔ `Monofont` is used for Web addresses.
- ✔ Sidebars, which look like text enclosed in a shaded gray box, consist of information that's interesting to know but not necessarily critical to your understanding of the chapter or section topic.

Foolish Assumptions

The world of money and taxes is rife with assumptions, foolish and otherwise. Here are some of the assumptions I've made about you:

- ✔ You're not aware of the variety of college saving options available to you, or you're aware but baffled by the number of plans or the way the plans work.
- ✔ You may have some idea of how much sending Junior to college will put you back, but you need more details.
- ✔ If you are saving for college, you probably feel as though you're not saving enough.

✔ You can't walk into a bookstore or surf the Internet without buying every book you see with a snazzy, eye-catching, strikingly-appealing, jaw-droppin' good-looking yellow-and-black cover.

✔ If you're not yet saving for college, you may feel that you don't have room in your budget for that expense. After paying your monthly living costs, you may have nothing left to save.

If you find yourself identifying with any of the above, then *529 & Other College Savings Plans For Dummies* gives you the information you need to start saving or kick your savings into high gear.

How This Book Is Organized

This book takes all the different components of college savings — from the necessity for it, through all the different sorts of savings plans, and finally to ways to augment with grants, loans, and scholarships — and breaks them down into easily digestible chunks — okay, *parts,* if you want to get technical about it. And each part is comprised of a few chapters. The following is a brief description of each part:

Part 1: Figuring Out the Cost of College — and How to Pay It

There's no question, the number is huge, but how huge is it? Sounds like the start of a bad joke, eh? Well, it isn't a joke, but dealing with the big cash question doesn't have to be *that* bad. After a brief overview of the scope of the book, this part looks at the current and projected future cost of postsecondary education, including vocational and trade schools, public and private colleges, two- and four-year institutions, and graduate and professional schools. It focuses on savings techniques, and finally, it lets you know who's available to make contributions into the savings pool.

Part II: Piecing Together Section 529 Plans

One of the recent entries into the college savings plan sweepstakes, Section 529 plans offer seemingly unlimited choices and high contribution limits (at least if you listen to the people who are trying to sell you their particular plan). This part dissects these plans, explaining how they work, why they work, and when they work, or don't, as the case may be.

Part III: Uncovering Coverdell Accounts

The new, improved, and renamed Coverdell Education Savings Accounts (formerly known as Education IRAs) have now become real players in the college savings arena, and more and more financial advisors, banks, and brokerages are touting their benefits. This part explores them in full detail, showing their good and bad points and explaining how and when they may, or may not, make sense for you.

Part IV: Filling In the Gaps: More Ways to Save for College

Saving for college has been around a lot longer than Section 529 plans or Coverdell accounts. So Part IV examines some of the more traditional ways to save for college and shows situations where these tried and true methods still may make sense for you. But what happens when all else fails and your savings come up a bit short? This part explains how the world of financial aid — loans, grants, and scholarships — works and how your college savings may factor into college financial aid decisions.

Part V: The Part of Tens

It's the part you've hopefully come to know and love. The *For Dummies* Part of Tens — this time with a college-savings twist. You like easily accessible top-ten lists? Here you go. The whole point of so-called "college savings plans" is first, to save, and second, to pay as little tax on your savings as possible. The chapters in this part give you hints on saving successfully, and tell you what you must do to dodge as many taxes as possible. The book includes one final element that's not technically a Part of Tens — it lists *way* more than ten things. But I thought I should let you know about the appendix, which gives you a more detailed look at the various Section 529 plans offered by each of the 50 states and the District of Columbia. The appendix gives you an apples-to-apples comparison of what is currently out there so you can make the best decision for your particular situation.

Icons Used in This Book

The icons that you come across in this book identify information or words of caution that you may find especially helpful.

You have a lot to remember when you're trying to slot your savings into the rules and regulations surrounding many of these college savings plans. This icon alerts you to important information that you don't want to forget, because it can often make the entire process of saving for college go a lot smoother.

If you're the type of person who always needs to know more than the basics, check out the information next to this guy. It points out information that you don't absolutely need to know to save for college (but you can always use it to impress your friends).

Life is rarely straightforward, and saving for college may be even less so. When you see this icon, you'll find a strategy that will help you get the most out of your savings or make it easier to put money away.

This book is littered with ideas of what not to do if you want to successfully save for college. When you find this icon, you've just landed on one of them.

Where to Go from Here

You can, if you want to and have the time, read this book from cover to cover, and it will give you a great view of how much, how, and where to save money for college. But if you don't have the time or the interest, you may choose to hop around from topic to topic, skipping those that don't apply at all to you and paying more careful attention to those that do. That's one of the great things about *For Dummies* books. You can get in and get out wherever and whenever you choose. If information that you need to understand a certain topic is covered elsewhere, the text will direct you, so you don't need to worry that you're missing basic information by skipping over a portion of the book.

Part I

Figuring Out the Cost of College — and How to Pay It

The 5th Wave   By Rich Tennant

"OH, HIM? HE'S SOME GUY FROM MUNCIE, INDIANA, LOOKING FOR A WAY TO PAY FOR HIS DAUGHTER'S COLLEGE EDUCATION."

In this part . . .

Any discussion about saving money, including one about saving cash for college, needs to begin with a careful look at your finances. If you can't figure out how much you're going to need and locate the resources available to you, all the information in the world will remain theoretical, not practical.

In this part, I help you check out your current financial situation — including your assets and, especially, your debts — and where you think you need to go — in terms of future college savings costs. I outline the costs associated with various forms of higher education, from piano-tuning vocational education to medical school. I provide tips on how to start thinking about meeting college costs, including the resources you currently have and those that you'll have down the road. Finally, I provide a plan so that you can examine how you're spending money now and find ways to trim your current expenses without butchering your lifestyle.

Chapter 1

Braving the New World of College Savings

*Y*ou may have just found out that you're pregnant. Maybe you're at the point where the college catalogs are beginning to accumulate on your dining room table. Or perhaps your family is somewhere in the middle, with your children out of diapers but not yet into calculus. Wherever your family falls in the age spectrum, one thing is certain: either in your immediate family or in your extended one, some people will want to continue their educations beyond that once-adequate but now insufficient stopping point of a high school graduation.

And therein lies a problem: Although your child can receive a primary and secondary education without incurring any added expense in your budget (unless you take into consideration your local parents' group's fundraisers), postsecondary education of any type isn't free for the asking. You must pay for the privilege of having your child attend college. If you've already explored the costs of a postsecondary education, you know that the numbers being discussed are large; if you haven't yet experienced the pleasure, rest assured that the amounts in question will likely take your breath away.

In solving any problem, you need to remain calm and focused on the task at hand. That's where this book may help — by making you methodically look at your lack of college savings, helping you leave your misconceptions about saving at the door, and showing you ways to actually begin saving. After you convince yourself that you're able to save something and you actually begin to put some money away, you've won a major victory; everything that follows will be easier. Just keep in mind that saving now will create opportunities and open doors for your children in the future.

Doing the Numbers

Up until now, crunching the numbers and figuring out what you think college will cost has usually been where you begin and end your exploration of the topic of how to pay for future educational costs. But after you resolve to start saving and you take the projected costs and create a plan to save for that amount, it's time to take this exercise a bit more seriously.

Figuring up the costs

Depending on the size of your family and your expectations, adding up the cost of a college education can be a fairly straightforward calculation, or it may become quite involved.

Be realistic, both about the capabilities and ambitions of your future student and your ability to pay.

Your straight-A daughter may have to scale back on her dreams of MIT if your budget, including amounts that you can add from your current earnings, only goes as far as your local state college (although not necessarily — she may want to seriously consider applying for some scholarship aid as outlined in Chapter 16).

Likewise, there's little point in your saving for an Ivy League education if your child has plans to open his own auto repair shop. And clearly, the more children you're sending to college, the thinner your resources may be stretched per child (although, depending on how closely spaced your children are in age, this situation may actually work to your advantage if you need to apply for financial aid, as can you find out in Chapter 17).

Finding resources to help you save

No matter how late you may begin to save specifically for future college costs, the entire weight of the enterprise doesn't necessarily need to rest solely on your shoulders, nor do you need to begin to save for college from nothing.

Chapter 3 helps you find hidden assets you may have available, to augment your college savings. It may also alert you to other resources you haven't even thought of — family and friends or even the student himself. Just because these are your children, you don't have to come up with the full amount of their college costs from your pockets alone.

Saving efficiently

Too many people equate saving for the future with current deprivation. For most people, living expenses currently equal, or even exceed, income, and they may not have money left over in the family budget for saving. Clearly, if you fit into this category, you're not going to be able to save unless you make some changes in your life. And although I would never advocate giving up your morning coffee and sticky bun every day as a savings technique, Chapter 4 shows you some relatively painless adjustments that will maximize the amount of money you can shave from your current budget while minimizing the effect on your life.

Exploring Section 529 Plans

Saving money is a good thing, or so the federal government would have you believe. Uncle Sam is prepared to back up that philosophy with a variety of savings programs that contain built-in tax incentives, some of which you may already be using (tax-deferred retirement plans, anyone?). One of the newest types of incentive savings plan is the Qualified Tuition Program, or Section 529 plan, which is designed solely for the purpose of saving for college or any other type of qualified postsecondary education, either tax exempt or tax deferred, depending on a number of factors. Like almost everything else the government cooks up, though, Section 529 plans aren't as simple to navigate as everyone selling these plans would have you think. Chapter 5 gives you the tools you need to understand how these accounts work and how you can best make them work for you.

Following the rules

Section 529 of the Internal Revenue Code is long, complex, and not for the faint of heart. Still, savings accounts that fall under its regulations can be a fantastic way to save for future educational expenses. To make it work, though, you have to understand its requirements; there's little point in setting up one of these accounts if you don't cross your t's and dot your i's just like the IRS wants. Remember, the IRS doesn't have a category of "close, but no cigar." Your account will either qualify under the regulations for tax deferrals or exemptions, or it won't. And if it doesn't, the consequences may be costly.

Making your money work for you

Creating a successful savings plan involves more than following the rules, although compliance with the rules is a big part. Chapter 6 shows you how to actually begin saving money and then put those savings to work for you.

You're a big factor in determining whether your savings program flies or falls. Your understanding of the various ways your savings may earn money and of the different investment options available to you is an important piece of creating the substantial amount of savings you'll need to see your children through college.

Choosing the best options

Even when you understand the rules, manage to regularly save major portions of your income, and discover how to manipulate the investment choices to your best advantage, events in your life may require you to make sudden changes in your Section 529 plan savings accounts. Life happens, whether you're prepared or not, and often the last thing you want to think about when it does is the effect on your investments. Chapter 7 alerts you to some planning opportunities you'll have with your Section 529 plan accounts and how to make corrections to your college savings when your life doesn't exactly follow the course you originally laid out.

Checking Out Coverdell Accounts

If the world of tax deferred/tax-exempt savings accounts were an ice cream parlor, Coverdell Education Savings Accounts (ESAs) would be a new and improved flavor, still not everyone's favorite, but just what you may want on a particular day. And, not surprisingly, many people, when shopping for a place and a way to save money for college, prefer Coverdell accounts, whether for their wider range of investment options, the account owner's increased level of control over the account, or the fact that certain expenses qualify for tax exemption under Coverdell rules that aren't under Section 529 requirements. Whatever your reasons, Coverdell ESAs may be just the flavor of account you want today.

Understanding the rules and regulations

Code Section 530, covering Coverdell ESAs, follows hot on the heels of Code Section 529 (those government sorts are sticklers for going in order). In it you find all the rules, regulations, and other assorted gobbledygook that govern these sorts of accounts.

But you don't have to mess with the Internal Revenue Code. In Chapter 8, you discover what rules you need to know to open an account, save money inside an account once it's been opened, and then make distributions from the account, tax-free or tax-deferred (depending on a number of factors), for qualified educational expenses.

Getting the most from your Coverdell account

You've probably discovered by now that successful savings involve far more than sticking your money in a passbook savings account at your local bank. And, while your investment options are seriously limited inside a Section 529 plan, you have far more latitude in investment decisions when you open a Coverdell ESA. In Chapter 9, you explore where you can open an account, what information you need to open that account, what sorts of investments you can put into an account, and how to decide what sorts of investments work best for you. Finally, you look at the nuts and bolts of what happens when you begin to make withdrawals from your student's Coverdell account to pay for qualified educational expenses.

Seeing if Coverdell accounts work for you

Saving now for future college expenses may seem like a no-brainer to you, but negotiating the ins and outs of any tax-deferred/tax-exempt savings plan isn't quite so simple. And, not to put too fine a point on it, Coverdell ESAs, while a valuable weapon in the arsenal of college savings accounts, may not be the right choice for you. Chapter 10 gives you some insights into what's involved in effectively managing a Coverdell account for your student and what pitfalls to avoid. Finally, if despite your best efforts you unintentionally land in a pile of muck, you find some strategies here to turn lemons into lemonade and perform some damage control.

But Wait! There's More!

People went to college long before there was an Internal Revenue Code, and parents and grandparents saved for college costs even when tax deferrals and/or tax exemptions weren't around. You can save money in lots of other ways, some of them even specifically for college. Even though they may not be as tax advantageous as Section 529 plans and Coverdell ESAs, they may make perfect sense in your overall savings plan. And if you're not able to save enough to cover the full cost, all is still not lost: Various scholarships, grants, and loan programs are available to cover any shortfall you may have between what you've saved and the cost of your child's education.

Rediscovering U.S. Savings Bonds

Whether you're able to save only relatively small amounts, you're uncertain about your potential student's future plans, or you love the safety and security found only in U.S. Savings Bonds, you may find that this is an attractive way to save for future college expenses and still take advantage of some tax exemptions on the interest earned on your bonds. Chapter 11 explains how you may be able to use certain U.S. Savings Bonds to pay at least some of your child's postsecondary educational expenses tax-free. It shows you who may invest, how you may invest, and how to allocate and report your earnings, both taxable and tax-exempt, when you redeem your bonds.

Saving for college the old-fashioned way

It may seem strange to even think this, but the trade-off for taking advantage of the income tax breaks available through Section 529 plans and Coverdell ESAs is that you're guaranteeing that you will use that money to pay for qualified educational expenses. If only all of life were so certain and so sure.

Many of you may be hesitating over how much to save in these plans, or whether to save at all, because of your great uncertainty over your child's future plans. When you save in traditional investment and savings accounts, you eliminate that uncertainty because you're not tied to using your savings in any one way. Of course, in exchange for that freedom to spend your savings as you will, you lose any opportunity to defer or exempt tax on your earnings, but if your world is an uncertain place, you may find that's a small price to pay.

In Chapter 12, you find out about different types of investment accounts, different options of account ownership and their consequences, ways to invest and manage a personal investment account, and, finally, the taxation of investment income.

Putting your faith in a trust fund

For most people, the phrase "trust fund" brings to mind visions of great wealth and privilege; in other words, it has nothing to do with you. And that picture couldn't be further from the truth. If you save money in any form, then you're a potential candidate to create and fund a trust. Chapter 13 explores some different types of trusts and explains why a trust may actually make sense for you in a college savings context.

Saving in your retirement accounts

Using retirement funds to pay for college probably isn't the best way to put money away for college. In certain limited circumstances, however (such as when parents are older or you face completely unplanned educational expenses), it may make some sense to access funds from a retirement account to pay qualified educational expenses. Chapter 14 explains the tax consequences when you use so-called retirement savings to pay for educational expenses, and it alerts you to some major considerations you need to factor into your decision.

Accessing your home equity

If you (or you and the bank) own your own home, you may be sitting on a larger nest egg than you ever considered. A combination of rising home values and shrinking mortgage loan balances has created a large pool of equity for many people, equity that may be made available to fund educational expenses. Chapter 15 illustrates how you may use your house to help put one or more children through college.

Identifying sources of free money

Not every potential student is an academic genius or a future first-round NFL draft pick, but you don't necessarily need to conclude that your child won't qualify for scholarships and grants.

Chapter 16 describes many sources of outright scholarships and grants. Some of them carry no strings whatsoever for your student (other than actually attending college), and others require some sort of payback, either upfront or after your child completes his education.

Borrowing to fill in the gaps

You're obviously reading this because you don't want to have to resort to borrowing money to pay for your children's college costs. And hopefully, you'll never have to touch the pages of Chapter 17. Still, if you do, it's not the end of the world. This chapter explains what types of financial aid are available and assesses the costs. It also peeks at some of the benefits and the downsides of borrowing money for college.

Maximizing Your Savings, Minimizing Your Tax

This book is, at its heart, about successfully saving and investing money for future college costs on the one hand and paying little or no tax on the other. And if that were the beginning and end of the matter, you'd be looking at a fairly straightforward task, one in which, if you followed all the rules, you'd achieve the desired result at the end of the game.

Unfortunately, you don't live your life in a vacuum, and many forces impact your ability to save adequately, to achieve reasonable investment returns on your savings, and to limit the amount of income tax you'll pay on those investment returns. You're operating on a field that is rarely level and that shifts and shimmies through no fault of your own. As a result, you need to be aware of how large and small changes, whether they're a result of government policy, market forces, or changes in your family's projected college cost needs, will affect your savings programs. And you need to be prepared to move with those changes — to adjust your savings programs to account for these other factors.

At the end of the day, your success will depend not only on how often you make deposits into your college savings plans or how large the deposits are but also on how well that money works for you. Your goal is not achieving a large balance in one or more college savings accounts. Your goal is watching your children begin their adult lives with good educations, marketable skills, and no college debt.

Chapter 2

Checking Out the Cost of College

- -

- -

Whether or not you went to college (and regardless of who paid for your education, if you did), the joy of planning and saving for that event for your children, your grandchildren, or even yourself and your spouse has to be tempered somewhat by the uncertainty of the financial costs involved. That uncertainty is the exact amount of the eventual bill because clearly cost is going up, up, up, and never down.

And there's the rub: How can you possibly know how much to save if you can't figure out how much college is going to cost?

In this chapter, I break down all the costs of education into their component pieces as well as compare different types of education. If you know that your prospective student plans to attend a prestigious medical school at the end of the rainbow, you need to plan accordingly. If, however, your budding student has a fascination with all things dead and tries to embalm the family pet before burial, you may be looking at a funeral services school, which costs much less than medical school. The point is that you need to be realistic about your expectations and about the talents and desires of the prospective student before jumping into your savings program. You want to save enough, but saving far more than you need for college is pointless.

Dissecting the Total Bill

Because tuition is usually the largest cost for college, many people make the mistake of saving *only* for tuition. But other costs, such as housing, books, and supplies, can account for a large chunk of college expenses — a large enough chunk that you should include those costs in your savings plan.

In this section, I let you know what costs you should start saving for, as well as give you an idea of how large a piece of college pie those costs are.

Although I cover the major costs of college in this section, they aren't the only costs you may encounter when sending your child off to college. Although I don't suggest that you start saving for a beer fund, be prepared to pay for other items, such as parking permits, transportation, health insurance, and a movie ticket or a new pair of jeans.

Tackling tuition

Tuition refers to probably the largest cost for college: the fees for actual instruction. For the academic year 2002–2003, the tuition costs for a state university reached as high as almost $10,000 for an in-state student and over $21,000 for an out-of state student, and many private four-year universities are charging over $28,000 *each year* for tuition alone!

If you're planning for a baby about to be born, who won't matriculate until 2021, and if tuition continues to increase at a rate of approximately 5 percent each year (which is what has been happening lately in the private universities), that highest annual tuition fee could increase to a whopping $24,400 for an in-state student at a public university, $58,300 for an out-of-state student at a public university, and $67,385 for a student at a private university — or over $97,600, $233,200 and $270,000, respectively for four years. If your baby thinks that carrying a briefcase is cool or asks for the professional doctor kit by age 2, tack on several extra years for graduate or professional school.

These numbers may seem insurmountable, especially if you're entering the savings game fairly late; however, some relief may be available. Only a small percentage of students (and their families) pay the top-dollar price. Not all universities charge in that price range, many offer huge amounts of outright grants and other forms of financial aid (other than loans, although those are available to all), and scholarships and grants from other sources may be available (see Chapters 16 and 17).

If you're fairly certain that your child will attend a public college, you may want to begin investigating whether your state offers a Section 529 prepaid tuition plan (described in Chapters 5 through 7) to help you pay for those upcoming tuition bills. Even if you aren't able to save for tuition costs in one of these plans, saving money in any Section 529 plan or Coverdell Education Savings Account (see Chapters 8 through 10) will allow your college savings to grow faster than conventional savings accounts.

Accounting for housing

You may come from a family who assumes that all those going on to higher learning will receive their postsecondary education at the local campuses, and you fully expect that, when your student reaches that point, he or she will be living at home. If so, you can probably skip this part, although you should be stashing some money away for good, reliable transportation, whether that means a car or bus or subway fare.

If, on the other hand, you suspect that your student won't be satisfied going to the local schools (or if your area is like mine and doesn't really have many postsecondary offerings), you need to add the cost of housing into your savings plan — either college-owned housing or local rental real estate.

College-owned housing

Most colleges provide some sort of room and board options in the form of on-campus or university-owned housing, and they gladly tack those fees onto the tuition bill. Because most university-owned housing is mandatory for all noncommuting students for at least the first year or two, if you plan on sending your child to college, these costs must factor into your savings plan. For 2002–2003, college-owned housing cost between $6,000 and $10,500 per year. Where your college falls in this range depends on a few factors, such as the following:

- ✔ **Location:** Generally, city schools tend to have higher housing costs than schools out in the country.

- ✔ **Size:** Generally, larger colleges tend to have higher housing costs than smaller colleges.

- ✔ **Number of students in a room:** If your child insists on having a room all to her lonesome, expect to pay a premium for that privilege. Generally speaking, the more students crammed into a single room, the less you're likely going to pay for your student.

Room and board charges paid directly to an eligible school (the school will be happy to tell you if it's eligible) can be paid by using tax-free distributions from your Section 529 and/or Coverdell plans (see Chapters 5 and 8).

Local rental properties

Although colleges and universities attempt to expand their student populations, many fail to increase their own housing to meet the increased number of students, which pushes more and more students into the local housing market. In areas where rental units are being added, this isn't a problem; the rental units increase at a rate equal (hopefully) to the number of students seeking housing. However, many older cities have very limited rental housing, and the increased number of students seeking it has forced prices up sharply. So, if you plan to rent an apartment or house for your student, costs become more variable, making it more difficult for you to predict how much you may need to save for your student's housing needs.

If you live close to the college your child attends, the easiest way to check local rental costs is by reading the classified ads and haunting the rental board in the college's housing office. If you're living further away from the action, the Internet can be the way to go. Many newspapers, both big and small, have Web sites, and those Web sites almost always include the papers' classified ads. The lag time between the ad appearing in the paper and the Web site being updated may prevent you from actually locating an apartment this way, but you can get a really great idea of what rental costs are.

The cost of a rental is only the cost of the rental — it may not include utilities (heat in the northern states and air conditioning in the southern states can both be very expensive), and it certainly doesn't include food. You need to add the cost of any utilities not included, plus either money for food or for a meal ticket at the university, in order to accurately compare your costs to the university's room and board plan.

Check the amount of room and board that the college considers to be a "qualified education expense." (You can often find this information buried on its Web site, or just phone one of the college's financial aid officers.) Money that you spend on rent to a non-university landlord can be paid by using tax-free distributions from your Section 529 and Coverdell plans (see Chapters 5 and 8); however, if you spend more than the college's estimated amount of room and board on a non-university landlord, you may want to pay the excess some other way. Distributions taken from your Section 529 and Coverdell plans in excess of "qualified expenses" are subject to income tax and a 10 percent penalty.

Factoring in books and supplies

Okay, so you know that you've enough saved for tuition and room and board, but the need for money doesn't stop once you unload the SUV on the first day of orientation. After your student is at school, he needs to buy books and other supplies, and he won't know which books and supplies he needs until after the first few days of school.

The costs for books and supplies aren't insubstantial. You need to figure on saving at least an additional $1,000 per year for books, plus $500 to $1,000 for other supplies, such as lab coats, protective glasses, notebooks, or even pens and pencils. In comparison to the tuition and room and board fees, this amount may not seem huge, but it's still substantial. Over the course of four years, that bill can be anywhere from $6,000 to $8,000.

Unlike tuition costs, which are set by the university, and housing and food costs, which are set either by the university or by the conditions in the local economy, you can somewhat control how much your student spends on books and supplies. Your student can purchase most books used and then resell them when he's through with them. Supplies, such as notebooks, don't need to have the university or college crest on them in order to function properly, and using the computer lab is always a cheaper alternative to purchasing a computer.

Provided that the books and supplies your student purchases are required by the college, these can be paid for using tax-free or tax-deferred distributions from either a 529 plan (see Chapter 5) or a Coverdell account (see Chapter 8).

Ignore this category at your peril. There is little point in saving enough money to send your student to the school of his or her choice, and then leaving him or her in the lurch, without the tools to completely access the education being offered.

Looking into the Costs of Various Types of Schools

No matter where your student decides to attend college, you have to pay the tuition and the books and supplies, and then you have to come up with some solution to the housing question. But because you may need a crystal ball to figure out where your child plans on attending college, the next piece of the puzzle isn't quite as straightforward — estimating the tuition and fees you need to save for. However, after you have an idea of what type of school your student plans on attending, or, if your up and coming student is either not yet born or just recently populating the planet, you have decided on what type of school you *hope* your student attends, you can begin some significant planning for the future.

To make that planning a little easier — short of a crystal ball — I give you some real numbers to work with in this section for each type of school your child may attend.

Enrolling in career and vocational training schools

Smaller, more specialized schools, such as career and vocational training schools, train students in very specific areas for very specific careers, such as funeral services, dental hygiene, piano tuning, or even bartending. The cost of these programs (which may exist entirely independently of or be attached to community colleges or even four-year colleges) tend to be much smaller than your typical college.

Figure 2-1 lists a few types of career and vocational training schools, their current and anticipated costs, whether they qualify for federal financial aid (see Chapter 17) and for available tax credits (see Chapter 16), and whether you can pay for them using funds from your college savings plans.

Type of School	Tuition and Fees (in Dollars)				Federal Financial Aid Eligible	Tax Credit Eligible	College Savings Plan Eligible
	2002–2003	2007–2008	2012–2013	2017–2018			
Broadcasting	19,500	25,000	31,750	40,500	Yes	Yes	Yes
Cosmetology	9,000–10,000	11,500–12,750	14,700–16,275	18,750–20,775	Yes	Yes	Yes
Dental hygiene	7,000–74,500	9,000–95,000	11,500–121,250	14,675–154,750	Yes	Yes	Yes
Funeral service	10,000–12,000	12,750–15,300	16,375–19,525	21,000–25,000	Yes	Yes	Yes
Gemology	7,600	9,700	12,375	15,800	Maybe	Yes	Maybe
Paralegal (12 month)	7,600–13,000	9,700–16,600	12,375–21,200	15,800–27,000	Some	Yes	Some
Piano tuning	11,500–23,000	14,500–29,000	18,500–37,000	23,600–47,200	Yes	Yes	Yes
Real estate	500–1,350	640–1,725	815–2,200	1,040–2,800	No	Yes	No

Figure 2-1: Career and vocational training school costs.

All current costs are approximate and are for the full length of the training. Future costs are estimated. Your costs may vary.

Taking community college and continuing education classes

Almost every city of any size has at least one community college, an institution of higher education that gives college level learning without the college-level price. In addition, many large universities have a division of continuing education that provides much the same function as a community college, including the low cost — just check out the cost comparisons between community colleges throughout the country in Figure 2-2.

Don't assume that because you can't afford an Ivy League college through the normal channels that you also can't afford to take courses in the continuing education division. Tuition at Harvard University in 2002–2003 is $27,448; per-course fees at the Harvard Extension are $475 for most courses.

School	Tuition (in Dollars)							
	*2002-2003 **2003-2004		2007-2008		2012-2013		2017-2018	
	In-State	Out-of-State	In-State	Out-of-State	In-State	Out-of-State	In-State	Out-of-State
Cape Cod Community College, Mashpee, MA**	3,180	9,360	3,940	11,595	5,150	15,150	6,730	19,800
Capital Community College, Hartford, CT*	1,764	5,292	2,300	6,900	3,000	9,040	3,940	11,800
Cincinnati State Technical & Community College, Cincinnati, OH*	1,950	3,900	2,550	5,100	3,330	6,660	4,350	8,700
Clinton Community College, Plattsburgh, NY**	2,860	7,150	3,550	8,850	4,630	11,575	6,050	15,130
Hibbing Community College, Hibbing, MN*	2,994	2,994	3,900	3,900	5,100	5,100	6,700	6,700
Western Piedmont Community College, Morgantown, NC*	1,136	6,304	1,485	8,240	1,940	10,775	2,550	14,075
Western Texas Community College, Snyder, TX*	960	1,110	1,250	1,450	1,640	1,900	2,150	2,475
Yakima Valley Community College, Yakima, WA*	2,088	7,296	2,725	9,535	3,575	12,460	4,660	16,300

Figure 2-2:
Yearly community-college costs.

All current costs are approximate and only for one year of tuition. Future tuition costs are estimates only. Your costs may vary.

Funds from all of your college savings plans can be used to pay either community college or continuing education tuitions, provided the school you attend is an eligible institution. However, in order to pay for housing using savings from these plans, you need to be at least a half-time student. Be aware of this, and vigilant; a mistake here will cost you not only income tax on the distribution but also a 10 percent penalty.

Going for a four-year public education

Each state has its own public university/college system. Because the universities are larger than the colleges and offer much more programming, they tend to be considerably more expensive than the colleges. If your student has a very clear idea of where she's going in life, it is going to be most cost effective if you can find that program at a state college rather than a state university, especially for in-state students. Check out Figures 2-3 and 2-4 for sample tuition costs for a number of state universities and colleges.

University	Tuition (in Dollars)							
	2002-2003		2007-2008		2012-2013		2017-2018	
	In-State	Out-of-State	In-State	Out-of-State	In-State	Out-of-State	In-State	Out-of-State
North								
University of Maryland — College Park	5,670	14,434	7,410	18,865	9,685	24,655	12,660	32,225
University of Vermont	8,994	21,484	11,755	28,075	15,363	36,700	20,075	47,960
Rutgers — New Brunswick, NJ	7,308	13,284	9,550	17,360	12,500	22,690	16,315	29,650
South								
University of Virginia — Charlottesville	4,595	19,805	6,000	25,900	7,850	33,830	10,260	44,215
University of Florida	2,581	11,595	3,375	15,150	4,400	19,800	5,760	25,900
University of Alabama at Tuscaloosa	3,556	9,624	4,650	12,575	6,075	16,440	7,950	21,485
Midwest								
University of Oklahoma	2,929	8,078	3,825	10,555	5,000	13,800	6,540	18,035
University of Michigan — Ann Arbor	7,806	23,738	10,200	31,025	13,335	40,550	17,425	53,000
University of Kentucky	3,975	10,527	5,195	13,760	6,790	17,980	8,875	23,500
West								
University of California — Los Angeles	4,225	15,886	5,520	20,760	7,215	27,135	9,430	35,465
University of New Mexico	3,170	11,436	4,145	14,945	5,415	19,535	7,075	25,530
University of Oregon	4,155	14,890	5,430	19,460	7,100	25,435	9,275	33,240

Figure 2-3:
Sample
yearly
tuition costs
at state
universities.

All current costs are approximate and only for one year of tuition. Future tuition costs are estimates only. Your costs may vary.

Unlike public elementary and secondary schools, public universities and colleges aren't funded totally by tax dollars (and may actually be funded very little by tax dollars). However, state-run colleges and universities are one of the best bargains around, especially for in-state students. Any state subsidy, no matter how small, is better than no state subsidy for keeping costs down, and this is reflected in the size of tuition bills.

University	Tuition (in Dollars)							
	2002-2003		2007-2008		2012-2013		2017-2018	
	In-State	Out-of-State	In-State	Out-of-State	In-State	Out-of-State	In-State	Out-of-State
North								
University of Maryland — Eastern Shore	4,128	8,612	5,395	11,255	7,050	14,710	9,215	19,225
Lyndon (VT) State College	5,252	11,168	6,865	14,600	8,970	19,075	11,725	24,930
New Jersey City University	5,063	8,663	6,620	11,320	8,650	14,800	11,300	19,340
South								
Virginia State University	3,312	9,738	4,330	12,725	5,660	16,635	7,395	21,740
University of South Florida	2,520	10,410	3,295	13,605	4,300	17,780	5,625	23,240
Alabama State University	2,904	5,808	3,795	7,590	4,960	9,920	6,485	12,965
Midwest								
Southwestern Oklahoma State University	2,138	5,031	2,795	6,575	3,650	8,595	4,775	11,230
Wayne (MI) State University	4,330	9,352	5,660	12,225	7,400	15,975	9,665	20,880
Kentucky State University	2,648	7,208	3,460	9,420	4,525	12,310	5,910	16,090
West								
California State University — Bakersfield	1,801	7,705	2,355	10,070	3,075	13,160	4,020	17,200
New Mexico Highlands University	2,092	8,669	2,735	11,330	3,575	14,810	4,670	19,355
Oregon State University	3,654	13,104	4,775	17,125	6,240	22,385	8,160	29,255

Figure 2-4: Sample yearly tuition costs at state colleges.

All current costs are approximate and only for one year of tuition. Future tuition costs are estimates only. Your costs may vary.

Getting your education in private

Public education may be the cornerstone on which our country is built. However, a vast network of private schools is available at every level, for those who can afford to pay. And because no college education is free (unless you look at the U.S. military academies, where the payment is in kind), all schools that don't rely on public subsidies are referred to as *private*. Private universities can refer to various types of institutions, from the Ivy League schools to hundreds of private four-year institutions throughout the country. Each of these colleges and universities offers a unique educational opportunity, as well as a unique price tag. Just check out Figure 2-5 for some estimates on private education.

Overall, prices are high, climbing higher every year, and no relief is in sight. Tuition and room and board fees are set by the college, and there is no public oversight. Furthermore, college presidents and trustees retain their jobs on the basis of how well their institutions are doing financially — if it takes tuition hikes to keep it that way, that's just too bad.

If your savings are a bit lacking when the time comes to start forking over tuition payments, the smartest way to look for a private school may be to shop by endowment (the amount of money that the school has invested, with the income available for building projects, professors' salaries, and tuition grants), rather than tuition ticket price. Schools with large endowments usually devote a large percentage of the earnings from the fund to outright grants, awarded on the basis of need.

University	Tuition (in Dollars)			
	2002-2003	2007-2008	2012-2013	2017-2018
North				
Drexel University (PA)	18,413	24,065	31,450	41,105
Harvard University (MA)	27,448	35,875	46,885	61,275
The Johns Hopkins University (MD)	27,890	36,450	47,640	62,265
South				
Tuskeegee University (AL)	10,824	14,145	18,490	24,165
Emory University (GA)	26,932	35,200	46,000	60,125
Duke University (NC)	27,844	36,390	47,560	62,160
Midwest				
University of Notre Dame (IN)	25,852	33,788	44,160	57,715
Colorado College (CO)	26,333	34,415	44,980	58,790
Northwestern University (IL)	27,229	35,590	46,510	60,790
West				
Brigham Young University — Provo, UT	3,060	4,000	5,225	6,830
Baylor University (TX)	13,614	17,795	23,255	30,395
Stanford University (CA)	27,204	35,555	46,470	60,730

Figure 2-5: Sample yearly tuition costs at private 4-year colleges and universities.

All current costs are approximate and only for one year of tuition. Future tuition costs are estimates only. Your costs may vary.

Going on to Graduate School

If your student has a burning desire to advance his knowledge for the sake of advancing knowledge, if he absolutely must find a way to cure the common cold in man or beast, or if the halls of academia beckon him professionally, your student may be on his way to graduate school, which is an additional cost to the four-year degree. Figure 2-6 shows you the costs of popular graduate school programs across the country.

Figure 2-6: Sample yearly tuition costs for graduate schools.

University	Tuition (in Dollars)							
	2002-2003		2007-2008		2012-2013		2017-2018	
	In-State	Out-of-State	In-State	Out-of-State	In-State	Out-of-State	In-State	Out-of-State
North								
University of Delaware	5,640	15,170	7,370	19,825	9,635	25,915	12,590	33,865
Harvard University (MA)	24,630		32,190		42,070		54,985	
South								
College of William and Mary (VA)	6,138	17,972	8,020	23,490	10,485	30,700	13,705	40,120
Emory University (GA)	26,770 (2003-2004)		33,165		43,345		56,650	
Midwest								
University of Michigan — Ann Arbor	12,522	23,558	16,365	30,790	21,390	40,240	27,955	52,595
Northwestern University (IL)	26,526		34,670		45,310		59,220	
West								
Brigham Young University — Provo, UT*	3,980	5,970	4,930	7,395	6,445	9,665	8,420	12,635
Stanford University (CA)	27,204		35,555		46,470		60,730	

*Tuition is for 2003-2004 academic year; in-state cost is actually cost for tithe-paying members of the Church of Latter-day Saints, while out-of-state cost is for all other students.

All current costs are approximate and only for one year of tuition. Future tuition costs are estimates only. Your costs may vary.

Pushing Forward to Professional Studies

Besides graduate school, professional schools are another alternative to students seeking education beyond a four-year degree. If your student has always dreamed of being a doctor, a lawyer, or even a veterinarian, or if you hope your student will be interested in professional studies, check out Figures 2-7, 2-8, 2-9, and 2-10 to get a better idea of how much extra money you need to start saving to send your student to medical, law, business, or veterinary school.

University	Tuition (in Dollars)							
	2002-2003		2007-2008		2012-2013		2017-2018	
	In-State	Out-of-State	In-State	Out-of-State	In-State	Out-of-State	In-State	Out-of-State
North								
University of Maryland	14,717	28,165	19,235	36,810	25,140	48,110	32,855	62,880
Harvard Medical School (MA)	30,500		39,860		52,100		68,090	
South								
University of South Carolina	12,960	37,552	16,940	49,080	22,140	64,145	28,935	83,835
Emory University (GA)	32,576 (2003-2004)		40,355		52,745		68,935	
Midwest								
University of Kansas School of Medicine	12,919	27,301	16,885	35,680	22,070	46,634	28,840	60,950
Northwestern Feinberg School of Medicine (IL)	34,998 (2003-2004)		43,355		56,665		74,060	
West								
UCLA School of Medicine (CA)	10,712	21,304	14,000	27,845	18,300	36,390	23,915	47,560
Stanford Medical School (CA)	33,063		43,210		56,475		73,810	

Figure 2-7: Sample yearly tuition costs for medical schools.

All current costs are approximate and only for one year of tuition. Future tuition costs are estimates only. Your costs may vary.

Checking out in-state versus out-of-state tuition

What makes a university or college public is the fact that, to a greater or lesser extent, funding for it comes from a public source: taxes. Although not every state provides huge amounts of assistance to its state schools, every state provides some amount of subsidy.

And because any state subsidy comes from the state's taxpayers, students who live in the state are given not only preference in admissions but also preferential tuition cost. This reflects that they, and their families, are already contributing through their tax dollars.

Even for out-of-state students, tuition at state colleges and universities often provides great value. The vast size of the state systems, their centralized administrations, and the typically lower salaries they offer their employees keep overall costs down. The top tuition price for an out-of-state student, while significantly higher than for an in-state one, is still substantially less than at many private four-year colleges and universities.

Tuition is the only variable between the cost to in-state students versus out-of-state students. All other expenses, including room and board, books and supplies, and so on, are the same for both.

Historically, the rate of increase in tuition and other fees has been more controlled in the state university systems than in private colleges, especially for in-state students. The annual budget is open to the public for comment, and political futures can rise and fall on the fate of a budget that increases too fast. Sometimes, though, state budget shortfalls can put pressure on state legislatures to increase fees at a more draconian rate with the hope that keeping other state services intact (and maybe not raising taxes) will keep the political fallout to a minimum. When states do increase tuition and other fees by a large amount, out-of-state students will typically feel the effects more than in-state students. Remember, in-state students, and their parents, are voters, and voters unhappy with the rate of tuition increases can effect some powerful changes.

Figure 2-8:
Sample yearly tuition costs for law schools.

University	Tuition (in Dollars)							
	2002-2003		2007-2008		2012-2013		2017-2018	
	In-State	Out-of-State	In-State	Out-of-State	In-State	Out-of-State	In-State	Out-of-State
North								
University of Maryland	12,148	22,890	15,875	29,915	20,750	39,100	27,120	51,100
Harvard University (MA)	30,520		39,890		52,135		68,135	
South								
University of South Carolina	11,120	22,516	14,535	29,430	18,995	38,460	24,825	50,265
Emory University (GA)	27,906		36,470		47,665		62,300	
Midwest								
University of Nebraska	5,760	13,075	7,530	17,090	9,840	22,335	12,860	29,190
Northwestern University (IL)	32,008		41,835		54,675		71,455	
West								
University of California Berkeley	11,027	22,731	14,410	29,710	18,835	38,830	24,620	50,745
Stanford University (CA)	31,230		40,815		53,345		69,720	

All current costs are approximate and only for one year of tuition. Future tuition costs are estimates only. Your costs may vary.

University	Tuition (in Dollars)							
	2002-2003		2007-2008		2012-2013		2017-2018	
	In-State	Out-of-State	In-State	Out-of-State	In-State	Out-of-State	In-State	Out-of-State
North								
Penn State University — University Park	10,304	19,682	13,465	25,725	17,600	33,620	23,005	43,940
Harvard Business School (MA)	31,800		41,560		54,320		70,995	
South								
University of North Carolina — Chapel Hill	11,794	26,749	15,415	34,960	20,145	45,690	26,330	59,715
Emory University (GA)	29,136		38,080		49,770		65,045	
Midwest								
Indiana University — Bloomington	11,204	22,408	14,645	29,285	19,140	38,275	25,010	50,025
Northwestern Kellogg School of Management (IL)	32,040		41,875		54,730		71,530	
West								
Arizona State University	11,508	20,028	15,040	26,175	19,655	34,210	25,690	44,710
Stanford University (CA)	33,300		43,520		56,880		74,340	

Figure 2-9: Sample yearly tuition costs for business schools.

All current costs are approximate and only for one year of tuition. Future tuition costs are estimates only. Your costs may vary.

University	Tuition (in Dollars)							
	2002-2003		2007-2008		2012-2013		2017-2018	
	In-State	Out-of-State	In-State	Out-of-State	In-State	Out-of-State	In-State	Out-of-State
North								
Cornell University (NY)	18,200	24,500	23,785	32,020	31,090	41,850	40,630	54,695
Tufts University School (MA)	30,151		39,405		51,500		67,310	
South								
Mississippi State University	7,216 (2003-2004)	21,577 (2003-2004)	8,940	26,730	11,685	34,935	15,270	45,660
University of Florida	11,724 (2003-2004)	31,785 (2003-2004)	14,525	39,375	18,980	51,465	24,810	67,260
Midwest								
University of Missouri	13,310 (2003-2004)	25,617 (2003-2004)	16,490	31,735	21,550	41,475	28,165	54,210
University of Wisconsin — Madison	15,843 (2003-2004)	23,874 (2003-2004)	19,625	29,575	25,650	38,655	33,525	50,520
West								
Oregon State University	12,385	24,036	16,185	31,415	21,155	41,055	27,650	53,660
University of California — Davis	15,836 (2003-2004)	28,081 (2003-2004)	19,620	34,785	25,640	45,465	33,510	59,420

Figure 2-10: Sample yearly tuition costs for veterinary schools.

All current costs are approximate and only for one year of tuition. Future tuition costs are estimates only. Your costs may vary.

Distance Learning: The Wave of the Future

Beyond brick-and-mortar colleges, which require your presence on campus for significant periods of time in order to graduate, there exists the world of online and low-residency programs (see Figure 2-11). Sometimes these programs function totally in the distance learning sphere; other times, they're divisions of regular institutions.

These programs are a godsend for adult learners, who are trying to juggle family and work commitments with their degree program. Many online courses provide all of your instruction and the additional resources you need (such as access to the library) either via the Internet or through the mail. The low-residency options require your presence one or two weeks each semester or one weekend each month. In either case, in exchange for a manageable amount of time, and a great deal of independent study, you receive a full semester's credit each and every semester.

Both distance and online programs offer a wide range of degree options, from associate through PhD, although not in all areas. The number of schools offering these programs is increasing rapidly as universities realize that the only way to increase their pool of students is to tap heavily into populations that are long past the traditional college age.

Figure 2-11: Sample full-time undergraduate costs for distance and low-residency learning options.

School	Tuition (in Dollars)							
	2003-2004		**2007-2008**		**2012-2013**		**2017-2018**	
	In-State	*Out-of-State*	*In-State*	*Out-of-State*	*In-State*	*Out-of-State*	*In-State*	*Out-of-State*
New School Online University, NY, NY	19,795	19,795	24,525	24,525	32,050	32,050	41,890	41,890
Skidmore College University Without Walls, Saratoga Springs, NY	10,850 (approx.)	10,850 (approx.)	13,440	13,440	17,565	17,565	22,960	22,960
Thomas Edison State College, Trenton, NJ	3,325	4,775	4,120	5,915	5,385	7,730	7,035	10,105
Union Institute & University, Cincinnati, OH	11,592	11,592	14,360	14,360	18,770	18,770	24,530	24,530
Vermont College Adult Degree Program	10,520	10,520	13,030	13,030	17,035	17,035	22,260	22,260

All current costs are approximate and only for one year of tuition. Future tuition costs are estimates only. Your costs may vary.

Chapter 3

Realizing All Your Resources

- -

In This Chapter

▶ Ensuring that parents explore all the funding sources

▶ Allowing relatives to make college contributions

▶ Delving into guidelines on gift taxes

▶ Finding ways for students to chip in

- -

*I*f you know approximately how much money you need in order to send your children through college (see Chapter 2 for more information on the costs of college), you may be suffering from sticker shock right about now. You may even be reading this while puffing into a paper bag, thinking that you'll never save enough money. And you won't, at least not until you pull your head out of your bag and begin to plan how to fund those future college expenses.

While you take a minute to catch your breath, let me ease your mind a bit — you may not be the only resource for your children's education. In this chapter, I introduce a variety of resources you can check out when putting your college savings plan together. You may find that you have more alternatives than you thought, but you may also see that you have some work to do. In either case, read through this chapter carefully, take note of the different resources, and discover which approach works best for your family and your situation.

If you feel that you may only be able to save a portion of your child's future college costs, and know that you'll be tapping into need-based financial aid programs down the road, be careful of how and where you save that money. Don't contribute your savings to any account that's owned by your child, such as an UGMA, UTMA (Chapter 12), or a Coverdell Education Savings Account (Chapters 8 through 10); 35 percent of the value of these accounts will be included as part of your expected family contribution under the U.S. Department of Education formula, whereas only 5.6 percent of your assets will be counted. Chapter 17 shows you how to avoid some pitfalls and maximize the amount of need-based financial aid you may qualify for.

Identifying How Parents Can Contribute

No matter how independent your child claims to be and no matter how colleges claim to promote and nurture that independence, the bleak reality remains: the school sends the tuition bill directly to your house for you to pay, and trust me, your child is more than willing to let you pay for it, too.

The financial aid system concerns itself primarily with the parents' ability to pay for college tuition (see Chapter 17 for more information on how schools determine your financial aid needs), and like the financial aid system, colleges look to your deep pockets when the tuition bills come out because, frankly, they want to get paid. You see, colleges count on two things — that you've been saving for your child's education and that, considering you're well into your prime earning years, you make more money than your child (unless you have a little tyke who is a sitcom darling on national television). In order to live up to those financial expectations, I give you some tips below to evaluate your assets and use your current income for your child's college tuition.

Accessing additional assets

Hopefully, you've been planning for the day your child heads off to school, and hopefully, you've been stashing away every possible penny in traditional savings or brokerage accounts (see Chapter 12), trust accounts (see Chapter 13), the new college savings plans (see Chapters 5 through 10), or some combination of those savings vehicles. I discuss all of these savings plans and more throughout this book, but be on the lookout for the following savings opportunities that you may have overlooked, especially if you find your traditional savings falls short:

- ✔ **Collectibles:** You may be surprised to find yourself with the cost of a college education forgotten amidst the spider webs in a closet or attic. I collected stamps as a kid. My brother, on the other hand, had a comic book collection that couldn't be beat. Others in my family have boxes of original Beatles memorabilia. These collections have the potential to turn into a small fortune. So check out those remnants of your childhood — they may be very rare and valuable.

- ✔ **Life insurance policies:** If you own life insurance (other than term), you may have a significant amount of cash value in that policy — cash that you can access by taking a loan against the value of the policy or by terminating the policy. Many folks purchase these policies to make sure their children are cared for through college in the event of a tragedy. Because you're still alive and kicking, what better use for the money now than to help pay for those very same college costs?

✔ **Scholarships from your employer:** Many larger employers offer scholarship opportunities to their employees' children. These scholarships are almost always merit-based (your children need to maintain their grades), and they're almost never enough to pay the full amount. Still, some scholarship aid is better than nothing, and you don't have to pay back this aid. See Chapter 16 for more info on scholarships.

✔ **Cash value in your home:** After focusing month in and month out on making sure the mortgage, taxes, insurance, and utilities are paid on your house, you may be astounded by the amount of value that's just sitting there in your house. In Chapter 15, I show you how to convert that value to funds that you can use to pay college expenses.

If you've been unable to save enough for your child's education, and the sale of your coin collection won't completely fill the gap, think carefully about how to apportion your savings. Split your savings equally between the number of years you'll be paying tuition bills — if you feel you'll be able to make up the balance each year with current earnings. On the other hand, if you feel that you'll have no choice but to borrow money in order to pay the balance, first spend down your child's savings, and then your own, as quickly as possible, postponing taking loans as long as you can. By reducing the amount of your family's assets, you'll increase the amount of need-based aid that your child may be eligible for.

Counting on your current income

Oh, if all of life followed fantasy closely, it would be a much simpler world. You would have all the money your child needs, ready to fully cover all the tuition, room, board, and expenses your son or daughter incurs. However, try as you may, when the day comes to start forking over those tuition payments, you may find yourself a little short in the college savings department.

Of course, the whole point of this book is to show you how you can save money for your children's college tuition, but if you're falling short of tuition, your current income could help fill those gaps:

✔ **Check to see whether the college has a payment plan.** Some colleges recognize the tuition crunch and offer payment plans. If you know this upfront, you can make arrangements to pay on such a schedule when the tuition bill comes in. Instead of going broke twice a year, you can ease the burden over the course of several months.

✔ **Consider diverting some money from other current savings programs to your current tuition needs.** The obvious place to look here is at your retirement plans, where you've presumably been putting away the maximum allowed each year. If you need the money right now to pay college expenses, you may want to explore the possibility of reducing your pension contributions right now, and reinstate your full contribution the day after graduation.

But before you reduce or even eliminate your pension contributions, be certain that you'll be able to make up the difference later. You can borrow for college, but you can't borrow for retirement.

✔ **Remember that your child doesn't live at home anymore.** If your child lives away at college, your household expenses decrease when he or she is at school. With judicious paring and careful budgeting (as shown in Chapter 4), you may find that coming up with the difference between what the college expects you to contribute and what you're saving is possible.

Accepting Help from Family

Although *your* child is the one you're trying to send to college, don't rule out the possibility that other relatives, like your parents or siblings, may be in a position, and may want, to help you out.

Families can be strange entities, and the larger the extended family, the more opportunities for really weird behavior. Although your pride shouldn't get in the way of having a family member fund all or part of an education, be aware of any strings that may be attached to the gift. At a certain point, the cost of any help to you and your family may become greater than the value of that gift. Weigh this price tag very carefully before you accept help.

Contributing to established savings plans

You may have already set up a Section 529 plan — see Part II — for your child, or a Coverdell Education Savings Account (ESA) — read all about it in Part III — or even both. If so, nothing in the rules that govern these plans prohibits other people from contributing to those accounts. If grandparents, your siblings, other relatives, or friends want to make donations to these plans, let them. Just be aware of the following:

✔ Limits are set on plan contributions in any given year, especially for Coverdell ESAs. These accounts are limited to a set aggregate contribution in each year, regardless of the source (see Chapter 8). If you've already made a contribution for the full amount for this year, Grandma and Grandpa need to find some other way to save for little Christopher's education for this year.

    ✔ Section 529 plans have total plan limits. Each state has its own ceiling on the total size of individual plans, and each state has the ability to raise that ceiling at will. Although the limits are very high and calculated to cover a four-year college education at the ritziest school in that state, you do want to be aware of where that ceiling is, especially as you begin to approach it (see Chapter 5).

    ✔ All contributions into college savings plans of whatever sort (whether Section 529 or Coverdell plans, eligible U.S. Savings Bonds, or trust or UTMA/UGMA accounts) are subject to the Gift and/or Generation-Skipping Transfer tax (see the section "Understanding the Tax on Gifts," later in this chapter).

Promising to pay

Unlike contributions into already existing plans, promises by Grandma and Grandpa (or anyone else) to pay for college are a bit more uncertain; between the time the promise is made and the time to keep the promise, much can, and often does, change.

Don't rely on promises. Every baby is adorable, and every grandparent (or other relatives) may want to do all that they can for that infant. But as time goes on, incomes may drop, health may deteriorate, or relationships may unravel, altering a relative's ability or desire to pay for college. If you've been relying on this promise, and not instituting a savings program of your own, you may be out of luck when freshman year rolls around.

Understanding the Tax on Gifts

Whenever you, your child's grandparents, or any other relatives make any contribution toward your child's education, a gift is being made to your child. And, because the IRS never leaves any good deed unpunished, that gift becomes subject to the Gift Tax and/or Generation-Skipping Transfer Tax (GSTT). Yep — right when you think you've done something nice for someone, the IRS has to slap some kind of tax on it. There is good news, however, and you can find it in the following sections, where I show you how to make the most of your goodwill by explaining the rules surrounding the Gift Tax and the GSTT.

If ever a topic defied easy explanations, it's the *transfer tax,* which is the slice the government takes when money is given from one person to another, either in a lifetime gift or an after-death inheritance, and which includes the Gift Tax and GSTT. You can easily go wrong when trying to figure out these taxes, and mistakes are costly to repair. If, after you read what follows, you have some gift tax or GSTT questions, please run, don't walk, to a qualified tax advisor, whether an accountant, a lawyer, or an enrolled agent (a person qualified by the IRS to advise clients on tax issues). The relatively small amount you may spend upfront for advice is peanuts in comparison to the amounts you may have to cough up if you don't play by the IRS rules.

Understanding the gift tax

If you, and your extended family and friends, are planning and plotting ways to see your child, or children, through college and beyond, you may begin a gifting program early in your child's life. Every year, every person is entitled to make gifts, tax free, to as many other people as he or she wants, up to the *annual exclusion amount*. This amount is adjusted periodically to reflect inflation. (The amount was $11,000 in 2003.) So, for example, if you have three children, you, your spouse, your parents, and anyone else who has the means and the desire, can each transfer $11,000 (or the current exclusion amount) to each of the deserving people on your list, without incurring any gift-tax consequences. Next year, you can do the same thing again.

Now, the IRS, in its infinite wisdom, realizes that handing a 7-year-old a check for $11,000 probably isn't a wise move, and this is one time (and maybe the only time) that you probably agree with the IRS. Accordingly, the IRS allows you to make gifts into financial vehicles, such as in trust (see Chapter 13), in UGMA/UTMA accounts (Chapter 12), in Section 529 Plans (Chapter 5), and in Coverdell Savings Accounts (Chapter 8), for your children (or grandchildren, or anyone else you want to make gifts to), that hold and maintain that money either for a specific period of time or a for specific purpose. No matter whether you gift cash, stocks or bonds, jewelry, or anything else, if you give up your interest in the property, the gift qualifies as a completed gift, and you can deduct the annual exclusion amount ($11,000) from the total value of the gift. Any amount you've gifted over and above the annual exclusion amount is now subject to the gift tax rules.

For example, if Auntie Elizabeth gives your child $20,000 in 2003, $11,000 is excluded from that gift, and $9,000 is subject to the gift tax. If Auntie Elizabeth and Uncle Bob (who are married to each other) each give your child $20,000, then $22,000 of their total gift qualifies as annual exclusion gifts (2 x $11,000), with $18,000 subject to the gift tax.

Splitting gifts

The IRS recognizes that many couples own assets individually, rather than jointly, and that the asset split between them many not be even. Just as married couples can elect (and most do) to file a joint income tax return, even though one spouse may earn the vast majority of the family income, they can also elect to treat at least part of their lifetime gifting as a joint gift, even if all of the gift is actually made by one spouse. If the proper election is made on your gift tax returns, one spouse can give the entire gift and then "split" the gift with his or her spouse. This is, not surprisingly, called *gift splitting*.

Suppose Auntie Elizabeth (who is still married to Uncle Bob) gives your child $40,000 on her own in 2003, and because Bob is still offended that you forgot he was allergic to nuts and you included them in your award-winning stuffing at Christmas 10 years ago (yes, folks, relatives such as this do really exist!), he gives your child nothing. If they don't take advantage of gift splitting, only $11,000 of the gift is excluded, and $29,000 is subject to the gift tax. On the other hand, if they elect to split the $40,000 gift (thus, each person "gives" $20,000), Auntie Elizabeth can exclude $11,000, and Uncle Bob can exclude $11,000. Then only $18,000 is subject to the gift tax. (Considering his attitude, Uncle Bob almost doesn't deserve to know such a neat trick.)

Getting excited about unified credit

The amount of the annual exclusion seems large, and it is — a great deal of wealth can be transferred without incurring a gift tax over the course of a lifetime. It seems somewhat unfair, however, that, if you or someone close to you is in a financial position to gift even larger sums, they should be penalized by having to pay a tax on the gift. The tax isn't small, either — gift tax rates are bracketed, but the top bracket was 49 percent in 2003. And because most people aren't as wealthy, as, say Bill Gates or Oprah Winfrey, that kind of hit would be hard to take. Ladies and gentlemen, may I introduce the *unified credit*.

Although a tax is assessed on every gift that is made over and above the year's annual exclusion amounts, you don't actually have to pay any gift tax until your lifetime cumulative taxable gifts have exceeded a certain level. The gift taxes assessed are then offset by the unified credit amount, or an amount that, when applied against the tax assessed, will eliminate or reduce the amount of tax owed. Through 2009, the unified credit for gifts stands at a lofty $345,800, which represents the tax on cumulative gifts of $1,000,000, not including any of your annual exclusion gifts.

To see how this works, let's go back to Auntie Liz and Uncle Bob, who each gave $20,000 to your child in 2003. Of that amount, $11,000 qualifies for the annual exclusion amount. The balance of $9,000 shown on each of their gift tax returns (gift tax returns may only be filed by individuals, not jointly) is subject to the gift tax. Because they've never given a taxable gift before, the gift tax on each $9,000 taxable gift is $1,620. Instead of writing a check to the U.S. Treasury for that amount, though, they then apply $1,620 of unified credit against their tax liability. Now they owe no gift tax in 2003, although they now each have only $344,180 remaining of their unified credit to use in future years.

Checking out the exceptions

You found this out in grammar class, and the same holds true for the gift tax — for every rule, you can find an exception. In the case of the gift tax, I discuss two exceptions below.

Section 529 plan exception

Section 529 plans, a relatively new item in the arsenal of college savings, are designed to harbor enough money to put a child all the way through college without any other assistance. Consequently, the amounts that are allowed in them are quite large (see Chapter 5). And, because you may have kids who are creeping up in age and approaching college far more rapidly than you may like, you may want to superfund your plan, pushing as much money into your Section 529 plan as fast as you can. And you can, without incurring a gift tax.

An exception to the annual exclusion rules has been made for Section 529 plans. You, or anyone you know, may put up to five years' worth of annual exclusion gifts into a Section 529 plan for the benefit of a specific person *in one year,* which means you can put $55,000 (5 x $11,000) in Junior's Section 529 plan in 2003 without being subject to any kind of gift tax. But wait — it gets even better. Gift-splitting rules still apply, so you can put $110,000 into a Section 529 plan for any beneficiary in 2003 without any gift tax consequences, split the gift with your spouse, and then file gift tax returns for the next five years, allocating one-fifth of the total gift (which equals $11,000 per donor) to each year.

However, during that five-year period, any additional gifts made to the same beneficiary are subject to gift tax treatment (remember, you've used up your annual exclusion amounts for five years). It probably would be a good idea if you didn't die during this period, either; any amounts gifted in anticipation of years that haven't happened yet will be pulled back into your estate and become subject to federal estate tax rules.

If your baby has just been born, and your crystal ball shows ample savings for his college education using normal methods, you probably don't need to worry about superfunding a Section 529 account. However, if you've waited until almost the last minute and still want to take maximum advantage of this savings plan, this gives you the opportunity. Likewise, if you have the money available now (perhaps you've just received an inheritance), but wonder if you might squander some or all of it if you wait, superfunding Section 529 plans for your children may make sense.

Qualified education expenses paid exception

Your children may be some of the fortunate ones. Maybe you, your extended family, and/or your friends can afford to just whip out your checkbooks when the time comes and write that check for Harvard, Notre Dame, or your local community college. If you have that luxury, you may be hesitating just a bit now because you suspect there may be gift tax consequences; but think again.

Tuition for another person which is paid directly to an educational institution, whether for primary, secondary, or postsecondary education, *does not* constitute a taxable gift, *does not* affect your annual exclusion amounts (you can still give that lovely, large birthday gift you were planning), and *does not* cut into your lifetime unified credit.

A word to the wise. If your child will be applying for need-based financial aid, tuition payments made on that child's behalf will count as untaxed income to the child on the next year's FAFSA application (see Chapter 17). If Grandma can afford to pay for only one year's tuition and you want to maximize need-based financial aid, ask her to postpone her tuition gift until your child's last year of college.

Figuring out the Generation-Skipping Transfer Tax (GSTT)

The Generation-Skipping Transfer Tax (GSTT) is yet another transfer tax (like the gift tax) that Congress devised to close a particular tax loophole: one generation (the grandparents, for example) bypassing their children in favor of their grandchildren when making a gift. That makes sense, but to Congress, it meant that they could only collect gift tax once on the value of that property, rather than twice — grandparents to parents, and then parents to children. The GSTT was instituted to deal with that problem.

The GSTT is, essentially, a tax calculated by figuring out how much the government would have collected had the transferred amounts gone first to your children, and then transferred subsequently to your children's children, and so on.

The GSTT is designed for the very wealthy; accordingly, you are entitled to a lifetime exclusion of transfers from this tax (over and above annual exclusion amounts, which are the same for the GSTT as they are for the gift tax), totaling $1,100,000 per donor in 2002 and indexed annually for inflation.

Because of the high GSTT exemption amount and the availability of annual exclusion gifts, for most of you, the GSTT will remain very far out on the radar. If, however, you're one of those grandparents who has undertaken to provide college education for your grandchildren (and you have more than a few of them), and if you've also decided to take advantage of various college savings plans that are now available, you may run up against this tax. If you plan to make large gifts into these plans (or into trust or any other financial vehicle), you need to contact your legal and tax advisors.

You should never ignore tax advice, but, in this case, missteps in the GSTT can cost you especially dearly — the top tax rate in 2003 was 49 percent. Because the GSTT is assessed in addition to any gift tax you may have to pay, the combined gift tax and GSTT on a gift to your grandchild can approach almost 100 percent of the total gift!

Seeking Out Student Sources

I know that our country has laws against putting children to work these days, but that doesn't mean you can never count on your children contributing to their own college tuition bill. For most of you, the economics of financing college is a whole-family project, not one dependent only on the pods. In this section, I show you how your children can take some responsibility for their futures, not only in studying and in obtaining good grades but also in trying to ease some of the tuition burden. Working to earn their own money and keeping their grades up to win awards and scholarship can help defray future college expenses, which means you have to save even less.

Begin discussions about college tuition with your children early. Their weekly allowance, which they'd probably rather spend on a new high-powered squirt gun or movie tickets, may never add up to an Ivy League education. But discussing college finances with your children and encouraging them to save their money raises their awareness of what things cost, including their eventual college education. These early discussions and the encouragement you give your children to save their money may pave their way to future sound financial decisions. As they get older, they may consider stashing a portion of any money that comes their way into savings accounts, hopefully for later college expenses.

Working part-time and summer jobs

You can't send your elementary student to work at the factory after school. As she enters middle and high school, however, her potential to make money to help defray college costs increases significantly. So start encouraging your college hopeful to get off the couch and get a job. Young teens can begin earning their own money with timeless neighborhood jobs such as babysitting, working as a mother's helper, lawn mowing, and snow shoveling. But your child can tap into even greater college money potential by working for an employer who

> ✔ **Provides a tuition-reimbursement program:** One of the most prized fringe benefits today is the tuition reimbursement plan, meaning that your employer essentially pays for some or all of the employee's tuition. Generally, larger employers (including many large retailers and fast-food

restaurants) offer these plans, and usually the plans cover only education expenses that apply to the employee's current job or that improve the employee's general job skills.

Other restrictions may also apply, such as limiting participation to full-time employees or to employees who have completed a certain period of service. However, if your child works for such an employer and meets all the requirements, she may be able to have her employer pay for at least a portion of tuition at a local college or university. Although the number of students who qualify for tuition reimbursement plans is small, if you (or your child) fall into this category, you could offset a significant portion of the eventual cost in this way.

✔ **Offers discounts:** Working for discount or retail stores may not sound glamorous, let alone lucrative, but most places offer discounts of some kind. Just think about all of the stuff that college kids need — school supplies, dorm outfittings, those crazy Yaffa blocks that seem to find their way into every college student's room, and so on. When you add up how much you can blow on the small stuff, remember that the money has to come from somewhere. And no matter who's paying the bill, you can reduce it significantly by getting it all on discount.

✔ **Teaches a marketable skill:** I began to work as a bookkeeper the summer I turned 13, my sister worked after school for my uncle the dentist, and my other sister worked during vacations for a jeweler. Beyond the fast-food restaurants and discount and convenience stores, teens can find summer or part-time jobs that provide them with a marketable skill or with experience in a field they may otherwise not have considered. Even working at jobs like lifeguarding can give teens skills and an experience that lasts much longer than a summer — your teens may have an easier time finding a job at school because of their experience or skill. In addition, if they can keep working while in school, they can further defray incidental and everyday costs that otherwise you or their college savings plans would have to fund.

Yes, nepotism is a dirty word — strictly defined, *nepotism* is when a relative is shown favoritism in getting a desirable position. However, I seriously doubt that most people consider typing up commercials at Uncle Dave's AM radio station a desirable position. So when it comes to getting your kids started earning money, it's a who-you-know-not-what-you-know kind of world, and asking your family and friends about any possible openings is a great way for your kids to find work.

After your child begins working, take that time to really emphasize what portion of college expenses you expect your child to contribute — whether it be the cost of books, incidentals, or a computer. Be clear about your expectations. Just like most of us, your child is more likely to reach a tangible goal than one that has no boundaries.

Going after scholarships, prizes, and awards

The option of scholarships as a way to fund a college education may seem so obvious, or it may appear to be unworkable for your student, but local, state, national, and corporate scholarships are available — some based on merit, others on need, and a few on a combination of both. Service groups in your town may offer them, your employer may offer something to children of employees, and the Daughters of the Revolution is usually good for something at graduation time. In addition, your child's university may also be a source for both merit and need-based grants. (Check out Chapter 16 for more details on scholarships.)

Many achievement awards have checks that accompany them, and no application process is usually involved. Many scholarships and grants, however, are accessed only through an application and/or a test. Encourage your child to apply to as many as he or she can, and take whatever tests are available. What may seem like a hopeless proposition could actually turn out well. For example, I laughed when my mother told me to take the Betty Crocker exam (I hadn't taken home economics since junior high school). But I won the prize! For more information about helping pay for your child's education, see *Free $ For College For Dummies,* by David Rosen and Caryn Mladen (published by Wiley).

Finding sources of available money and determining what your child may qualify for isn't as tough as it may seem. Check with your child's guidance counselor for lists of what's out there locally. Your child can access the application guidelines for most national scholarship contests via the Internet. Finally, don't be afraid to approach the financial aid office of any school — prior to application, after admission, or while your student is actually attending classes — to see what scholarship award may have your student's name written all over it.

Chapter 4

Sharpening Your Savings Techniques

At some point early in your children's lives, you need to calculate how much you think that you'll need to see your children through school and figure out who's going to be paying when the time comes. Essentially, you're defining the size of the problem.

Now, your biggest concern is finding a solution. Because, as much as you realize you need to save money, you're not saving money! You're sure you have the will, the desire, and the need — you just seem to be lacking the cash. This chapter dissects your life and your spending habits (just a little bit). It shows you that adding more money to this equation isn't the only way you can ever increase the amount of cash you save. Although finding additional money is always nice, you can use a variety of methods to carve some savings out of what you already have.

Focusing on the Family Budget

You can call it a budget, a financial plan, microeconomics, or a good excuse to pig out on a pint of ice cream every month, but whatever name you give it, the most important part of the family economic dynamic isn't *how much* money you have, but rather how you *spend* the money you have. And if you focus attention on budgeting, you can gain control over your family's finances and find that extra money you need to start saving for college.

The mechanics of your family's budget are fairly straightforward — you bring in a certain amount of money, through work, entitlement programs such as Social Security or other pensions, or investments. From that money, or income, you need to pay for the basic needs of your family — housing and utility costs, food, clothing, transportation, insurance, and so on — and for the frills your family has come to expect — cable television, vacations, and fancy gifts at birthdays and holidays.

While that sounds simple enough, you may find that your family's needs and expectations slightly exceed your income. You may also want to save a significant piece of your income each month, but when the end of the month comes, you find that you're a bit short. If you find yourself in either situation, thinking that saving money for college is impossible, put that pint of ice cream back in the freezer and check out my tips on how to dig for the dollars you need in your monthly budget to start saving for college.

Eliminating most of the fat

The first step in gaining control over your family's finances is not to cut off the cable television or the Internet connection or take the family dog to the pound. You need to take a step back and look at the big picture — you need to know not only how much money you have coming in but also how much is going out and where that money is headed.

Making lists of where you are now

Before you can start making changes to your family's finances, you need to understand what you have right now, at this moment. Sit down and make a list of your monthly income and, if your income tends to be seasonal at all, your yearly income (and then divide that by 12). List all your income, from every source. Don't declare this account or that resource as off-limits. Every income item needs to be on the table (no, the IRS isn't looking over your shoulder).

Your next list needs to be those payments that you absolutely, positively, need to make, including the following:

- Rent or mortgage (plus necessary repairs)
- Food
- Utilities (*not* including cable)
- Insurance (life, disability, medical, homeowners/renters, and car)
- Car and other transportation costs
- Student loan payments

  ✔ Taxes

  ✔ Charitable contributions

  ✔ Annual clothing costs for your family

Once again, if amounts change seasonally, add up a year's worth of bills and expenses and then divide by 12.

Third, you need to catalog so-called discretionary items — entertainment costs, travel, cable or satellite television, Internet access, gym memberships, private school tuitions, and so on. Depending on your family, this list can be quite extensive.

Finally, take a good look at how much you pay each month on outstanding consumer debt (plus the total amount you owe). Make sure you add your credit-card payments to your lists of expenditures, as well as any bank fees that you may pay on your checking account.

Try to be as accurate and honest as possible when preparing these lists. It's one thing to lie to your accountant, but lying to yourself really doesn't help here.

After you have all your lists prepared, you'll be able to see where your money goes and how much of it you actually fribble away.

Carving away the truly wasteful

With your income and current spending patterns laid out in front of you, you probably won't have any trouble spotting the expenditure items that are really, really wasteful. Right at the top of the list are bank and finance charges. You may consider these charges to be minimal, but adding those minimal costs up can be another story. Check out the following examples of potential fees you could face, depending on how you manage your money:

  ✔ **Minimum balance penalty:** Some banks assess fees if your checking account carries a balance below the minimum for the month. For example, if my checking account balance drops below $750 in any month (even it's $749), my bank hits me with a $7 per month fee.

  ✔ **Insufficient funds penalty:** I don't know of any bank that doesn't slap a fee of at least $20, if not more, on bounced checks.

  ✔ **Credit card interest:** Carrying a balance on your credit card can cost you between 10 and 20 percent (or more) per year for the loan of that money in interest alone.

  ✔ **Over-limit fees:** Most credit card companies charge a fee if you go over your credit limit — like a bounced check, I don't know of any credit card that charges less than $20 each month for going over the credit limit.

> ✔ **Late-payment fees:** If your payment check doesn't arrive on time, it'll probably cost you at least $20 for the month. (Late payments also decrease credit-worthiness and increase the cost of later loans to you.)

Table 4-1 paints a picture of how these fees can add up for a typical family.

Table 4-1	Truly Wasteful Spending			
What You're Paying	**Monthly Amount (Good Credit History)**	**Annual Amount**	**Monthly Amount (Slightly Flawed Credit History)**	**Annual Amount**
Bank finance charges	$7	$84	$12	$144
Credit card interest	$25 ($3,000 debt @ 10% a year)	$300	$62.50 ($5,000 debt@ 15% a year)	$750
Late mortgage payment	$25 (5% of $500 payment)	$300	$50 (5% of $1,000 payment)	$600
Over-the-limit credit card fee	$29	$348	$35	$420

Not only can bank and finance charges waste your money, but consider the following examples:

> ✔ Paying health club dues to a club you haven't attended for over a year
>
> ✔ Continuing a newspaper subscription that you just haven't gotten around to canceling
>
> ✔ Hitting the coffee shop for a cup o' joe in the morning because you don't get up early enough to make your own
>
> ✔ Going out for dinner or lunch rather than eating at home

Wasteful spending can be curbed if you take the time to assess your spending. I'm not advocating punishing your family by getting rid of a health club membership, but I am advocating ridding yourself of expenses that you don't need or put to use. Add up what you waste each month. Start getting payments in on time, maintaining the minimum balance in your checking account, making coffee at home, or canceling memberships or subscriptions that you don't use so that you can begin saving that money for college.

Reorganizing what's left

If you've crossed off all of the wasteful spending, or if you had no wasteful spending to begin with, you can still lower your total expenses each month. Check out what's left of your expenses and see whether you can take advantage of additional ways to save that I discuss in the following sections.

Lowering your debt

The biggest piece of most budgets is the amount folks pay to their mortgage company, their car finance company, and their credit card companies. Many people are surprised to find that they pay more than they need to in many of these areas. Check out the following ways to reduce your monthly debt:

- ✔ **Consider refinancing your house.** Look at your current housing, car, and credit card payments. You may be able to consolidate all these loans into one mortgage, and leave your mortgage closing with one monthly payment that's significantly less than the total of all debt payments you had been making. While this isn't true in every case and is dependent on interest rate fluctuations and the current value of your house, it's certainly worth an afternoon or evening of your time to investigate.

- ✔ **Consolidate your student loans.** If you're currently paying off student loans, and you haven't yet consolidated them, you may find that now is the time. Depending on the amount you owe and current interest rates, you may be able to significantly lower your monthly payment.

- ✔ **Liquidate your assets.** Another way to lower debt payments is to liquidate assets that you may have and pay down your debt. If, for example, you have shares of stock that aren't increasing in value, it may be well worth it to sell the stock and pay off your credit cards.

- ✔ **Lower your credit card interest rate.** If you can't retire your credit card debt entirely, negotiate with your credit card companies for lower rates. You'll need a history of timely payments; one late payment will muddy the water considerably — two or more, and they'll probably just laugh. If your current company won't negotiate, go shopping. Many banks are eager for your business, often with introductory rates as low as 0% for three, six, or nine months. Transfer your high-interest balance, and pay it off before the introductory rate expires.

- ✔ **Trade down when you trade in.** Take a close look at your car and the size of your car payments. When getting a new vehicle, consider something less than a Mercedes even if the dealer says that you can afford it. He's trying to put his own kids through college, but your responsibility extends only as far as your own offspring — not his.

✔ **Consider debt consolidation.** If you're *really* burdened by debt, and can't find *any* reasonable way out (robbing a bank isn't reasonable), making an appointment with a reputable credit counselor isn't the worst idea. Counselors can often negotiate deals with your creditors that you won't be able to get on your own, and through their services, you may be able to eliminate hundreds of dollars from monthly credit card and other loan bills. If you consider this option, remember that this may damage your credit-worthiness. Of course, it may also help: If you're so deeply in debt that you need to consult with one of these services, you're probably also missing payments, making late payments, and otherwise messing up your credit rating. In the long run, your creditors will likely be relieved to see you gaining some control over your finances.

Trimming other costs

Clearly, you need electricity, water, telephone service, heat, and so on. And, for most of you, these costs are not negotiable — the utility companies have cultivated a world of monopolies, and in most cases, no bargains are to be found as far as price per unit goes. However, you may be able to reduce costs within your own household, and these are well worth exploring.

I give you a few ideas in the following list to get you thinking about ways you can reduce other monthly costs:

✔ **Ask for a lower rate.** Telephone and heating oil companies are highly competitive. Don't hesitate to shop around, and ask your current company to meet, or beat, a competitor's lower price.

✔ **Pay for only what you use.** Don't pay for more cable and/or satellite service than you need or can use. Cut back to a place that still provides the programming that you want but doesn't give you a whole lot of extras that you rarely use.

✔ **Practice energy conservation.** Upgrade your house with energy- and water-efficient appliances and improvements. Many of these have small upfront costs (energy-efficient light bulbs and low-flow toilets, for example) but pay off in huge savings over their lifetimes.

✔ **Comparison-shop for insurance.** Seek out the most competitive price for all your insurance needs — life, disability, homeowners/renters, car, and medical (if you pay for your own.) Many folks can trade a costly whole-life policy for a much less expensive term-life policy. Your life insurance coverage can remain the same for a fraction of the cost.

✔ **Trim the grocery bill.** You can slash your grocery bill by using coupons and store affinity cards and by shopping on sale. Also, don't forget that house brands are almost always less expensive than the national brands, and for many items, the quality remains the same. Just because you've always used a certain brand doesn't mean you have to continue to use it. The manufacturer won't punish you for disloyalty.

You'll be most successful in your trimming program if you don't slash costs willy-nilly. If you're content with how you're living right now, cutting out the funds to do the things you love will only create a savings ogre, one that sucks the joy out of your life in exchange for money in the bank.

Changing Your Perspective — Watching Your Savings Grow

Saving for any purpose, whether for college, retirement, a new home, or that dream vacation of a lifetime, isn't a punishment, nor does it need to be a deferral of pleasure. Some people (and you all know someone like this) squeeze every penny until it squeals and never seem to have any fun. Who can forget Ebenezer Scrooge, after all? He began to live only after he stopped clutching his money quite so tightly. And he is, of course, the epitome of the saver — the miser.

Well, he's a fictional character, and plenty of savers out there still know how to have a good time. And maybe they even have a better time, because at the end of the evening, they know they have the money to pay the bill.

Saving money can and should be neither painful nor pleasurable; it should just be, and you should view putting cash into your savings plans and accounts in the same way as you view paying your other bills. I don't particularly like paying bills, but I do get great satisfaction from knowing that my bills are paid.

Paying yourself first

You've probably heard this advice more than once but never put it into practice: Pay yourself first. As you look at your income, you should carve a portion of that income out and earmark it for savings.

That money needs to be physically segregated from the rest of your income (so you're not tempted to dip into it, even a little, for that extra something you've been wanting to buy). Only after you've subtracted it and put it elsewhere should you figure out how much money you have available for all your other expenses, which need to fit into this smaller amount. If, after putting aside your savings amount, you can't pay the rest of your monthly bills, you need to change something — find a cheaper mortgage, eat out less frequently, or buy fewer books. The choice is yours. The only item that isn't on the table for negotiation is your savings amount.

Systematically saving

You can successfully save if you put the same amount of money into some sort of savings account each and every week or month (depending on when your income is paid to you). Even if the periodic amounts may seem small to you, Table 4-2 illustrates how those savings can add up to considerable nest eggs at the end of one, five, ten, or twenty years.

Table 4-2	Systematic Savings (at 5% Interest, Compounded Weekly)			
Amount per Week	1 Year of Savings	5 Years of Savings	10 Years of Savings	20 Years of Savings
$10	$532.96	$2,952.26	$6,742.58	$17,829.41
$25	$1,332.39	$7,380.65	$16,856.46	$44,641.38
$50	$2,554.78	$14,761.30	$33,712.91	$89,282.76
$100	$5,329.57	$29,522.60	$67,425.83	$178,565.52

Earmarking certain pieces of income for savings

Most people not only receive their normal income, paid at regular intervals, but they also have periodic injections of additional cash, whether it's in the form of overtime wages, significant salary increases, holiday bonuses, gifts and/or inheritances, or even income tax refunds. (I can't begin to tell you the number of times people have told me that they use additional withholdings on their pay as a way to save money.)

If you've been doing your job and dissecting your budget, you've probably already figured out how to live comfortably on what you earn on a regular basis, and you're also, hopefully, now saving systematically and regularly.

So what should you do when a little extra money comes your way? Of course, from where I'm sitting, the answer is obvious. Save, save, save. You've figured out how to live nicely without it, and you won't miss it, so put it in a safe place and forget about it!

Ah, but I can see ideas of a vacation, a new piece of jewelry, or redoing the kitchen dancing through your head. Obviously, if your household budget hasn't included money for some glaring need (perhaps your roof is leaking) and you've just been waiting for some extra cash to pay for that project, you can divert at least some of that money for that purpose. But if you've managed to pare your spending to a place where you're managing beautifully with what you have, take a big chunk of that extra money and sock it into your savings plans. What's out of sight is also out of mind, and these additional funds may be just the ticket to beef up a somewhat anemic college savings or retirement account.

Educating yourself about investing

There can be no question about it: The world of investing can be a scary place, and the days when stockbrokers did your buying and selling have mostly gone the way of record albums and eight-track cassettes. Investing is now a do-it-yourself operation that can present many pitfalls for the unwary. Before you even think about sticking your big toe in the investing pool, you need to make sure you have a handle on the following.

Know what you're buying

Your success with any investment rests squarely on your understanding of what you're buying. Know what you're paying for, whether it's an individual stock or bond, a mutual fund, or even a certificate of deposit. You wouldn't purchase an orange without first making sure it wasn't rotten; don't assume that every security being sold and touted by the so-called experts is as solid as Fort Knox. Do your own research and make your own decisions.

Understand and be able to live with risk

After you move beyond bank savings accounts, certificates of deposit, and mutual fund money market accounts, you enter the world of ever increasing risk. Whether you invest in individual securities or in mutual funds (which are nothing more than pools of individual securities), the price of those securities can rise (which you hope for) and also fall (which you dread).

Risk is inherent in the investment world. Whether you buy small pieces of companies (stocks, or equities) or lend companies and/or governments money (bonds, or debt instruments), your money is only as secure as the company or companies you've tied it to, as well as the general economic conditions both in the United States and around the world.

In other words, if you can't even contemplate that your savings may be worth less next week, or even next year, than they are today, you may want to reconsider plunging your money into a junk bond fund. (Junk bonds are loans to companies that Wall Street has serious doubts about, so they're considered risky.) Instead, you may want to consider a mutual fund that purchases nothing but U.S. Treasury bonds and notes (very, very safe).

If you own an investment that's keeping you awake at night, there's no crime in selling it, whether at a profit or a loss. Even if you don't sell a security at its absolute height, you need never apologize for making a profit. Likewise, if your investment is leaking value, remember that this isn't a sinking ship and you're not the captain. Jump overboard and live to invest another day.

Balance risk and expectations against future monetary needs

Not every great investment is a great investment for you. If you want to gamble on which company will be the next Microsoft or IBM, you need to have the luxury of time to allow that company to develop and grow. You may need to be patient; many start-up companies struggle initially, and the big payoffs, if they do develop, develop over time.

If you're going to need to make that next tuition payment in the not-so-distant future (within the next five years), you may want to temper your level of risk, keeping a larger portion of your savings in cash and cash equivalents such as money market funds or certificates of deposit. I'm not saying that you can't invest your teenager's college savings funds in Wonder Widget, Inc.; you may want to only invest a small portion of those savings in it, and keep the majority of your money invested in less risky ventures.

Identify the cost

Just because you invest directly with a mutual fund company or through an Internet brokerage doesn't mean that you're going to avoid paying anything for the privilege of investing your money. Face it: People aren't in this business for their health; they're in it to make money. And they make a lot of it. And as far as purchasing individual securities, the cost of each transaction is usually right there on your confirmation slip.

Still, identifying exactly what a mutual fund costs you may be difficult because the management costs may be buried deep inside the prospectus. Search for it. A company may charge its fee based on a percentage of the value of the assets within a fund, or it may charge a percentage of income collected. Know how the fees in your accounts are calculated, and then factor that into total return for that fund.

Choose your mutual funds carefully. Excessive fees can eat into your savings as easily as market declines. The end result, less money in your account, is the same.

Read the fine print about total returns

Every mutual fund company offers literature about how well its fund has performed against other similar funds and about the percentage of increase (or decrease, but those numbers tend to be in much smaller print) the fund has realized over time. The literature probably also touts the expertise of the fund manager (who chooses what to buy and what to sell within the fund).

Unless your fund's manager is an expert crystal-ball reader, these numbers are of historic value only. Mutual funds tend to follow the trends of the overall stock and bond markets, and their fortunes rise and fall in concert with the markets. Past performance isn't an indicator of how the fund will do for you, and the bygone wizardry of a fund manager may never be repeated.

Taking advantage of giveaways

You get something for nothing very few times in life, and money-back offers from credit cards and from retailers may or may not qualify as one of those times for you. Still, if you can take advantage of an offer without spending any additional money to do so, well, you would be foolish not to.

Credit card offers

Many credit cards are now offering a rebate equaling 1 percent of your total purchases towards a Section 529 plan (see Chapters 5 through 8) for yourself or your child. This plan may be in addition to, or instead of, other incentives that credit cards often offer, such as air miles, travel insurance, rental car insurance, and double warranties.

If you don't handle credit cards well, this may be an offer you want to avoid. The 1 percent incentive will be more than swallowed up by any interest or other fees the credit card company will charge you.

On the other hand, if you use a credit card anyway, you may want to investigate changing card companies to avail yourself of the offer. Doing so won't put your child through school; however, every dollar that someone else puts into your savings plan is one less dollar that you need to find.

Upromise and BabyMint

In a unique twist on the credit card theme, Upromise and BabyMint have devised a scheme by which they sign up retailers, manufacturers, restaurants, and various sorts of service providers who gift a percentage of your spending into a general account maintained by Upromise or BabyMint. The funds in these accounts can then be invested in a Section 529 plan. For example, a major gasoline company may offer you 1 cent per gallon, an office supply store may give 2 percent of your total purchases, and the return on a new car or home could be in the hundreds.

Granted, these are all small amounts by themselves, but just as your small weekly deposits of savings add up over time, so do these. Depending on how many of the associated stores and products you use and how much you spend, your savings here could be substantial. You can find out all the details on the companies' Web sites at www.upromise.com and www.babymint.com.

Dealing with Debt

Your debt probably hinders your plans to save money for college the most. You may find it difficult to justify putting money into a college savings account when you feel swamped by debts that need to be paid, and you may feel like you need to pay off all of your debts before you begin saving for your child's college education. Fortunately for you, you don't need to eliminate all debt before you begin to save. To show you how to save for college while drowning in red ink, discover the difference between good debt and bad debt and begin saving right now, regardless of your debt situation.

Understanding good debt and bad debt

The good news: Some types of debt are good, are factored into your monthly budget, and shouldn't hinder you from saving for college. The bad news: Some types of debt are bad, should be paid off as quickly as possible, and hinder you from saving for college.

Clearly, you're not planning on paying off your entire mortgage before you start saving for college, at least if you intend for your children to begin college before their hair turns gray. And you probably feel the same about your car payment, which is factored into your budget as a transportation cost, and any student loans that you may still have outstanding.

Even after you finish paying off the loan amounts for your house, your vehicle, and your education, those items should still have value to you. And from a credit-worthiness standpoint, since most credit rating companies expect you to have some form of this debt, the fact that you have these sorts of loans actually makes you more attractive as a potential borrower than having no loans at all (provided that you make your payments on time). This is *good debt:* debt that you plan for, budget for, and manage appropriately.

On the other hand, your credit cards (if you carry unpaid balances from month-to-month), your rent-to-own accounts, your layaway accounts, in fact, all of your so-called consumer debts are considered bad debt, and you should reduce or completely eliminate them if possible (see the section "Eliminating most of the fat," earlier in this chapter, for ways to reduce and/or eliminate your debt). *Consumer debt* is money that you have borrowed to purchase something that is either a consumable (like groceries) or something that has a very limited life (last year's clothes, perhaps, that your teenager won't wear this year because they're no longer fashionable). Basically, after you buy things in these categories, they cease to have any monetary value.

Now, I'm not saying that you shouldn't buy food or clothing, or even that new television set. You do need to eat, after all, and watching television is still a relatively cheap form of entertainment. What you shouldn't be doing, though, is borrowing money to satisfy these needs. And that is exactly what you do when you carry balances on your credit cards. You're not only paying interest on last night's dinner, but you also may still be paying for last year's holiday gifts and your wedding dress from ten years ago.

However you dig yourself out from under your debt, you need to also break yourself of the credit card habit. Stop thinking that, just because you still have credit available, you should feel free to indulge yourself in anything that crosses your path. If you can't use your cards responsibly and pay them off in full every month, then it's time to make a plastic salad. Sliced and diced credit cards in a glass bowl can make an attractive focal point in a room, and they also serve as a powerful reminder of spending habits run amok.

Saving while in debt

Being in debt doesn't preclude you from saving money for college. Sure, it makes doing so more difficult, but the following strategies can make saving for college, while paying down debt, more manageable.

✔ **Understanding the difference between needs and wants:** *Needs* fulfill a necessary function ably, but *wants* add other elements, at a price. For instance, you need a new television. The television you need is the one tucked away on the bottom shelf: 27 inches, color, and with a remote. But the one you want is on center display: It has picture-in-picture, surround sound, and who cares how many inches it is — it's as big as the wall you plan to put it on! However, the one you *want* also costs much more than the one you actually *need.* Buying the one you need can make you just as happy, can fulfill the need for a television, and can ensure that you don't break the bank or borrow money for it (like using your credit card) and have to pay it off in installments.

As you slice away at your consumer debt and hopefully finally retire it, nurture the habit of looking at every potential purchase and expenditure from a need-versus-want perspective. Although denying yourself everything that you want may, in the end, be self-defeating and make you miserable (you're not a monk, after all, and never took a vow of poverty), constant self-indulgence will prove equally disastrous.

✔ **Learning to defer gratification until you can afford it:** No matter how badly you want that new television (whether the stripped down or deluxe version), don't buy it until you've saved enough to pay for it. Most folks see a television as a necessity, but doing without for a period of time won't kill you, and you may actually use the extra time you have to rediscover old hobbies, visit with friends, or otherwise pleasurably spend time. When the time comes to plop your hard-saved cash down on the store counter, you're likely going to be more pleased with the less expensive TV than you would be with the bells-and-whistles model that you paid for with your charged-to-the-max piece of plastic.

✔ **Using credit as a tool, not a weapon:** Consumer credit is not, by definition, a bad thing, and used properly, it can be a valuable tool. Paying for purchases using credit cards negates the need to carry large amounts of cash, allows you to pass unmolested through the checkout line at the grocery store (I'm not keen on giving out all of my personal information to someone I've never met), and at the end of the month or the year, you get an easy way to track your spending habits. Use it improperly, though, and it becomes a weapon that destroys your finances and demolishes good intentions. Be responsible: If you can't pay your credit bill in full every month, destroy your cards and use cash instead. Budgeting cash will allow you to insert a line-item for savings.

Saving Throughout the Ages

Saving money for college, beginning the instant you know you have a child on the way, is certainly the most effective approach. However, if you couldn't or didn't save money for your child's education back then, you may be behind in the savings game.

But it's never too late to begin saving for your child's education. In the following sections, I discuss the best ways to start saving today for your children's education, regardless of their age.

Beginning at birth

Saving for future events in your child's life should begin no later than the day he or she is born, but you shouldn't be the only one putting money away for that purpose. Your child eventually can help fund his college accounts, too. Use the occasion of your child's birth to open up one or more college savings plans and an account in your child's name, into which you can deposit any gifts he or she receives at birth. You can add birthday gifts and other such sums to it regularly, until your child is old enough to begin making his or her own deposits. There's no better way to show your child the benefits of saving than to have a ready-made example with his or her name on it.

Putting small sums of money aside in your child's name (with you as custodian) is great, but you may want to consider depositing larger sums into an account in *your* name (perhaps as trustee for your child, but using your Social Security number to open the account) or even using that money to start a Section 529 plan for your child. Teaching your children about money is key if they're to become successful adults, but if your child will need any sort of need-based financial aid down the road, the value of the accounts held in his name will be counted more heavily than one in your name (35 percent for your child's account against a maximum of 5.6 percent for yours).

While your child is still young, you may want to consider investing in high-growth stocks, as opposed to bonds or even money market funds. True, the risk is higher than with other sorts of investments, and you may actually see the value of your investments drop. Time, though, is on your side; traditionally, money invested in the stock market has outperformed other investments, and if you have the time (usually anything longer than five years) and a stomach that can handle the risk, your investments will probably appreciate significantly.

Getting in gear during the teen years

If you begin your child's college savings accounts at birth, by the time he or she is a teenager, you should have a tidy sum inside those accounts. Still, you're edging ever closer to that magic matriculation date, and some of your investments may not have been gold-plated. It's never too early to start saving, but it's also never too late: It's time to start superfunding your Section 529 plan, if you can.

Regarding the money you have managed to save, it doesn't matter if your investments have done spectacularly or have tanked: Now is the time to begin moving at least a portion of the value of your investments into less-volatile areas, such as bond and money market accounts. As each year passes, continue to decrease the amount you have invested in riskier stocks, and increase the amount you maintain in bonds, certificates of deposit, and money market funds. Although the potential for growth in these accounts is limited, so is the potential for loss, and at this stage, you want to know that the money you've saved is secure for your child's education.

If the writing is on the wall, and you're realizing that your child is going to need some amount of financial aid, this is also the time to start moving assets away from your child. If you have a Coverdell account for your child, you may want to convert it into a 529 plan at this point. If you choose this option, as Chapter 10 explains, the original Coverdell beneficiary must also be the 529 designated beneficiary. If you decide not to roll over the Coverdell funds into a Section 529 plan, now would be the right time to use the money in the account to either buy a computer or pay for some extra tutoring. At this point, anything you can do to give your child an academic edge may pay off in the long run; many scholarships are awarded based on merit, rather than need, and money spent now in strengthening academics may pay you back many times over down the road.

You may have been saving in a 529 plan, but your investments have done so poorly that they're now worth less than the amount you initially put into an account. If you want to keep the option of financial aid open, now may be the time to close that 529 plan that has you listed as the owner. You can then gift the funds over to your parent or another relative, and have that person open a 529 plan for your child. Because there are no earnings in the account to tax, the fact that you've just taken a nonqualifying distribution won't matter (no income tax, and no 10 percent penalty), plus you may pick up a valuable itemized deduction on your own income tax return. If you think this scenario may work for you, check with your tax advisor first.

Finding out it's never too late to start saving

Obviously, if you wait until one year before college to set up a college savings account, you probably won't have as much in it as parents who begin saving the day their child was born. You could let that knowledge defeat you: Why bother saving anything if it's too little, too late? But you can fight back.

Forget a Coverdell account at this point (unless you're able to roll over an existing Coverdell account from another child to this one). But a Section 529 plan is still the best bet. Many prepaid tuition plans will be closed to you (they require that you begin making contributions by the time your child reaches a certain grade, which you've probably already passed), but all of the savings plans are open, available, and just waiting for your money.

And, although putting money into a tax-deferred or exempt account six months before the first tuition payment is due may not make sense, remember that your child will be attending college for the long haul, and that money could earn a considerable amount inside that account before the last tuition payment is due. Consider making your first payments using current income, or Stafford or PLUS loans (see Chapter 17), and save money in your child's Section 529 plan for his later college, or even graduate-school, years.

No matter when you start, or how much you manage to accumulate, saving something is better than saving nothing. That something may mean the difference between your child being able to attend college or not, or being faced with massive debt or a smaller, more manageable amount.

Part II
Piecing Together Section 529 Plans

The 5th Wave   By Rich Tennant

"I understand different States offer different versions of a 529 college savings plan. What do you offer for a state of desperation?"

In this part . . .

Section 529 plans are all the rage in the world of college savings — and with good reason. These plans provide all sorts of tax-exempt and tax-deferred incentives to save for higher-education expenses, both at the federal and state level, and they're available to everyone, no matter how much money you earn or what your relationship to the future student is. And Congress seems to be always tinkering with these plans, providing everyone with more options and greater gifting opportunities. What more could you want?

In this part, I cover all the rules and regulations surrounding 529 plans. I provide the nuts and bolts on how to open an account (or two or three, depending on your needs). And I also show the ways to plan ahead to create the best financial result for your family with your Section 529 accounts and avoid the pitfalls that dot the road.

Chapter 5

Laying Down the Basics of Section 529 Plans

*E*ven though you probably have come across the terms "Section 529 plan" and "qualified tuition program" (QTP, for short) many times, you still may not really know what they mean. Everyone seems to be selling one, so these plans clearly must be the best thing since sliced bread and bologna, right?

In fact, Section 529 refers to a part of the Internal Revenue Code (how's that for sexy?) regarding the rules and regulations concerning qualified tuition programs. And, despite the fact that the phrases may have become so familiar that the words just drip easily off your tongue, these rules are quite complex and must be followed exactly.

Qualified tuition programs covered under Section 529 of the Internal Revenue Code are, quite simply, programs that allow you to save money or purchase tuition credits for future college expenses for a specific beneficiary in an account that is administered either by the state (yours or any other — some states allow residents of other states to participate in their plans) or by a specific college or university. You may see them called either Section 529 plans or qualified tuition programs — they're one and the same.

In this chapter, you find out what qualified tuition programs under Section 529 of the Internal Revenue Code are, how they work, why they're great, where they could be improved, and how they may be changing in the future.

Discovering the Parts of 529 Plans

Although you may come across many variations of 529 plans, all have the following component parts:

- **The plan owner:** The *plan owner* is the person who sets up the plan (and who, presumably, makes contributions into it, although other people can make contributions into a plan that isn't their own). You must be at least 18 years old to be a plan owner, and depending on the plan that you're interested in starting, you may need to be a resident of the plan state.

- **The designated beneficiary:** The *designated beneficiary* is the potential student for whom the plan owner (who doesn't need to be related to the designated beneficiary in any way) intends to provide a postsecondary education. The plan owner names this person when he or she sets up the account. You can change the designated beneficiary over the lifetime of the account, but the account must always have a designated beneficiary. Like the plan owner, the beneficiary may have to be a resident of the plan state to qualify as a designated beneficiary.

  With any luck, the person that you name as your designated beneficiary will grow up, in time, to also be a *qualified student* (see the "Making sure your student qualifies" section, later in this chapter).

- **The plan administrator:** The *plan administrator* is the state or educational institution under whose auspices the plan exists. In many cases, especially in prepaid tuition plans, the plan administrator is also the plan manager (see the next item in this list). The plan administrator lays out the rules that are specific to that plan, including how much may be contributed, what sorts of investments are allowed, when contributions may be made, and whether plans are open to only resident owners and beneficiaries, or if all may participate.

- **Plan manager:** Many Section 529 plans (particularly savings plans) are invested in a variety of mutual funds. Because states aren't in the mutual fund business, they farm this work out to mutual fund companies. These companies (and states that actively manage investments) are the *plan managers*; they're responsible for the actual investing of your money.

Figuring Out the Qualifying Criteria

Section 529 plans seem to be wrapped in qualification after qualification, but don't allow these endless lists of criteria discourage you from using 529 plans. Instead, check out how I break down those lists of qualifications so that you can easily identify whether your plan, your student, and your student's expenses meet the myriad criteria associated with 529 plans.

Funding for the professional student

You may have already investigated one or more Section 529 plans and discovered the dollar limitation that is built into each state's plan. The limits are very high, especially for the Section 529 savings plans (which can reach toward $300,000 in a single plan, depending on what state's plan you use). But if your designated beneficiary is headed for great things — such as years of graduate or professional education beyond a bachelor's degree — the limits built into a single state's Section 529 plan may not be enough to cover your costs.

If you suspect that perhaps your son or daughter is heading for medical or law school after college and nothing but an Ivy League school will do, you can fund Section 529 plans in more than one state, even if your total contributions across all plans, regardless of state, equal more than the limit for any single state. Remember, the wording in Section 529 is specifically vague, and the limits are imposed at the state level, not the federal. So long as you do not fund plans in excess of what your designated beneficiary will use during his or her postsecondary education, having more than one plan in more than one state is perfectly okay.

Making sure your plan qualifies

In order for a Section 529 plan to qualify under the IRS's rules, it must meet the following criteria:

✔ Contributions may be made only in cash, including checks, money orders, or payroll deductions, but not in stocks, bonds, or real estate.

✔ After a contribution is made into a specific plan, you may not direct the investments. You may, however, change plans once each year.

✔ You may not pledge the value of the account as security against any sort of loan.

✔ The plan or program in which you invest must provide each designated beneficiary a separate accounting.

✔ You can't contribute more into an account, or group of accounts, for the benefit of a single designated beneficiary than the beneficiary will use in the payment of qualified higher education expenses. You have to try to estimate this amount.

When you make a contribution to a Section 529 plan, you're not allowed any federal income tax deduction for the amount of your contribution (unlike many sorts of retirement plans, which defer income tax not only on the accrued earnings in the account but also on your contributions). Depending on what state you live in (and if you use its plan), you may get a current state income tax deduction for part or all of your contribution each year.

After your money is safely tied up in a Section 529 plan, interest that you earn on it isn't taxed until *distributions* (amounts of money you take out of the plan to pay your student's expenses) are made to your designated beneficiary. And, if you use distributions from these plans to pay the qualified education expenses of a student at an eligible educational institution (these are the IRS's words, not mine), accrued earnings generally aren't taxed at all (see the exceptions outlined in the section "Exceptions to tax-free distribution rules," later in this chapter).

In other words, a Section 529 plan allows you to save for college, and it exempts or defers income tax on the accrued earnings until the designated beneficiary begins taking distributions from the plan.

At this point, you may be thinking that the only educational institutions that these plans are qualified to pay for are colleges and universities. Not true. Qualified institutions include all postsecondary schools that are eligible to participate in U.S. Department of Education financial aid programs, including many vocational and technical schools, community colleges, and even some apprenticeship programs. Eligible institutions don't need to be located in the United States; many foreign colleges and universities qualify. The standard here is that the schools must be eligible; they don't actually have to participate in these financial aid programs. Check with the institutions you or your student are interested in to be sure that they qualify.

Making sure your student qualifies

Strangely enough, the things you think of when the phrase "qualified student" comes to mind (grades, commitment, drive, and so on) have absolutely nothing to do with the IRS's definition. For the purpose of Section 529 plans, a qualified student must meet the following criteria:

✔ He or she needs to be the original designated beneficiary of the plan or, in the case of a tax-free plan rollover (see the section "Transferring and rolling over plans," later in this chapter) to another beneficiary, must be a member of the same family as the original beneficiary in one of these listed relationships:

- Spouse

- Child, grandchild, or great-grandchild (a lineal descendent)

- Stepchild, stepmother, or stepfather (but no stepgrandchildren)

- Brother, sister, stepbrother, or stepsister

- Father, mother, or grandparents (a lineal ancestor)

- Niece or nephew

- Brother or sister of your mother or father

- First cousin
    - An in-law, either mother, father, sister, brother, son, or daughter
    - Husband or wife of any person on this list
 ✔ He or she must actually be an enrolled student at a qualified educational institution.

Making sure expenses qualify

When I went to college, a fancy car, a nice apartment, and spring breaks in exotic locations were part of the package for many of my classmates. (My package included public transportation, shoe leather, university housing, and vacations in lovely downtown Baltimore — watching traffic going to the Orioles games was very exciting!) Of course, this was before the days of any qualified tuition plans, let alone Section 529 plans, so the question of what was a qualified expense and what wasn't never entered the discussion. It was more a question of what your parents could afford and were willing to spend.

Things have changed a little in the intervening years. Now, although all the extra perks are still the norm for many students, parents (and other relatives) who fund Section 529 plans need to be very conscious of what constitutes a qualified higher education expense and what doesn't. (Trips to Cancun, unless part of your child's specific university program, and a sports car won't make the grade.) Table 5-1 lists qualifying higher education expenses.

Distributions from 529 plans that pay for *nonqualifying* expenses *will* qualify for income tax on the earnings portion (not on the amount of your contribution into the plan). Your student will also pay an additional 10 percent tax on the income, otherwise known as a penalty, unless she qualifies for an exception (see the section "Exceptions to tax-free distribution rules").

Table 5-1	Qualified Higher Education Expenses for 529 Plans	
Type of Fee	*Full-Time Student at an Eligible Institution*	*Part-Time Student at an Eligible Institution*
Tuition	Yes	Yes
Room and board (paid directly to educational institutions)	Yes	If enrolled half time or more, yes; otherwise, no
Room and board (paid directly to other landlord and grocery store)	Yes, to extent allowed by budget amount set by school	If enrolled half time or more, yes, to extent allowed by budget amount set by school; otherwise, no

(continued)

Table 5-1 (continued)

Type of Fee	Full-Time Student at an Eligible Institution	Part-Time Student at an Eligible Institution
Fees (as required by the institution)	Yes	Yes
Books, supplies, and equipment (including computers)	Yes, to extent allowed by school	Yes, to extent allowed by budget amount set by budget amount set by school
Expenses of a special-needs beneficiary necessary for enrollment at an eligible institution	Yes (regulations defining qualifying expenses are still pending)	Yes (regulations defining qualifying expenses are still pending)

All eligible schools are now required to provide you not only with the price of what you will pay them directly (tuition, fees, and often room and board) but also the total cost of what they expect an academic year to cost. This is called the *budget,* or the total cost of attendance, and includes tuition, fees, room and board, books, supplies, insurance, transportation, and miscellaneous items. Remember, even though the total budget amount may be higher, only the expenses in Table 5-1 are qualified for payment from a Section 529 plan.

Qualified expense limitations

The amount of qualified expenses you may be able to use Section 529 plan distributions to pay for are limited if you fall into any of these categories:

- ✔ If your qualifying student receives tax-free educational assistance (outright grants and scholarships), the amount of expenses that would otherwise qualify will be reduced by the amount of the tax-free aid.

- ✔ If your qualifying student is also the beneficiary of a Coverdell Education Savings Account (see Chapters 8 through 10) and receives distributions from that plan, all qualified expenses need to be divided proportionately between the two plans. You can't double dip, or take the full amount of qualifying expenses from each plan.

- ✔ If you want to take the Hope and/or Lifetime Learning Credits on your income tax return, you need to use taxable income to pay for at least a portion of your student's qualifying expenses. See Chapter 17 for a discussion of what expenses qualify for these credits and how they work.

Exceptions to tax-free distribution rules

Beginning in 2002 and currently scheduled to end after December 31, 2010 (the "sunset provision"), distributions made from Section 529 plans for payment of qualifying educational expenses are free from federal income tax (state income tax rules may differ — check with your state). The federal government has found an effective way to provide incentives for you to send your children to college; however, it has also built in many safeguards to make certain that you don't abuse its kindness.

When taxable distributions do occur, the federal income tax is paid by the designated beneficiary, not by the contributor(s) to the plan (rules regarding state income tax vary by state). Often, the rules aren't clear, even to the IRS, or your situation may be ambiguous. Don't hesitate to seek advice here.

The following are instances where the designated beneficiary may be required to pay a federal income tax on distributions from a Section 529 plan:

- ✔ **Using plan distributions to pay nonqualifying expenses:** If the designated beneficiary takes a distribution but doesn't use it to pay qualified expenses, he or she is basically out of luck. The accrued earnings on that distribution will be taxed at normal income tax rates, plus an additional 10 percent for trying to pull the wool over the government's eyes. The news here is not all bad, though; if only a part of the distribution is used to pay nonqualified expenses, the entire distribution isn't tainted. Only the earnings on the portion that didn't pay qualified expenses will be taxed.

- ✔ **Terminating a plan, because the designated beneficiary chose not to continue his or her education or because some money is still left in the plan after completing that education:** When a plan is terminated (rather than rolled over into another plan or beneficiary), the earned income that's distributed, whether to the designated beneficiary or the plan owner, along with the original contribution amounts is taxable. In addition, it's subject to the 10 percent additional penalty. Likewise, if the plan contains more cash than the designated beneficiary will use for qualified higher education expenses, the income portion of that excess distribution is taxable, and the 10 percent additional tax applies.

- ✔ **Taking plan distributions from an institutional plan before January 1, 2004:** If you set up a plan with a specific college or university or a consortium of colleges and your designated beneficiary begins to take distributions before January 1, 2004, for qualified expenses, he or she will have to pay the income tax on the accrued earnings, but not the additional 10 percent. Unfortunately, the tax-exempt distribution rules for institutionally administered plans don't come into play until January 1, 2004; fortunately, because institutional plans only came into being in concept in 2002 and in actuality in 2003, not too many people should be affected.

✔ **Distributing funds on account of the death of the designated beneficiary:** If you need to distribute funds to a beneficiary's estate or to someone other than the designated beneficiary of the plan, due to the death of that beneficiary, the earned income portion of the distribution is taxable; however, no additional 10 percent tax is assessed.

✔ **Making distributions due to the long-term disability or impending death of the designated beneficiary:** In much the same way as insurance companies can now prepay life insurance policies to terminally ill patients without any adverse tax consequences, the IRS now allows distributions from Section 529 plans to be made to terminally ill beneficiaries and to beneficiaries with a long-term and indefinite disability. The earned income portion of these distributions is taxable, but no 10 percent additional tax is assessed. You do need to provide the IRS with a doctor's note to qualify for this exemption.

✔ **Using the Hope or Lifetime Learning Credits:** To the extent that you use certain qualified educational expenses to qualify for the Hope and Lifetime Learning Credits (see Chapter 16), those expenses will no longer qualify for tax-free treatment, even if you paid for them from your Section 529. The earnings portion will be taxed, with no additional 10 percent tax; again, no double dipping is allowed.

✔ **Receiving education benefits that are excludable from gross income:** If you're fortunate enough to receive qualified scholarships, veteran's assistance, funds from employer tuition-reimbursement plans, or other tax-free benefits (excluding gifts, bequests, or inheritances), the earnings on Section 529 plan distributions are taxable only if the amount of the 529 plan distribution is less than or equal to the amount of other tax-free educational assistance. There is no 10 percent additional tax. For example, if your student's qualified expenses equal $20,000, he receives a $20,000 tax-free scholarship, and you make a $20,000 distribution to him from his Section 529 plan, he will pay income tax on the earnings portion of the 529 plan distribution, but no penalty, even though none of the distribution is being used to pay qualified educational expenses. From the IRS's standpoint, it's enough that it would have been used for that purpose if your student hadn't received the scholarship.

Contributing to a 529 Plan

Contributing to a 529 plan may seem quite simple — you write the check or get the money automatically withdrawn from your checking account, and those funds get deposited into the 529 plan. That much may be true, but you still need to review the restrictions in this section so that you know who can contribute to 529 plans and how much can be contributed so that you avoid — as much as possible — any complications, such as the tax man.

Figuring out whether you can contribute

Anyone can set up a Section 529 plan (whoever creates an account under Section 529 is considered the plan owner). You don't need to be a parent, grandparent, or even a doting aunt or uncle. You don't need to meet any relationship test. You can even set up a plan and name yourself as the designated beneficiary if you're planning on going back to school.

In fact, the rules regarding who may contribute are so broad that you really need to consider only one major factor before you open a Section 529 plan: Make sure that you have a designated beneficiary (who already must have a Social Security number) in mind and, if he or she's not a sure thing, one or two beneficiaries in reserve. Section 529 wasn't devised to allow you to save money tax-deferred for any other purpose (you have your retirement accounts for that). If, at a later date, your named beneficiary turns out to be a less than sterling student or decides to forgo higher education altogether, you may change your designated beneficiary through a tax-free rollover into a new account or just by changing the name of the designated beneficiary on the account (see "Transferring and rolling over plans," later in this chapter). The new beneficiary, however, must be related to the original one, as described in the section "Making sure your student qualifies," earlier in this chapter.

Estimating how much you can contribute

In establishing Section 529 of the Internal Revenue Code, Congress and the IRS didn't set express limits on how big these plans could be. They had a tacit understanding that higher educational expenses couldn't be accurately gauged and that annual increases bore no relation to the rate of inflation or any other such economic measurement. If they truly wanted to be responsive to the needs of many to be able to sock enough money away, they knew the plans had to be nonrestricting in their contribution limits but not so open-ended that people could stash fortunes away inside these plans.

The IRS set no specific dollar limits on the amount of money you may contribute into an individual plan, either annually or over the life of the plan. Instead, it limited the amount you could contribute to the amount of qualified expenses your student is going to need for higher education. This is where you'll have to do some guessing. Although there is no dollar limit, if you contribute more than your student will eventually spend on qualified educational expenses, the deferred earnings on any amounts that you contribute over and above will be taxed when you distribute them. The earnings are also subject to an additional 10 percent tax.

Before you consult your crystal ball regarding how much you think you should contribute, you need to take into consideration Gift and Generation-Skipping Transfer Tax issues and individual state contribution limits.

Gift and Generation-Skipping Transfer Tax considerations

Section 529 plans were devised to allow all people, regardless of their annual income, to save very large sums for higher education expenses. Because there are no annual contribution limits, you may be tempted to sell the family farm and put all that cash into one or more plans. If this sounds reasonable to you, you need to remember that contributions that you make into a plan for any person (other than yourself or your U.S. resident spouse) are subject to the gift and/or Generation-Skipping Transfer Tax (GSTT) rules (see Chapter 3).

The gift tax regulations include one unique provision, applicable only to Section 529 plans. You may contribute up to five years' worth of annual exclusion gifts ($55,000 in 2003, or 5 x $11,000) in one year. If you're married, your spouse can do the same, enabling you to push $110,000 into a plan for one designated beneficiary in a single year (for more info on gift splitting, see Chapter 3). Should you choose this option, you must file gift tax returns for each one of the five years, claiming your annual exclusion gifts. Furthermore, any additional gifts that you make in the five-year period are then subject to the gift tax or GSTT.

Gift and Generation-Skipping Transfer Tax returns (Form 709) aren't for the weak of heart. Find a professional with expertise in this area (many pros don't have it). Mistakes here are costly, and if they're discovered after the death of the donor (that's you), they're impossible to fix. Don't take that chance!

Contribution limits imposed by the states

The federal government doesn't impose any specific dollar limitation on the maximum contribution into Section 529 accounts for a specific beneficiary. But the code section is intentionally vague. And most plans are administered by the individual states: They have far more definite ideas as to the actual dollar amounts necessary to see your children through four years of college.

State-imposed contribution limits vary by state, and the state law that governs your account will be the state in whose plan(s) you are investing, not the state in which you live. Thus, you can invest money in a high-limit state, even if you live in a low-limit state. Also, be aware that states have the ability to change their limits (and often do), increasing them as tuition costs climb.

You really need to shop for plans. Although every state has plans either established or under development, some states limit participation in their plans to state residents, and some states offer a variety of different plans. Some states give you a current income tax deduction or tax credit for contributions into their plan, and some, but not all, follow the federal rules and treat the earned income portion of withdrawals as tax-exempt. The appendix in the back of this book lists state plans at the time of publication. In addition, you can access every plan through its sponsoring state's Web site or through college saving Web sites such as www.savingforcollege.com.

Don't rely totally on Web sites for information regarding a specific plan. If you have any questions or see conflicting information, contact that plan manager, who will have the latest info on the plan in question.

Contribution limits aren't per account, but per designated beneficiary. Your designated beneficiary may have more than one Section 529 plan set aside for his or her use; however, the total aggregate account size in all plans in a particular state can't exceed the limit for the state in which the plan resides. States don't share info, though, so if you begin to bump against the ceiling set by one state, you can open a plan in another state. Just make sure that all the money in all of your plans is used to pay qualifying expenses for your student; the income portion of any excess will be taxed and penalized.

Picking Your Plan

I will never forget my high school American history class, where the only lessons I carried away with me were multicausation and that the story of the United States was the ongoing push/pull between the federalists (those who wanted a strong central government) and the states' rights supporters.

Section 529 plans clearly illustrate that the discussion is far from over. The code section is a federal one, the application is almost entirely on the local level, and every state's rules are slightly different. So this is where things get interesting. You know that, in theory, this type of plan makes sense for you and your family, but you're not quite sure what type of plan you should invest in and where.

Discovering the different plans

Not all Section 529 plans are alike. They all have different contribution limits. Some plans allow only residents of their states to participate, while others open their plans up to everyone.

There's an even larger difference in plan types, however. Original 529 plans were all done on the basis of prepaying tuition; the more common savings plan (which is what most people think of when they think of 529 plans) is a later addition, designed for greater flexibility but perhaps more risk.

Prepaid tuition plans administered by the states

Prepaid tuition plans, as the name suggests, are just that: the purchase of tuition to a particular school or group of schools ahead of when your student will attend. The state (in 2003, about one-third of states had a prepaid tuition option) or a particular school may administer them (see the next section, "Prepaid tuition plans administered by educational institutions").

In general, prepaid tuition plans, or contracts, allow you to purchase future tuition at current costs. For example, assume that your son will be attending a local state university in 2006, where current tuition is now $4,000 per year, but which you expect will cost $5,000 per year by the time he attends. You have $16,000 available (you just sold one house and didn't plow all the proceeds back into a new one, perhaps), and you invest it in a prepaid tuition plan while tuition is still just $4,000 per year. If you purchase the equivalent of four years of tuition at its current cost (4 years x $4,000 = $16,000), when your son is ready to attend school, the proceeds from the plan will pay all of his tuition costs (4 years x $5,000 = $20,000). By purchasing $16,000 worth of tuition now, you expect to receive $20,000 worth of tuition down the road.

If, on the other hand, he chooses to attend a college or university whose tuition costs at the time you invested in the plan were greater than $4,000, the plan will pay a percentage of the higher tuition equal to your original contribution's value against the other school's higher cost. If he attends a school that cost $10,000 at the time the plan was purchased (but that now costs $16,000 per year), the prepaid tuition plan would pay 40 percent of the cost of his tuition at the time he entered the higher-priced school, or $6,400 per year. In this scenario, your initial $16,000 investment in your son's education reaps you $25,600 worth of tuition when he actually attends.

With a prepaid tuition plan, your money is guaranteed to buy a certain amount of tuition. You don't need to buy all the tuition at one time — you can buy any part of one or more years — but whatever amount of money you put into this type of account is guaranteed to buy as much tuition in the future as it would on the day that you put it in.

Just because you think that you're buying a sure tuition payment at the end of the rainbow, don't bank on it. Many states don't absolutely guarantee full tuition payments at the time your student attends, even if that's what you thought you purchased. And because the entire rationale of prepaying tuition is based on the assumption that the amount of income earned on your investment will at least equal the increase in college tuition, many states have found their prepaid tuition plans to be a losing proposition. If the value of your investment isn't keeping pace with tuition inflation, most states do provide a state remedy so that you probably won't need to find additional cash to pay for the shortfall between the actual value of your investment at the time you need to cash it in to pay for tuition and the real cost of tuition. Every plan is different, and plans (and state legislatures) can change funding provisions as the need arises. Stay current, and don't invest in any plan until you have read, and understood, the most recent plan provisions.

Whether or not your state plan carries a guarantee, Section 529 prepaid tuition plans are trying to ensure a certain payback at a certain time. Because of this, these plans carry several restrictions that Section 529 savings plans don't. Check these restrictions carefully. Among the limitations are the following:

- ✔ Most plans carry restrictions as to who may participate. Usually either the owner of the account or the designated beneficiary is required to be a state resident at least at the time the account is established.

- ✔ Most plans carry restrictions as to what colleges, universities, and community colleges are covered by the plan. Generally, the state schools are covered; tuition coverage at private colleges and universities within the state is spotty, and tuitions out of state, while not entirely out of the question, can be problematic. You need to check what schools are covered before signing up for a particular plan.

- ✔ Many prepaid tuition plans cover only tuition costs. Room, board, and other fees have to be paid at the time your student is attending, from current income or other savings, like a 529 savings plan.

- ✔ Most prepaid tuition plans have a limited enrollment/contribution period each year. If you plan on or are currently investing in a plan, don't miss your window of opportunity.

- ✔ The contribution limits for prepaid tuition plans are significantly lower than for Section 529 savings plans; if you're attempting to use a 529 plan to transfer a lot of money to a designated beneficiary and to defer or avoid income tax on the earnings, the prepaid tuition option may not be the best vehicle for you.

- ✔ If you need to cancel the plan for any reason, be aware that normally fees are charged for terminating the account. In addition, many plans limit the amount that you receive on cancellation to either your contribution amount (less cancellation fees) or your original contribution plus some small percentage of income.

- ✔ Distributions on behalf of the designated beneficiary currently are counted as being totally available to pay tuition, and thus may decrease financial aid eligibility (see Chapter 17).

Prepaid tuition plans administered by educational institutions

If you know for certain and beyond any reasonable doubt that your child or grandchild is going to attend a certain school in the future (your alma mater, perhaps, because you've already donated the fieldhouse and the science lab?), an institutional prepaid tuition plan may be just the ticket for you.

Since 2002, educational institutions have been allowed to offer their own prepaid tuition plans. These plans are essentially the same as state-run prepaid tuition Section 529 plans, except that individual institutions (or consortiums of colleges and universities) administer them and the contributions that you make are restricted to use at that particular college or university or that particular group of schools. Make sure that your institution has a plan already in place; not many schools have signed on at the time of this writing.

The rules governing these plans are the same as for the state-run plans. Contribution limits vary from school to school, depending on current tuition costs.

Like all other 529 plans, those administered by an educational institution are transferable; if your designated beneficiary decides to attend a different school, you can transfer your account to another plan administrator (see the section "Transferring and rolling over plans," later in this chapter). In addition, if your designated beneficiary chooses not to attend school at all or receives some sort of free ride, you can make a tax-free rollover and name a new designated beneficiary, so long as the new beneficiary falls under the allowed relationship rules (see the section "Making sure your student qualifies," earlier in this chapter).

Savings plans

Savings plans are probably what comes to mind when you think of 529 plans. The Section 529 savings plan option broke open the world of college savings, offering truly huge tax advantages to the wealthy and the not so wealthy.

A Section 529 savings plan is, in many regards, an investment account. Although states may establish the rules, most of these state-sponsored plans are actually administered by mutual fund companies, or fund managers. Having a fund manager in charge of your money has many benefits, including the fact that these companies hire investment professionals, who you hope will wring a better return out of your money than the state will.

That's the theory, anyway, and for several years in the 1990s, when the stock market soared, it was the practice, as well. These funds far outperformed anything the states could do (the states tend to be extremely limited in the investments that they can make with your contributions into a prepaid tuition plan). The fact that you may have had to pay a broker's sales commission to enter the fund and that you were also paying annual management fees to the fund manager made little difference. Your investment was increasing in value. Though your actual contributions into the plan may have been modest in size, visions of college *and* graduate school began dancing in your head.

Stock markets don't always soar, however, and investment markets that are staggering under the weight of years of unsound economics, burgeoning budget deficits, rampant unemployment, and questionable accounting practices tend to affect all mutual funds, including Section 529 funds, negatively. Many investors have watched the value of their savings plans shrink well below their initial contribution amounts. And now, adding insult to injury, the fund managers, who make their money even when the markets are doing poorly, haven't chosen to waive the fees they charge to manage these accounts. Imagine!

Still, if you envision your son or daughter giving the Latin valedictory address at Harvard at some future date, saving in a prepaid tuition plan isn't going to fill the bill for you. Section 529 savings plans offer several advantages over their prepaid tuition relatives.

✔ Maximum allowable account size is usually far greater, between $200,000 and $300,000 per designated beneficiary (depending on the state in which you are investing and adjusted periodically as tuitions and other expenses rise).

✔ The value of the plan is counted as an asset of the owner, not the student, when applying for federal financial aid. When applying for financial aid, if the plan owner isn't either the parent or the child, the amount of money in the plan isn't included at all in the federal financial aid formula; it may, however, be counted in other formulas the colleges use to determine additional need-based financial aid awards.

✔ Distributions from Section 529 savings plans can be used for all qualified higher educational expenses, not just tuition.

✔ When planning how much to contribute to your Section 529 plan, you don't need to project costs only for undergraduate school; these plans can be used to pay for graduate schools, as well.

✔ If your savings haven't produced any earnings at all (your plan is worth less than the amount you put into it when you begin to take distributions), you may claim a loss on your income tax return in the year in which you finally fully distribute the plan. When the amount you have been able to distribute over the years is less than the total of your contributions (your basis), you may deduct the difference between your cost and the amount distributed as a miscellaneous itemized deduction on Schedule A of your Form 1040. This provision adds insult to injury: Not only has your investment lost money, but your deduction will be reduced by 2 percent of your adjusted gross income.

Guaranteed savings plans

Although all Section 529 plans are created equal under the terms of Section 529 of the Internal Revenue Code, clearly the states don't agree with that, severely limiting the size of traditional prepaid tuition plans in comparison to savings plans. Also, the U.S. Department of Education hasn't figured out that it should treat plans the same. Instead it gives preferential treatment to savings plans while determining that distributions from prepaid tuition plans are a financial resource that reduces need on a dollar-for-dollar basis, thereby limiting financial aid packages and the awards of outright, need-based grants.

In an effort to address these disparities, a few states have started a movement to meld the two types of plans into a hybrid: the guaranteed savings plan. Guaranteed savings plans follow all the rules and requirements of Section 529 of the Internal Revenue Code and qualify for the same preferred tax treatment as prepaid tuition plans and savings plans.

Each state that offers these plans at the time of this writing (Colorado, Ohio, Pennsylvania, Tennessee, and Washington) has a slightly different take on the same theme: a guaranteed return on your investment, based either on current tuition rates in that state or a stated interest rate, recalculated each year.

So far, this strategy appears to be working. For federal financial aid purposes, plan assets are being counted as the account owner's assets (not as the student's), and distributions from plans to pay qualified higher educational costs aren't considered a financial resource of the student.

The guaranteed savings plan is a sane response to burgeoning college costs, assuring low risk and reasonable (although not spectacular) growth of your savings while not tying you to the more limited contribution amounts of pre-paid tuition plans.

Contribution limits in these plans are generally the same as for savings plans administered by those states (except for Washington State, whose plan appears to limit contribution amounts to four-year tuition at an in-state public university — much more in keeping with a prepaid tuition plan limit).

Weighing the 529 plan features

The only thing that is certain about any of these plans is that everything that has come before is subject to change. New plans are being developed, contribution limits are always on the move, old restrictions are removed, and new ones are added. If ever there were a moving target, Section 529 plans would qualify. Still, you should be looking for certain things and trying to get answers to certain questions before putting any money into any fund.

Checking how your state income tax is affected

Section 529 plan contributions often are income-tax deductible, either in whole or in part, on your state income tax return. Often that tax deduction is limited to state residents who participate in their home state plans, but some states give a deduction for a contribution into any plan. You need to check.

You also know that distributions to the designated beneficiary of a plan, to the extent it is used for qualifying higher education expenses, are tax-exempt at the federal level. Many states follow the federal rules and offer tax exemption to the earnings on distributions from their own in-state plans. Other states exempt the earnings from any plan. Finally, some states aren't yet on the bandwagon, taxing the earnings from any plan, in-state or out.

You also should be aware that some states (those who don't follow the federal rules) may tax the deferred income earned in accounts when you make a federally tax-free rollover from one state's plan to another's. If you invest in an in-state plan and receive a deduction on your state income tax return(s) for your contributions, and then roll your account over to an out-of-state plan, you may also have to add back, or recapture, your prior deductions and pay income tax on them. If the change of plan is advantageous to you otherwise, you may just have to pay the tax and move on.

Many states lack an income tax altogether. If you live in one of these states, feel free to invest in any state's plan, because your own state doesn't provide any income tax benefit, either on contributions or distributions.

However, some states have a dividends and interest tax that taxes only — you guessed it — dividends and interest. Because the earnings on Section 529 plans consist of primarily dividends and interest, if you make a nonqualifying distribution, the earnings may be liable for this particular tax. Be familiar with the tax law governing your state and the state where your plan is located.

Transferring and rolling over plans

In the good old days (pre-2002), transferring between plans held for the same beneficiary just couldn't be done. But beginning in 2002, along with the new, tax-free distribution rules, you now can transfer amounts between 529 plans held for the same beneficiary, although you may not make a tax-free transfer more than once in every 12-month period for a single beneficiary.

Say that you have a 529 savings plan for your daughter. The plan hasn't done as well as you would like, and your daughter is going to a state university in a few years. You decide to transfer your savings plan into a Section 529 prepaid tuition plan in your state. You can buy four years' worth of tuition with the amount currently in your savings plan. Because you've kept the same beneficiary on the new plan as was on the old, the transfer is tax-free. Should your daughter decide that she wants to attend college at a neighboring state school, you can transfer your 529 prepaid tuition plan for your daughter to the new state, but you must wait for 12 months before doing so.

Tax-free transfers may be made from any type of Section 529 plan to any other type, between states (so long as residency requirements are respected), and even from Coverdell savings accounts to Section 529 plans.

You may also transfer or roll over an account tax-free to a new beneficiary at any time, if you meet the following requirements:

- ✔ You must complete the account transfer or rollover to a new beneficiary within 60 days from the date the money actually leaves the first account (the original distribution date).
- ✔ The new beneficiary must be a member of the same family as the original beneficiary, within the permitted relationships.

Finally, even if you don't roll over an account to a new account, you're permitted to change the designated beneficiary on any account at any time without any tax consequence if the new beneficiary is a member of the same family as the original beneficiary.

Opening accounts with funds from an UGMA/UTMA account

From the perspective of a child's well-being, UGMA (Uniform Gift to Minor Act)/UTMA (Uniform Transfer to Minor Act) accounts may be the worst idea since Al Capone decided not to pay his taxes (see Chapter 12). Many of you, though, when faced with the desire to start gifting away substantial amounts of wealth (especially in the rampant stock market of the 1990s), set up these accounts for your children and grandchildren. At the time, when they were babies, putting securities into these custodial accounts seemed like a great idea. The kids couldn't touch the money (at least not without the permission of the custodian), and it would be there, waiting for them, when they reached college age. What a deal — providing college money for the kids and shrinking your personal estate at the same time.

Now, though, those babies aren't babies anymore; they're getting close to those magic ages when all that money becomes theirs, and they're still incredibly young. For years, they may not know about these custodial accounts, but when they reach age 18 or age 21, they'll definitely find out about them. They'll also discover that everything in there is theirs, to use wisely or to fritter. Unfortunately, your child may be the type to fritter.

Surprise! If you want to add at least a layer of deterrent to your child's ability to squander all, or a portion, of what you've saved in an UGMA or UTMA account, you can transfer the money in an UGMA or UTMA account into a Section 529 plan if you are the UGMA/UTMA custodian. A few different restrictions will be in place, though:

✔ The funds you contribute aren't really yours — they're funds currently being held in custody for a minor child. Accordingly, although you are the plan owner until the child turns 18, at 18, the plan owner becomes the child. In other words, moving this money into a 529 plan doesn't allow you to regain control over these savings

✔ You may not choose any designated beneficiary other than the child whose UGMA/UTMA account originally funded the plan, and once the designation is in place, you may not change it.

✔ When the plan reverts to the child's ownership at age 18, he or she can take whatever distributions he or she wants, regardless of whether the money will be used for educational expenses. If the money is not used for qualified expenses, however, income tax on the earnings, plus the 10 percent penalty, will be assessed.

Using UGMA/UTMA accounts to fund 529 plans makes the money more expensive for a child to access to buy that sports car or take that trip (because of the addition of the 10 percent penalty on top of the income tax owed), but it doesn't make it impossible. Hopefully, the additional cost will make the new account owner think twice before spending the money unwisely.

Opening multiple accounts

As a plan owner, you may open as many Section 529 plans as you want, in as many locations as you can and that make sense for you, provided you have enough designated beneficiaries to go around. You may not have more than one designated beneficiary per account; however, a designated beneficiary may have more than one account set up for him or her. If you're purchasing prepaid tuition but your prepaid tuition plan covers only tuition, also investing in a savings plan often makes sense. When your student finally begins his or her college career, you'll have money in the savings account to pay all the qualified expenses the prepaid tuition plan won't.

If you come from an incredibly generous family, you may want to be certain that the aggregate amount in all the plans for one designated beneficiary does not exceed the amount of qualified expenses that beneficiary is likely to incur. Excess contributions trigger income tax and a penalty on the income portion of the balance not used for higher education expenses. However, if you do find yourself in this situation, you may want to consider changing the designated beneficiary on one or more accounts. You can even transfer it to yourself and retrain yourself in a new field or pursue a long-held interest.

Assessing the risk

Very few things in life are sure, and most 529 plans belong in the "not sure" category. Anytime you put money into securities other than savings or money market accounts, you put your nest egg at risk. Investments can fall in value as easily as they can rise, as many a dismayed investor has found.

The riskiest of all Section 529 plans are the savings plans, although not all savings plans carry the same level of risk. These plans are tied most closely to the stock and bond markets and will enjoy the same bumpy ride. The gains can be spectacular (in a strong market and with a good plan manager); the losses can be devastating. Seeing the value of your savings decrease is never easy. Watching your child's education seeping away is especially difficult.

Both guaranteed savings plans and prepaid tuition plans are much safer than savings plans, as they're usually tied to specific investments that are less volatile. Many prepaid tuition plans may invest only in state obligations (read municipal bonds), which have a fixed rate of return over their lifetime, although bond prices can fluctuate. Although your gains will not be huge, provided that you hold on to your tuition certificates or your guaranteed savings account and redeem these accounts only to pay qualified expenses, you should do all right.

Still, tuition costs often rise higher than the return on the modest investments these accounts are allowed to make. If the earnings in an account don't keep pace with tuition hikes, the state administering the plan may discount the amount of tuition you think you've purchased. You may think that you've funded four years of tuition, but you actually end up with only three.

Most states without a guarantee have provisions in place to make up any deficiencies between the earnings in their plan and the actual costs. Some states may devote lottery monies, while others may take a percentage of unclaimed property and devote this to the shortfall. Very few states without a guaranteed return on prepaid tuition plans or guaranteed savings plans lack any contingency plan at all. Carefully investigate the plan you're thinking of investing in for these safeguards.

Finally, some states absolutely guarantee that the tuition you think you're prepaying is actually going to be paid, in full, to the extent that you've purchased it. These gold-plated plans often have residency requirements for the plan owner, the plan beneficiary, or both. Check carefully.

Now, because states actually administer so many Section 529 plans, you may be wondering whether the states can liberate money you contribute into any plan and divert it to another function. The answer is unequivocally no! Money that you put into any Section 529 plan is segregated from all the other money that states collect or hold. It is segregated from all tax revenues, and the state (or plan manager) must account for it at all times. Siphoning money away from a registered account (because that's what these accounts are) is theft, even if it's done by the state.

Chapter 6

Applying Section 529 Plans to Your Household

*I*f you decide that a Section 529 plan makes sense for you and your family (see Chapter 5), the next step is putting theory into action and actually opening and funding a Section 529 plan.

In this chapter, you find all the information you could want on how, exactly, you go about doing that. You figure out how to choose the plan that's right for your situation (every plan fits someone's life, but not every plan may be right for you) and how to fund it. And, after your plan's funded, you find out how closely you should watch your investments and when you may want to consider changing them. Finally, you see what happens when the magic day arrives and you finally start making distributions from your plan to pay for the qualified educational expenses of your student.

Finding the Best Plan for You

When you're looking at most things, the cookie cutter approach almost never works, and that is especially true of financial planning and college savings. No two families are exactly alike, and what works best for your siblings and your friends and their families probably won't be what works best for you and yours. You can make your Section 529 plan(s) a success for your family, but first you need to consider exactly what your needs are.

Creating a 529 checklist

Just like shopping for groceries, clothes, or a house, you'll be most efficient in choosing a plan when you know exactly what you need before you ever look at what's being offered. Plans that have features you don't need but lack qualities that you do may work well for some people, but not for you.

Here is a checklist that you should have answers to before you start looking. Keep in mind that your answers today don't necessarily need to be your answers tomorrow; these plans are flexible and can be changed as needed.

- ✔ **Who will be your designated beneficiary?** Your plan choice may vary depending on the age of your student. You may also choose differently for your child who has a lifelong membership in the Future Doctors of America than for your child who lives with his head in a car engine.

- ✔ **Where does he or she anticipate attending school?** If your designated beneficiary is an infant or young child, she obviously can't express her college preferences — even if you have taught her every word of your alma mater's fight song. But don't despair — this is where your expectations come into play. You choose; you can always change it later.

- ✔ **What do you anticipate the cost will be of that choice at the time your student will be attending, not only for tuition but also for all other expenses?** Now it's time for you to do some homework, checking out all the expenses listed in Chapter 2 and figuring out where your child's choice slots into that equation.

- ✔ **Given your current income and future earning potential, is your student likely to qualify for need-based financial aid when the time comes?** If there's no way that you'll ever be able to pay the full amount, looking at how different types of plans are counted in the federal financial aid formula may make one plan preferable to another.

- ✔ **What state do you live in, and does your state give tax benefits either for contributions to its own Section 529 plans or for distributions from its own plans?** Does it give tax benefits to contributions and/or distributions from other states' Section 529 plans?

- ✔ **How much can you reasonably put away into a 529 plan on a regular basis, without unduly strangling your family budget and dooming you to a life of beans on toast?** You want to save as much as you reasonably can, with the emphasis here on "reasonably." You still have to live now. If you're happiest when you're squeezing the buffalo on a nickel so hard you can hear it squeal, go for it. But if life without the prospect of an occasional movie or dinner in a nice restaurant (fast food doesn't count here) seems like an endless, dark existence, you may want to save a little less and budget a set amount for current little extras.

✔ **Who's your successor-designated beneficiary (see Chapter 5 for relationship test), and who's your successor owner (see Chapter 7 for instances where that might happen)?** And will your successor beneficiary and owner meet residency restrictions your plan may have?

With completed checklist in hand, you can select a plan and begin saving.

If your and your student expect that he or she will attend either a state college or university or a community college, the first place to look is at prepaid tuition options in your own state or the state in which your student plans to attend school. But, if you see only private options, out-of-state public universities, or a graduate/professional school career in the future, you may want to look only at savings plans run by the mutual fund companies.

Looking at state-run plans

At the time of this writing, 529 plans include thirteen state-run prepaid tuition plans, five guaranteed savings plans (two of which are also prepaid tuition plans), and one plan that isn't qualified under Section 529 (Massachusetts U.Plan) but which really falls within all the other parameters and has many of the same tax advantages of state-run 529 plans. Of these plans, only Alabama and Massachusetts have prepaid tuition plans open to all, and Colorado is the only state that opens its guaranteed savings plan to everyone; all other state-run plans are restricted to resident donors, resident beneficiaries, or both.

Read the fine print carefully; plans may have restrictions beyond residency. Many limit the age at which you can set up a plan for a specific beneficiary, so you may be out of luck in a particular plan if your student is in high school already and you haven't yet begun. They may also restrict when distributions must start and when you must complete your distribution schedule.

Rates of return on prepaid tuition plans haven't kept pace with annual tuition hikes, and many prepaid tuition plans are running huge deficits and teetering on the edge of insolvency. States are dealing with this in one of three ways:

✔ **Charging increasingly large premiums for each tuition contract or unit you buy:** For example, you may have to pay 150 percent of the current cost of one year's tuition to buy one year of future tuition.

✔ **Decreasing the amount of tuition you thought you bought:** For example, you may think that you bought four years but may receive only three.

✔ **Closing the plan to new enrollments:** West Virginia, for example, closed new enrollments in its plan due to a $16 million deficit. The state has said that it intends to honor all contracts that have been purchased.

Most plans are backed by the full faith and credit of the state (which means they'll cover any losses, so you're not at risk) or by contingencies written into the statutes governing their plans that require action by state legislatures, the governor, or some other stopgap to plug the holes. But not all plans have backup plans in place. Once again, you need to read the fine print carefully.

Table 6-1 lists the prepaid tuition and guaranteed savings plans currently available. This is only a place to start. Plans can be added and dropped, and new enrollments and/or new contributions can be suspended at any time. Check with your state, or the state whose plan you're considering, for up-to-date information when you're ready to enroll your student.

Table 6-1   Prepaid Tuition (PT) and Guaranteed Savings (GS) Plans, by State

State	Plan Name	Plan	Tuition and Fees	Other Qualified Expenses	2003 Maximum Contribution
AL	Prepaid Affordable College Tuition Plan (PACT)	PT	Yes	No	$15,629
CO	Stable Value Plus College Savings Program	GS	Yes	Yes	$235,000
FL	Florida Prepaid College Plan	PT	Yes	Additional plan available	$25,724
IL	College Illinois!	PT	Yes	No	$30,342
KY	Kentucky Affordable Prepaid Tuition (KAPT) *	PT	Yes	No	$68,885
MD	College Savings Plans of Maryland – Prepaid College Trust	PT	Yes	No	$31,992
MA	U.Plan	PT	Yes	No	***
MI	Michigan Education Trust	PT	Yes	No	$24,252
MS	Mississippi Prepaid Affordable College Tuition Program (MPACT)	PT	Yes	No	$17,487

State	Plan Name	Plan	Tuition and Fees	Other Qualified Expenses	2003 Maximum Contribution
NV	Nevada Prepaid Tuition Program	PT	Yes	No	$12,250
NM	The Education Plan's Prepaid Tuition Program	PT	Yes	No	$18,360
OH	Ohio CollegeAdvantage Savings Plan	GS	Yes	Yes	$245,000
PA	TAP 529 Guaranteed Savings Plan	GS	Yes	Yes	$290,000
SC	South Carolina Tuition Prepayment Program	PT	Yes	No	$21,828
TN	Tennessee's BEST Prepaid Tuition Program	Both	Yes	Yes	$235,000
TX	Texas Guaranteed Tuition Plan	PT	Yes	No	$65,391
VA	Virginia Prepaid Education Program (VPEP)	PT	Yes	No	$34,593
WA	Guaranteed Education Tuition of Washington (GET)	Both	Yes	No	$26,000
WV	SMART529 Prepaid Tuition Plan **	PT	Yes	No	$18,320

* Contributions and new enrollments suspended until at least July 2004
** Closed to new enrollment as of Dec. 31, 2002
*** Current cost of tuition and fees for 4 years at highest-cost participating institution

In addition to prepaid tuition and guaranteed savings plans, some states also offer savings plans that they administer themselves. Most of these state-administered savings plans limit their investments to fixed income securities (bonds). And, because states aren't in the business of making money off your investments (other than by taxing the money that you do make), the fees associated with these plans tend to be very small. Investing in a state-run savings plan is fairly low risk but also provides a fairly small return on your investment. If you feel that you'd like to be a bit more daring with 529 funds (and you need to see at least the possibility of big gains in their value), you'll probably need to invest in plans administered by the mutual fund companies (see the section "Considering mutual fund plans," later in this chapter).

Finally, if you like the idea (and relative safety) of prepaid tuition plans but don't see your child attending a public university or don't live in a state that offers a plan, you may want to consider investing in an institutional prepaid tuition plan, which I discuss in Chapter 5.

Considering mutual fund plans

Most prepaid tuition plans only cover tuition (and mandatory fees). But higher educational costs only begin with tuition (see Chapter 2). All the other college costs need to be paid for, too. Whether you go the prepaid tuition route or want more choice in investments and schools where you can use that money, you may want to explore the Section 529 savings plans. These savings plans are established by the states, which then contract with *mutual fund companies,* companies whose sole business is putting money to work to make more money. And this is how these companies market themselves: They hold up their expertise and flexibility (as opposed to some employee at the state treasurer's office who can buy only certain sorts of bonds) and lure you in with pictures of past performance dancing in your head.

The truth is that mutual fund managers are pros, and if there is a way to make money in the stock and bond markets, they're very likely the ones who will figure it out. They are not, however, infallible, and many a fund has plunged in value even as the general markets have risen or stayed the same. Those past performance numbers show only how the fund has done in the past — they don't predict how any fund will perform in the future.

No matter how well, or poorly, a particular manager has done, the fact remains that if you want to invest in a Section 529 savings plan, you're almost definitely going to have to deal with the decisions of at least one mutual fund manager over the lifetime of the account because the vast majority of states farm out their investing to these companies.

Before you jump right in to a professionally managed savings account, you need to remember a few things:

- ✔ **Professional money managers don't work for free, nor are they cheap.** Management fees associated with Section 529 savings plans that are managed by mutual fund companies are notably higher than fees charged by state-managed plans. Fees widely vary; check carefully and be prepared to pay even when your account isn't gaining in value. The fund companies don't drop their fees out of the goodness of their hearts.

- ✔ **Many mutual fund plans can't be purchased except through a broker or a financial planner.** If the fund that you want can be accessed only in this way, you need to know that you're going to spend a substantial amount in order to join. Not only will you have the fund fees, but you'll also be paying a broker's commission. As you flip through the appendix in the back of the book, any fund that states it's sold only through a financial advisor has this extra fee tacked on.

✔ **Mutual fund companies make money on large accounts, not small.** Although the amount required to start in any fund varies not only by state but also by mutual fund company, many companies require a sub-stantial initial investment. You may find that you need to have between $1,000 and $3,000 just to open an account. Carefully check the plans you're interested in for minimum opening deposit amounts.

✔ **Just because a professional is managing your money doesn't mean that you can just sit back and relax.** *You* are ultimately responsible for the well-being of your 529 account, and you need to be ready to make changes when whatever the plan manager is doing is clearly not working.

Most mutual-fund managed plans, while administered by a specific state, aren't restricted in any way to only state-resident owners or beneficiaries (Kentucky, Louisiana, and New Jersey are the only exceptions at the time of publication). This lack of restrictions allows you a great deal of latitude when shopping for a plan, especially as more states rework their tax laws to allow tax-exempt distributions from out-of-state plans (most plans don't tax the income portion of qualified distributions from their own plans owned by in-state residents). You need to be careful, though, and make sure that your state not only currently follows these rules but continues to follow these rules. As states struggle to close budget gaps, the untaxed money from 529 distributions may be attractive additional sources of income. If your state changes the rules regarding income taxation of out-of-state plan distribu-tions, you may want to relocate your plan to your home state.

Opening a Plan

After you complete your research and decide what plan you want to invest in, you can obtain an application, complete it, and send it off with a check to open your account. Applications for all plans are available by mail; many states also can provide you with online application forms and downloadable forms (for the Internet savvy). If you're investing in a plan that may only be purchased through a financial advisor, obtain the application directly from that person (who'll probably be more than helpful in filling it out, as well). Be sure to also obtain, and keep, a prospectus for your plan and the plan agree-ment, which outlines all the rules and regulations governing your plan.

No matter what state's plan you invest in, whether you're investing directly with the state or through an advisor, the application process is quite straight-forward. As Chapter 5 discusses, you need to provide the information for the plan owner, the designated beneficiary, a successor owner, and parent or guardian information (if the designated beneficiary is a minor child).

Funding a Plan

After you complete your application and send it off, you need to get down to the serious business of making your 529 plan grow. And, although you'd like to think that the stock and bond markets will rocket skyward, multiplying the value of your initial investment so rapidly (and securely, of course) that you'll never have to add any more money to your account, you really do need to be sensible here. Unless you can sock away the full amount your student is likely to need when you set up the plan, you have to make additional contributions in order for this to work. Opening a plan and making an initial investment are only the start of saving enough to send your designated beneficiary to school. Consistent savings is the rest of the equation.

You can add money to a 529 plan in three ways: write a check (or money order, cashier's check, or travelers' checks), schedule automatic withdrawals from your bank account, or make contributions through payroll withholdings.

Writing a check

This contribution method may seem like a no-brainer, but for many people, it's the most difficult type of saving to do. Writing a check and actually depositing it into an account where you won't be able to pull it back out without incurring a penalty takes discipline. I know — I'm guilty of writing many a check only to tear it up months later, knowing that the money that I set aside for savings is now long gone and spent elsewhere.

If you invest in certain prepaid tuition plans (see Chapter 5), though, you may not have much of a choice. Some plans don't allow contributions except during a small window of time each year. Others, however, are happy to set you up on a payment plan (remember, in a prepaid tuition program, you purchase a set amount of tuition to a specific class of postsecondary schools).

Writing a check may work best for people whose income is variable throughout the year. If you work only in the summer and collect unemployment benefits every winter, you may want to make all your contributions in the summer, when the money is rolling in.

Although writing a check takes the most discipline, it also gives you the most control.

Automatically scheduling bank withdrawals

You may think of money in very concrete terms. The dollars and cents in your pocket have a certain look and feel, and even checks are tangible. But, most money never takes physical form; instead it whizzes around the world as bits and bites of computer wizardry. You may already use this technology, if you have direct deposits to your bank account or pay bills and fund other savings accounts in this way. Two basic types of transfers are available:

- ✔ **Wire transfers** are made on a one-time-only basis, using the Federal Reserve Wire system. You may find that this is the best option for you when opening a Section 529 account. Wire transfers can be made at any time of the banking day.

- ✔ **Automatic fund transfers** are made using the American Clearing House (ACH) system. (No, you aren't entering a sweepstakes, and no celebrity with a six-foot check is going to ring your doorbell.) These transfers are generally made on a periodic basis (every week, every month, however you choose), on a specific day of the week or month that you choose. The money transfers first thing in the morning, before the bank opens.

When setting up an ACH transfer, be certain that the money that you're transferring is really in your account. If you get paid via direct deposit on the first of every month, set up your transfer for a few days later (leaving yourself the luxury of a long weekend between receipt of the money and subsequent transfer). Often, money deposited isn't available to you to use until the next banking day, after the bank is sure that the money isn't going to be yanked back. Also be aware that, if you set up your ACH transfer on a specific day each month, the money transfers on that day provided it is a day the bank is open. If your day falls on a weekend or legal holiday, the money transfers on the first day *after* (never before) your scheduled day that the bank is open.

In order to set up an ACH transfer, you need to provide your plan administrator with a copy of a check from your account. The face of the check provides all the information necessary to put automatic withdrawals into motion (as you can see in Figure 6-1).

If you're already familiar with automatic fund transfers, you know how easy they are to use and how painless payments are when made in this way. If this is all new to you, you may need a little time to become comfortable with the idea. After an automatic transfer is in place and functioning, you may wonder how you ever managed without it.

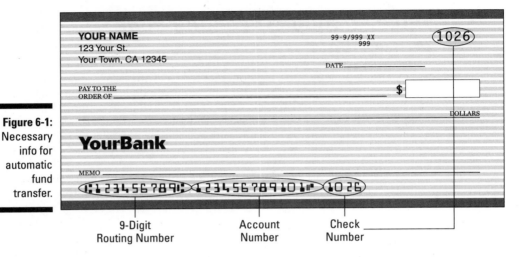

Figure 6-1:
Necessary
info for
automatic
fund
transfer.

9-Digit
Routing Number

Account
Number

Check
Number

Making contributions through payroll withholdings

Contributions through payroll deductions aren't available to everyone, but more companies are offering a payroll deduction for 529 plans. This option works just like all the other payroll deductions that you may be familiar with, such as medical insurance premiums, flexible spending accounts for medical and dependent care expenses, and tax-deferred retirement savings. Payroll withholdings offer several benefits:

- **Automatic state tax benefits, where applicable:** If you live in a state where contributions into your state plan(s) are tax-deductible, the adjustment for state taxes is made on your paycheck rather than waiting for a refund at the end of the year.

- **Flexibility:** Most people procrastinate when faced with a call to a mutual fund company or a state agency to change amounts being transferred; however, a trip down to the personnel office of your company to make a change is easy — and on company time.

- **Automatic cessation of fund transfers when employment ends:** No one wants to contemplate losing a job, but it happens. When it does, you may want to consider halting contributions into a Section 529 plan, at least until you've found a new job. If you fund your plan through payroll withholdings, the fund transfers stop when your paychecks stop.

Managing Your Investments

You know, of course, that you're not allowed to direct the investments of a Section 529 plan once your money is safely stowed in a particular plan (see Chapter 5). You do, however, have choices about where you put your money initially, and if your investments aren't doing well, you can move it once in every 12-month period without a penalty for a nonqualified withdrawal.

Selecting an investment strategy that works for you

One of the biggest complaints about early Section 529 plans (all of which were prepaid tuition plans) was the straitjacket component: These plans might have been guaranteeing tuition payments, but they weren't big on flexibility. Your major choice was whether or not to participate; once you opted in to the plan, your ability to choose investments ended.

Section 529 savings plans were created as a response to that perceived inflexibility. They've traded guaranteed tuition payments for your increased ability to select a wide variety of investment options. Of course, now that you have choices, you need to understand them to make good decisions for your money and for the future education of your designated student.

The element of risk

In the world of investments, nothing is a "sure thing." If you have retirement and other investment accounts that have risen and fallen with the financial markets, this comes as no surprise to you. If, however, this is your first serious venture into the wide world of investing, the inherent riskiness of it may come as a shock to you. No investment should ever make your hair stand on end; if it does, you may want to consider changing it.

Mutual funds are made up of either *equities* (stocks) or *debt instruments* (bonds) or a combination of both. When you purchase a stock, you're actually buying a piece of a particular company; when you buy a bond, you're lending money to that company. The income from stocks (which you receive either as a dividend or by receiving more for your stock when you sell than you paid for it) derives from the income from the company. A company that fails to earn more money than it spends rarely issues a dividend. Bond income represents interest payments on the loan you've made to that particular company.

It's all very simple in theory but may be more complicated in practice. The prices of stocks can rise and fall on the basis of rumor rather than solid financial data. Prices are often inflated on hopes and promises rather than on reality. Likewise, a fixed payment on a bond may seem secure, but if the company that has borrowed the money is on less-than-sound financial footing, the actual amount of the loan could be at risk.

To successfully invest in any mutual fund, whether it's in a Section 529 plan, a retirement plan, or just as an independent investment, you need to determine what level of risk you're willing to take. If you have trouble sleeping when the stock market is on a roller coaster, you may want to invest in bond funds (which are generally more stable in price than stock funds but which can offer a more moderate rate of return). But, if you can shrug your shoulders even when the stock market is exploring the depths, and just continue on with your life, investing in an aggressive stock fund could be just the ticket for you. The higher amount of risk should lead to a higher total return on your investment over time, if you have the patience to wait out market downturns.

Short-term versus long-term investing

When you invest in a Section 529 plan, you clearly have an idea that, at a certain time, a certain someone whom you know and probably love will head off for some sort of postsecondary education. That is, after all, why you set up the plan in the first place and why you put that person's name on the line labeled "designated beneficiary." So, whether that designated beneficiary has just been born or is already in high school, you have some idea when you might need to access this money that you've been saving.

This is where timing issues come into play. One major factor in dealing with risk is allowing yourself enough time to come back from a bad market. If you're in a market downturn but your designated beneficiary is only just starting kindergarten, you probably have enough time to sit out this particular market cycle. If you just hang on, your investments should come back to where they started and then begin to increase in value again. You do need to be patient, though. Remember, losses are only really losses when you cash out of a plan; until then, they exist only on paper.

As your designated beneficiary closes in to the magic scheduled time of distribution, you may want to think carefully about the level of risk in your current plan and begin to decrease it. Even though a more conservative approach (moving an increasingly large portion of your overall savings into bond funds and money market funds) limits the amount your investments will grow, you want to be sure that, when you need the money in order to make qualified distributions, the money is there.

Age-based management

If you don't feel that you're a savvy enough investor to make timing decisions on your own or if you don't want to have to keep track of when you should be making changes, many Section 529 savings plans have an age-based management feature that you may opt to use.

Essentially, all this option does is allocate your investment among stocks, bonds, and cash (money market funds, actually, because no money in a mutual fund ever just sits around doing nothing), depending on the current age of your designated beneficiary. When the beneficiary is very young (preschool or younger), your mix may, in fact, be entirely stocks. As he or she ages, the mix slowly moves away from stocks and toward bonds and cash.

Every 529 plan that offers an age-based management option allocates among stocks, bonds, and cash a little differently, and the ages at which shifts begin to occur aren't exactly the same, either. Investing isn't a precise science.

Management through asset allocation

In addition to age-based management, many plans also offer *static investment options,* or access to funds where the asset mixture stays the same over time. You may have a choice of a fund that's 100 percent stocks, one that's 100 percent bonds, or any mixture of the two. In addition, your plan may offer a mutual fund that invests only in foreign investments. Or your plan may offer a mutual fund that works like a money market fund: In a money market fund, your initial investment is protected (it won't decrease in value), but your growth in the fund is limited to the amount of interest currently being earned in money market accounts.

Choosing to invest through asset allocation can be a double-edged sword. When you invest in this way, you essentially take on the responsibility for shifting from higher-risk funds to lower-risk funds as your student ages. You will need to be the person in charge of timing changes in investment strategy, and if you don't end up with a brilliant result, the fault will be yours. Of course, if your strategy pays off (and you know it will — that's why you're doing this), your market savvy will become the stuff of family legend.

On the other hand, investing through asset allocation makes tremendous sense for people who aren't certain when (or even if) their designated beneficiary is going to begin his or her postsecondary education. If you have doubts about the future plans of your current designated beneficiary, maintaining flexibility through asset allocation allows you to continue on with a successful investing strategy long after the time age-based management would have begun changing your investment mix to a lower-risk, lower-return one. If you find yourself in this position, you may want to continue to manage through asset allocation, at least until your current beneficiary begins to make some concrete plans or you change your beneficiary designation to someone else.

Identifying and changing a strategy that has gone haywire

It's sad to say, but not every child attends college or the college of your choice, not every savings plan works (the road to hell being paved with good intentions), and not every investment strategy miraculously causes your money to grow rapidly and safely. Life is littered with good planning that has failed, for one reason or another. The beauty of Section 529 plans is that they do not staple you into one box but rather allow you to make changes, within reason, as your life's circumstances change. (Chapter 7 discusses changes in beneficiary designations and savings shortfalls and overflows in detail.)

Investment strategies that fail to live up to their advance billing are a big reason why many savings plans fall short of the mark. Investment returns aren't guaranteed, and your investment in a fund is only going to do approximately as well as the general market. When the markets rise, so will the value of your investment; when they fall, so will your account value.

Section 529 savings plans don't come with a safety net. There are no state guarantees of your contribution amounts *or* the amounts that may have accumulated from interest and dividends. If you contributed $10,000 last year, it may be worth only $8,000 this year, and it'll buy only $8,000 worth of qualified educational expenses for your designated beneficiary.

Be aware of the performance of your funds over time. You can exchange a fund that isn't living up to your expectations for another fund, either within the same plan or as a rollover of your current plan to a different Section 529 plan of any type. If you find that your investments have lost value and that there is no way that you'll be able to save enough for your designated beneficiary's education at an Ivy League school, you may opt to roll over all or part of your current savings plan into a prepaid tuition plan that will pay tuition at a state college or university. If any balance remains in the original 529 plan after you purchase all your prepaid tuition contracts, you can distribute it to the designated beneficiary to pay qualified expenses that aren't covered by the prepaid tuition plan.

If your Section 529 savings plan investments are doing poorly and you choose to make a change, you need to know that you may make a tax-free rollover from one plan to another only once in a 12-month period. If you change plans more frequently, any transfers after the first count as taxable distributions, subject to both income tax on any income and the 10 percent penalty. Of course, if the value of the plan has dropped below the amount you have contributed to it, this may not be a problem, as there won't be any income to tax or penalize. See Chapter 5 to find out the tax consequences of a loss.

Whatever your tolerance for risk, don't stay with an investment that continues to do poorly. Set a limit for how much you're willing to lose from your account (10 percent, 20 percent — it's your money, your limit, and your choice). When your investment starts to approach that lower number, it's time for you to start doing some research again and to make a decision.

Taking Qualifying Distributions

You've saved, you've invested, and amazingly enough, your investments have grown. Now, your designated beneficiary is ready and raring to head off to college, and you actually have the money you need. What could be better?

In the somewhat odd world of Section 529, where taxability doesn't follow the ownership of the account (remember, you own the account even if you had to file gift tax returns for giving the money that's in the account away to the Section 529 plan), the beneficiary (not the owner) bears all the income tax consequences of distributions made to, or on the behalf of, him or her.

Depending on the state and the type of plan you own, distributions are made directly from the plan to the school (this most likely occurs with a prepaid tuition plan) or to you or your designated beneficiary. If checks are being written to you or your beneficiary, make sure that you create a good paper trail, showing exactly what qualified expenses were paid with the distribution amounts. Remember, it's not enough that you have a qualified student and that student is actually attending an institution of higher learning; you also need to use the distributions from your 529 plan to pay those expenses.

Assuming that (a) your designated beneficiary is now a qualified student and (b) that student is now incurring qualified expenses, you now need to figure out just how much of a distribution you should make from your Section 529 plan. In calculating this number, here's what you need to do:

- ✔ **Estimate how much the qualified expenses are likely to be, not only this year but also for the remainder of this student's education.** If you think that your savings may be a bit short, spending them all in one or two years may make sense if you need to make up the balance by using current income. Spread them out over the lifetime of the diploma or degree your designated student is working toward. If you think that your student may qualify for need-based financial aid (see Chapter 17), spending down the amount in the 529 plan in the first year or two may be to your advantage down the road.

- ✔ **Explore what other resources are available to make up any gaps in funding.** If you don't have the total cost of all qualified expenses sitting in your Section 529 plan, you'll probably have to pay some portion of qualified expenses from your current earnings. If you also have a Coverdell Education Savings Account for your student, a portion of qualified expenses may be paid from there, as well (see Chapter 9).

- ✔ **Consider any outright grants and scholarships that your student may be entitled to.** To the extent that any sort of scholarship, fellowship, or grant money is available, it always offsets qualified tuition expenses first. The income portion of any 529-distribution amounts that are not used to pay qualified educational expenses is generally treated as taxable income to the recipient.

✓ **If you want to take the Hope or Lifetime Learning Credit, you need to pay at least some qualified expenses using real, taxable income.** This includes wages, taxable interest and dividends, rental income — you get the picture. You have to admit that this idea makes sense; you really shouldn't get a tax credit for expenses that you paid with tax-exempt income.

If, at the end of the day, you've taken too large a distribution from your Section 529 plan, well, the world as you know it doesn't really end. To the extent that the distribution exceeds the amount of qualified education expenses, the income portion on the overage will be taxed at the designated beneficiary's tax rate, which is usually lower than your own. In addition, unless the excess distribution amount is one of the qualified exceptions outlined in Chapter 5, the student will also pay an additional 10 percent penalty on the income portion only of the nonqualified amount.

Taking nonqualifying distributions from a Section 529 plan will cost your beneficiary money, but the sky won't fall in. Just don't make a habit of it.

What Does Uncle Sam Have to Say?

Section 529 is a federal code section under the Internal Revenue Code. It's not surprising, then, that the IRS has some input into documentation and reporting requirements. Always keep in mind that the IRS is not in the business of making the laws or implementing policy (Congress is supposed to do that); its job is to enforce the laws that are on the books.

Reporting contributions: Income tax versus gift/GST tax

Very little in Section 529 qualifies as easy to understand — but this does. There is no current federal income tax deduction for contributions made into a Section 529 plan. You don't need to disclose to the IRS that you have a Section 529 plan on your income tax return (your Form 1040, 1040A, or 1040EZ). It doesn't matter how much money you earn; if you have the money to put into a plan, you can contribute it, no matter your income.

Finally, there's no limit to how much you can contribute in a single year or how many plans you can fund. If you have six potential students you want to put through college, you can. You can even fully fund a plan, any plan, and as many plans as you want, in one lump sum, up to the stated plan limit, in a single year, although you may have gift and/or Generation-Skipping Transfer (GST) tax considerations.

The rules regarding reporting contributions for gift and GST tax returns are a bit more complex, and you may decide early on to seek professional advice. Smart choice! However, here's a quick overview:

✔ If you make gifts of less than $11,000 in 2003 to any one person (including the contribution you make into a Section 529 plan for that person), even if that gift isn't to your child, you don't need to file a Form 709, the U.S. Gift (and Generation-Skipping Transfer) Tax return.

✔ If you make contributions into a Section 529 plan of between $11,000 and $55,000 for a single designated beneficiary, you need to file a Form 709 for this year, and for the next four years if you make any additional gifts in those years. In each year, you show the total amount of the gift and the amount of the gift eligible for annual exclusion status. If the amount that you give is less than $55,000, then you will report one-fifth of the total amount in each year. You make this election on the tax return itself, which is due at the same time as your income tax return. You need to make the election only once, in the first year; in the subsequent four years, if you don't make other taxable gifts, you're not required to file a Form 709 for those years. If you're gift splitting with your spouse, both of you need to file a Form 709 in the first year, and both of you need to make the election for spreading the gift over five years.

✔ If you make contributions into a Section 529 plan in excess of $55,000 in any single year for any single beneficiary — or $110,000 if you can split the gifts with your spouse (see Chapter 3) — you can still elect to spread $55,000 over five years. The balance of the amount over $55,000, though, is entirely taxable in the year the gift is made. Be certain to make the proper election on your gift tax return to get the five-year treatment.

✔ When you contribute an amount that's in excess of the annual exclusion amounts to a 529 plan for a beneficiary who isn't your child, you need to know where this person fits on the generational scale, for Generation-Skipping Transfer Tax (GSTT) purposes. If the person is your relative, this is easy to figure out — your children's children constitute one generation skipped, your niece's child is one generation skipped, and so on. If the designated beneficiary is not related to you, the generations are calculated by using your age as the benchmark as follows:

  • For someone born not more than 12½ years after you, he or she is considered to belong to your generation and is therefore not a skip person.

  • For someone born between 12½ and 37½ years after you, he or she is considered to belong to the same generation as your children and is therefore not a skip person.

  • For someone born between 37½ and 62½ years after you, he or she belongs to the same generation as your grandchildren. Gifts made into a Section 529 plan also qualify for GSTT treatment.

Gifting tuition outright versus gifting into a Section 529 plan

In one of the oddities of the Internal Revenue Code, you can make tax-free gifts of an unlimited amount of qualified tuition (although not room, board, or any of the other expenses that are qualified under Section 529) to any student without being shackled by annual exclusion amounts.

If you discovered the joys of Section 529 late in your designated beneficiary's secondary school career, you may find that the amount you need to fully fund a Section 529 plan will exceed your annual exclusion amounts, even with the five-year election and gift-splitting. In such a case, pushing all the money he or she will need for all qualified educational expenses into a Section

529 plan might trigger a taxable gift. To avoid this, you may choose to put only a smaller amount, the amount that your beneficiary might realistically spend for qualified educational expenses other than tuition, into a Section 529 plan. The amount that you'll need to pay tuition alone can be paid, without limitation and without any gift tax consequences, directly to the educational institution when the tuition needs to be paid.

Unlimited gifts of tuition can be made for tuition at any school, from preschool through graduate school, if you write your check to the school and not to the student (or his or her parents).

Whenever you make a gift larger than your annual exclusion amount to anyone who is more than one generation removed from you, that gift becomes subject to the gift tax *and* the GSTT rules (Chapter 3 has info on these taxes).

Reporting distributions

After you figure out the contribution reporting requirements, you need to know how and where to report distributions, both qualifying and nonqualifying, for income tax purposes.

When you receive any distribution from a Section 529 plan, the plan manager is required to furnish to the person receiving the distribution (or the person on whose behalf a distribution is made) a Form 1099-Q by January 31 of the following year. On this form, you'll see the total distribution in Box 1, the earnings portion in Box 2, and your basis (the amount you contributed over the years) in Box 3. Box 2 and Box 3 added together should equal the amount in Box 1.

The good news is that, although you'll receive this form, you determine what, if any, of your distribution is taxable. If you know for a fact that the total distribution made to you paid for qualifying educational expenses (if the plan wrote the check directly to your college or university, that's a safe bet), then all you need do is keep the 1099-Q safely stored with the rest of your tax information so that you can defend your position if any question arise later.

If, however, you know that some or all of the distribution was not used for qualifying expenses, then you need to sit down, do some calculations, and arrive at the amount of taxable income you should include on the line labeled "Other Income" on your Form 1040.

For example, say a student received a distribution from his parents' Section 529 plan for $20,000. He also received a scholarship in the amount of $2,000. His qualifying expenses at his university were $15,000. Box 2 of his 1099-Q shows $3,500, while Box 3 shows $16,500. To arrive at his taxable income from this distribution, he must make the calculation shown in Figure 6-2.

Figure 6-2:
Figuring out taxable income from a 529 distribution.

Total qualifying educational expenses	$15,000
SUBTRACT: Scholarship amount	− 2,000
Net qualifying educational expenses	$13,000
Total distribution from Section 529 Plan	$20,000
SUBTRACT: Net qualifying educational expenses	−13,000
Total nonqualifying distribution from Sec. 529 Plan	$7,000
Ratio of nonqualifying to total distribution	$7,000/$20,000 = 35%
Taxable portion of nonqualifying expenses	$3,500 × 35% = $1,225

Because, in this example, the parents have distributed more than the amount of qualified educational expenses to their student, he pays tax on the earnings portion of the nonqualified distribution. In addition, he also pays the 10 percent penalty on the earnings included in the amount of nonqualified distribution he would have received if he didn't have the scholarship (in other words, he's not penalized for someone giving him free money).

Current income tax law contains sunset provision

Congress giveth but is afraid to giveth too much. Members of Congress aim to win popularity contests every two or six years, and the distant future, they figure, will look after itself.

Accordingly, the tax-exempt status of distributions from Section 529 plans used to pay qualified educational expenses is set to fade into the sunset on December 31, 2010. After that date, unless the deadline is extended or the tax-exempt status is made permanent, all earnings from Section 529 plans, regardless of what they're used for, will be subject to income tax on the beneficiary's income tax return in the years that distributions are made.

My son won't reach college age until 2013. Although I'd like to think that Congress will act rationally and reasonably about this matter, I also know that budget deficits can only burgeon so much before an atmosphere of fiscal responsibility takes over. I'm not banking (literally) on being able to make tax-free distributions to my son; on the other hand, Section 529 plans are a wise choice even without the tax exemption for earnings. Long-term tax deferrals allow my money to grow faster than if I had to pay tax on earnings as they were earned, and my son will almost certainly pay tax in a much lower tax bracket than I do. It's not quite as beautiful as tax exemption, but as a scenario, it's still hard to beat.

Reporting for purposes of future financial aid awards

Just like no two Section 529 plans are identical, the response to how these plans affect financial aid awards varies widely and by type of plan.

Currently, distributions from prepaid tuition plans seem to have the most adverse effect on need-based financial aid packages, as each dollar you take as a distribution is currently offsetting one dollar of potential aid. The states are clearly looking at prepaid tuition plans as a direct reduction in the cost of attending an institution, and not the plan owners' assets, and are assessing payment ability accordingly.

Savings plans are currently being treated completely differently under the federal formula used to determine need-based aid eligibility. They are considered an asset of the plan owner and are therefore counted as a parent asset if the parent is the account owner and as a student asset if the student is the account owner. A plan that is owned by Grandma Ida, for example, is not even looked at when the student applies for federal financial aid, although it may be if the aid is coming directly from a specific college.

Because your student needs to apply for financial aid for each academic year that he needs assistance, the receipt of any nonqualifying distributions from a 529 savings plan in one year may result in a smaller need-based aid award in the subsequent year or years. It appears however, that, so long as distributions are made only for qualifying expenses (and therefore the student doesn't need to declare any income from the distribution on his or her income tax return), the distributions won't affect subsequent aid eligibility under current rules.

Chapter 7

Weighing the Pros and Cons of Section 529 Plans

*I*f you discover anything in your research about Section 529 plans, it's probably that there's no such thing as a simple answer and that sometimes these plans won't suit your needs at all. A 529 plan also isn't for you if your income is very low and you pay tax at the lowest rates, because your student will probably receive full grants. Likewise, if your student is going to give Einstein a run for his money, he may receive a free (or partially assisted) ride to some fabulous institution and won't need the full amount of your savings.

For the rest, though, Section 529 plans, either by themselves or in concert with other college savings devices, may make a great deal of sense. In this chapter, you find out the benefits of having a Section 529 plan. However, because no plan is perfect, I also alert you to some potential problems of these plans and show you how to work around them.

Pondering the Pros of Section 529 Plans

In Voltaire's *Candide,* Dr. Pangloss is forever talking about "the best of all possible worlds." Well, in the best of all possible worlds, 529 plans are a wonderful, marvelous creation that can pay all qualified postsecondary educational bills (and may even cure the common cold if invested correctly). In any number of scenarios, if you pick the right plan and the right investment strategy for your student, you and your student win. It's as simple as that.

Higher returns than traditional savings and investment accounts

Saving money is the name of the game, but saving efficiently (and accepting help when offered) is the best way to go about it. Although the federal and state governments won't actually start a savings account for you or put money into one that you've opened, they do provide tools to help your savings grow.

Section 529 plans offer three ways by which your savings can grow faster than they would if you invested them in an ordinary investment account or in your local savings bank:

- ✔ Tax deferrals (postponing when you pay tax)
- ✔ Tax exemptions (not paying any income tax at all on earnings)
- ✔ State income tax deductions (sometimes being able to exclude your contributions from your income in the year that you make the contributions)

Here's how it works. George and Hannah, who are Maryland residents, have a baby in 2003. They don't have any savings in the bank, only the money that they currently earn, so they know that paying college costs 18 years down the road may be tough. George and Hannah think it's wise to start planning now.

They do their research and begin implementing their decisions as soon as the baby arrives. Their first decision is to open a Section 529 plan, and their second is to opt for four years of paid tuition in Maryland's prepaid tuition plan, which offers not only tax-free qualified distributions but also tax-free contributions. They both attended the University of Maryland, and they feel they received a fine education. It seems like a good choice for their baby.

George and Hannah know that the next 18 years are going to pass quickly and that their son will be heading off to the University of Maryland (or any other college or university, but they're loyal alumni, so Maryland seems the obvious choice) in 2020. By religiously making their payments into the plan, they know they'll have four years' worth of tuition credits when the time comes. They expect that their son, who they expect will be a motivated student, will complete his degree in four years, graduate, and start his working life with a reasonable job in a reasonable company.

Figure 7-1 shows a comparison of how well George and Hannah will do by investing in Maryland's prepaid tuition plan as opposed to just saving in the bank for college expenses. Several options are included — prepaying the entire amount in a lump sum, using a 10-year payment plan with annual payments, a 5-year payment plan with monthly payments, and a 17-year payment plan with monthly payments. All comparisons assume that Congress will make the tax-free nature of distributions permanent, that Maryland will continue to provide tax deductions for contributions (and won't alter the terms of its plan in any way), and that college tuitions and outside investments will both increase by 5 percent each year.

Figure 7-1: Comparing saving in a Section 529 prepaid tuition plan with saving in an ordinary investment account, using Maryland (MD) income tax rates.

Description	Using Section 529 Plan			Not Using Section 529 Plan		
	Total Amount of Contribution	Income Tax Paid on Earnings Used to Fund Plan		Amount of Contribution + Investment Return @ 5%	Income Tax Paid on Earnings Used to Fund Plan, Plus Investment Income in Year Earned	
		Fed (25%)	MD (4.8%)		Fed (25%)	MD (4.8%)
2003 lump sum payment	$25,022	$6,256	$0	$25,022 +33,417 $58,439	$14,610	$2,805
10 yearly payments of $3,395	$33,950	$8,488	$0	$33,950 +30,047 $63,997	$15,999	$3,072
5-year monthly payment of $499	$29,940	$7,485	$0	$29,940 +32,074 $62,014	$15,504	$2,977
17-year extended monthly payment of $216	$44,064	$11,016	$0	$44,064 +25,458 $69,522	$17,381	$3,337

Although the tuition will be the same, whether or not Hannah and George have a Section 529 plan, the amount of money they have to supply will not. Even if they fund a savings account with exactly the same amount of money as they fund an equivalent 529 plan, they'll have to pay federal and state income tax annually on income being earned. In addition, although no federal income tax deduction is allowed for contributions made into a 529 plan, Maryland provides one (as do many other states). In fact, if Hannah and George put their money into a traditional savings or investment account, they may pay between $10,000 and $12,000 more in tax in the years leading up to college than they would have if they'd funded a 529 prepaid tuition plan.

This example uses fairly generous rates of investment return and relatively moderate rates of tuition increase. Real life rarely follows planned examples exactly. If you're not using a Section 529 payment plan, you may need to adjust your budget and your savings accordingly.

Figure 7-2 illustrates how your money may grow in a 529 plan and how the same amount of periodic savings (whether you use weekly, monthly, or quarterly deposits) will cost you more if you put it into conventional investments outside of a 529 plan. As in Figure 7-1, which shows how the numbers work if you save the same amount each month, all numbers assume a 5 percent annual rate of return, and federal income taxes are calculated at 25 percent. No adjustment is made for state income tax (each state is individual in this regard), and most savings plans don't carry residency restrictions.

Savings per Month	$200 per Month		$300 per Month		$500 per Month	
	Sec. 529 Plan	Ordinary Account, after Tax	Sec. 529 Plan	Ordinary Account, after Tax	Sec. 529 Plan	Ordinary Account, after Tax
Year 1	$2,466	$2,450	$3,699	$3,674	$6,165	$6,124
Year 2	$5,058	$4,990	$7,587	$7,486	$12,645	$12,476
Year 3	$7,783	$7,631	$11,675	$11,447	$19,458	$19,079
Year 4	$10,467	$10,374	$15,701	$15,561	$26,168	$25,934
Year 5	$13,658	$13,221	$20,487	$19,832	$34,145	$33,053
Year 10	$31,186	$29,184	$46,779	$43,777	$77,965	$72,961
Year 15	$53,681	$48,454	$80,522	$72,681	$134,203	$121,136
Year 18	$70,131	$61,883	$105,197	$92,824	$175,328	$154,707

Figure 7-2: Comparing saving in a Section 529 savings plan with an ordinary investment account.

Figure 7-2 clearly shows that, over time, you'll save much more money if you don't pay tax currently on your earnings. If you live in a state that has a state income tax on investment income but that follows the Section 529 federal rules, the disparity between the Section 529 funds and the ordinary investment funds becomes even greater. Regardless of what your total rate of return is (and no one has any accurate idea what it will be until it's actually earned, although it could be much higher or lower, depending on market conditions and how aggressively you invest), saving money costs you less when you can save in a tax-deferred or tax-exempt account.

Flexibility of funding

Suppose that you're like George and Hannah — settled in one place with no plans to move — and you'd like nothing better than to see your children graduate from one of your state's colleges or universities. In that situation, investing in your state's prepaid tuition plan (if it has one) makes wonderful sense. But you don't have to be like George and Hannah in order to take advantage of a 529 plan, because there are not only state-run prepaid tuition plans but also savings plans and college-run prepaid tuition plans. So, if you're saving for the day your child goes to almost any sort of postsecondary school, some 529 plan out there should fit your needs, whatever they are.

Take, for example, Lisa and Sean, who have a newborn and a 15-year-old for whom they haven't begun saving. Because they're always on the move from one state to another, they don't think that investing in a prepaid tuition plan will work for them because of residency requirements built into so many of them. They also like having very few restrictions on where their children can attend postsecondary school. They decide to invest in a 529 savings plan.

With two children of very different ages to save for, Lisa and Sean can open Section 529 plans for each of them but fund the plans unequally, putting more into the older child's account to beef up savings there and then superfunding the younger child's account after the older child finishes his education. If any money is left in the older child's account after his education is complete, Lisa and Sean have the option of making a tax-free rollover (see Chapter 5) of the remaining balance into the younger child's account.

No taxes to pay (at least for now)

Saving money is saving money, whether you put cash into a savings account or cut needless expenses. Section 529 plans help you to do both. While you're busy stashing as much away as you can, you're also, at the very least, postponing any income tax reckoning. You may be eliminating it altogether.

When your distribution program finally begins, any tax on accumulated earnings within the plan is paid by the person to whom, or for whose benefit, the distribution is made. So if you make the distributions for your benefit, you pay the tax; if your designated student is someone else (and it usually is), that person is responsible for any income taxes owed. Currently, as Chapter 6 shows, the income portion of distributions that pay qualified educational expenses aren't being taxed at the federal level at all, and many states are following suit. Congress may choose to make that exemption permanent, but even if it doesn't and the provision sunsets in 2010, you and your student will still realize great tax savings by using a Section 529 plan.

For example, suppose that you manage to save $200 per month for 18 years in a 529 account, and that money invested earns a 5 percent rate of return. If you don't pay any tax, Figure 7-2 shows that you'll have $70,131: your contributions of $43,200 and interest and dividends of $26,931 that you've earned over the 18 years. If you take a qualifying distribution in the first year of college of one-fourth of the total, your distribution will be $17,533, of which $10,800 is your contributions (and therefore not taxed, because you've already paid federal income tax on them), and $6,733 represents the income portion of the distribution. If the distribution is made for the benefit of your student for qualifying expenses (and if the sunset provisions described in Chapter 6 are allowed to expire), your student will show $6,733 as income on his income tax return. If your student pays tax at a 10 percent rate, the income tax on that amount will be $673. If the remaining money in the account continues to earn 5 percent per year and the student continues to be taxed on the income portion of all qualifying distributions for the next three years, the total tax paid by the student over the four years of distributions totaling $75,699 will be only $3,253.

On the other hand, suppose that same $200 was invested each month in a traditional savings or investment account (see Chapter 12) and that account earns 5 percent per year in income. Because the income is taxed in each year that it's earned, after 18 years, the account value is only $61,883 ($8,248 less than the 529 account funded with the same amount of money). The amounts available to be distributed to the student are also less. If remaining balances continue to grow at 5 percent per year over the four years of college, the distribution amounts are $15,471 in the first year, $16,066 in the second, $16,680 in the third, and $17,326 in the fourth, for a total of $65,543, or $10,156 less than the total distributed from the 529 account. And, if the parent (not the child) owns the account, the income earned in each year is taxed at the parent's rate (usually higher than 10 percent), not the child's.

This example clearly shows the benefit of tax deferrals, even when the income portion at distribution time isn't completely tax exempt. The fact that you've postponed paying tax lets your money grow faster than if you pay tax yearly on your earnings. The tax-deferred account allows larger distributions to your designated beneficiary for exactly the same dollar cost to you.

Working Around the 529 Shortcomings

Tax deferrals, higher investment returns, and funding flexibility are all powerful motivators, and they may be just the enticements you're looking for when shopping for a way to invest your savings for college. But all good things carry a price tag, and Section 529 plans are no exception here.

A 529 plan can carry some unexpected, sometimes unavoidable, and often less-than-optimal consequences, such as in the following circumstances:

- If you save too much or too little

- If the plan owner or the designated beneficiary dies

- If your designated beneficiary decides, for whatever reason, not to continue beyond high school

- If you need to rescue the money you've saved to pay for one of life's surprises that often hit you in the face when you're least expecting it

If you're aware of what can happen ahead of time, however, you may be able to minimize the damage.

Finagling financial aid implications

The impact that owning a Section 529 plan has on the amount of financial aid available to your student has been the topic of much discussion. And if you aren't able to save the entire amount you need, you and your student will have to fill out the dreaded U.S. Department of Education's Free Application for Federal Student Aid (FAFSA) form to determine eligibility for federal financial aid based on the federal methodology. You may also have to complete other aid forms required by individual colleges, who calculate your needs completely differently, using the institutional methodology.

Information that you provide on the FAFSA determines how much your family is expected to contribute to your student's education. If the cost of that education is higher than your expected family contribution (EFC), your student is eligible for low-cost loans, possibly need-based grants, and/or scholarships. See Chapter 17 for more info on EFCs and the FAFSA.

No matter how you slice it, if you're the owner of a 529 plan and you, your spouse, or your child is the designated beneficiary, your financial aid award will be affected. The extent to which it's affected depends on several factors:

- **The type of plan you own:** A prepaid tuition plan is counted far more heavily in the financial aid formula than a Section 529 savings plan, and it will reduce your student's financial aid award on a dollar-for-dollar basis because it is considered upfront as a direct reduction in the cost of attendance.

- **The amount of the taxable earnings portion of the annual distribution:** To the extent that a distribution has a taxable component that is shown on the student's income tax return, 50 percent of that amount (after being adjusted for the student's income protection allowance) will be included in arriving at the family's expected contribution, regardless of whether the distribution is made from a prepaid tuition plan or from a savings plan. Currently, tax-free distributions are not included on the FAFSA; however, no regulations prohibit the U.S. Department of Education from requiring disclosure of even tax-free amounts in determining need or changing its view on the asset classification of 529s, and it may choose that path in the future.

- **The value of the plan if it's owned by a parent:** If you own the plan for the benefit of one of your children, the current value of it needs to be included as a piece of your net assets on your student's FAFSA even if the Section 529 plan is not for the benefit of the child applying for aid. Although you don't have to list your assets separately, you may be required to substantiate any number that appears on the FAFSA.

> ✔ **The relationship between the plan owner and the plan beneficiary:** If you're the owner of a savings plan and your child is the beneficiary, a maximum of 5.6 percent of your 529 plan is factored into your student's expected family contribution. If you're the owner and you (or your spouse) are the beneficiary, that percentage increases to a maximum of 35 percent if you have no other dependents, less if you have dependent children. If you own a plan for the benefit of a grandchild or a nonrelative, the value of your plan is excluded from any aid calculation.

If, after FAFSA has calculated your student's expected family contribution, the amount available to you in your Section 529 isn't adequate to meet the contribution amount, you may need to explore other funding sources, including scholarships (see Chapter 16), federal work-study funds, and student loans (see Chapter 17).

When the plan owner dies

Dying is not something you (or anyone) want to contemplate, and especially not before completing the job you've started: educating your children. But sometimes it happens. If it happens to you, you want to be certain that you've left all your affairs as tidy as you can. And that includes your 529 plan.

Different government agencies differ in opinion on who actually owns the assets in a Section 529 plan, and they have conflicting rules. As a result, the death of a plan owner can have some interesting, and sometimes unfortunate, consequences. Remember, should you fail to plan adequately, the Section 529 plan(s) that you own could become part of the residue of your estate and be disposed of in accordance with either the terms of your last will (if you were smart and wrote one) or according to the laws of *intestacy* (what happens to your stuff if you die without having a valid will) in your state.

Should your family members find themselves dealing with the aftermath of your death, you won't be around to help them to sort it out. Make sure that your affairs are in order now, and then make certain that they stay that way.

Transferring plan ownership

All plan applications have a section to designate a successor account owner; many have an additional section to designate an alternate successor account owner. Don't ignore these sections, and remember the names you write in the spaces. If one of your choices for successor owner dies or moves to another state (for states where an owner must be a resident), update your account information with your plan manager. Whoever is deemed the plan owner at any given time can change the beneficiary designation. Be certain that whoever is on your list for successor ownership of your 529 account has the same plans in mind as you did when you established the account.

This advice may seem simple and obvious, but many a plan has come to grief through death and divorce. Take, for example, David and Lilly. David, a widower, has a daughter from his first marriage, for whom he has set up a Section 529 plan. When he marries Lilly, he names her as his successor plan owner. David and Lilly go on to have two children of their own. Five years later, David dies suddenly, and Lilly becomes the plan owner.

As a result of David's death and Lilly's assuming ownership of the 529 account, she's now in control of the assets. She and David's daughter have never seen eye-to-eye, and Lilly decides to change the beneficiary designation to one of her children. Because Lilly's children are half siblings to David's daughter, this beneficiary change is allowable. The money David saved to send his own daughter to college is now being used to send David and Lilly's child to school, and David's daughter needs to fend for herself.

Keep your successor owner designations current. Check them at least annually, and never put off until tomorrow what you can do today. There's no fixing this mess after it happens.

If you're not sure whom you'd like to name as your successor owner, you can set up a specific trust and name the trust as successor owner. Provided the trust is a resident in the state where you also live (for Section 529 plans that have a residency requirement), it should qualify as a successor owner. You do need to find trustees who will honor your wishes, including successors in case one or more of your named trustees is not able to serve, but once you have that all in place, you'll never worry about a successor owner designation again. Consult an attorney to draw up the trust instrument, and make sure that it follows all the necessary rules and regulations for your particular 529 plan.

Gift/GSTT Consequences

If you've been able to superfund your Section 529 plan, taking advantage of the five-year election explained in Chapter 5, where you give up to $55,000 per donee in a single year and then plan to spread those gifts out over five years, you need to read this.

Section 529 plans have a unique place in the rules and regulations surrounding Gift and Generation-Skipping Transfer (GST) tax. After you put the money into the plan and designate a beneficiary, it counts as a completed gift. From the perspective of the Gift and GST rules, you've given up "all right, title, and interest" in the money. Except you really haven't. Provided the money you've gifted goes into an account that you own, you remain the plan owner and are therefore in control of the assets. You can change the investment strategy (but not the investments themselves), and you can even change the beneficiary, to the point of terminating a plan entirely and taking the money back. You will pay a penalty, but you'll have your money back. So much for giving up "all right, title, and interest."

Still, because the IRS considers the gift a completed transfer, you're entitled to use your annual exclusion to gift money into these accounts (see Chapter 3). And, when you die, because you've given the money away previously (even though you really haven't), it's not counted in your estate, even though you are (or were, because you're now dead) the plan owner.

The only piece that may be pulled back into your estate and counted for estate and/or the GST tax is that amount that you superfund (see Chapter 3). If you die during the five years that constitute your election period, any amounts for which you haven't filed a gift tax return yet, if you were required to file one, are included in the value of your estate.

For example, Moe sets up 529 accounts for his two grandchildren. He puts $55,000 into each one in 2002 and makes the election on his 2002 Form 709 (U.S. Gift and GST Tax Return). He doesn't make any other gifts to the kids in the following years, so he isn't required to file any more gift tax returns. Moe passes away in 2004. Because he was alive during only three of the five years of his election period, his estate tax return must include $44,000 (2 years x $11,000 annual exclusion x 2 grandkids), even though the money is safely tucked away inside the 529 plans. The money for the annual exclusion amounts that would have been made had Moe not died doesn't return to his estate; only the value does for the purpose of calculating Moe's estate tax.

Estate tax consequences

With the exception shown in the preceding section, when a five-year election has been made in order to jump-start a Section 529 plan and then the plan owner dies before the end of the five-year period, there are no estate tax consequences for the plan owner. Even though you may be considered the plan owner while you're alive, the account carries sufficient restrictions to give the appearance that you lack total control over the account, even before your death. None of the assets appear on your estate tax return, and your estate pays no additional tax due to your ownership of these plans.

Death of a designated beneficiary

Sometimes the unthinkable happens, and the person for whom you've been saving money all these years dies. In these situations, the rules governing Section 529 nonqualified distributions, rollovers, transfers, and terminations ease, although they don't entirely disappear.

If a distribution was made to the beneficiary, or to his estate after his death, and the distribution wasn't entirely used for qualified educational expenses, the income portion of that amount is taxable to the student or his estate on the appropriate income tax return. Because it was clearly not the student's intention to use the money for nonqualified expenses, the 10 percent penalty is waived.

And that is usually the only tax consequence to the designated beneficiary, or to his estate (assuming that he does not have a taxable estate, because the distribution does become part of his estate). Because you remain the plan owner (and therefore nominally in control of the plan assets), what happens next with the remaining money in the account is your call.

You have a plan that has no designated beneficiary (as I explain in Chapter 5, having a designated beneficiary is a requirement of 529 plans), so you need to name a new one or terminate the plan. As in any change of a designated beneficiary, you can merely change the designation in an existing account, add the funds from the old account to a different existing account for a new beneficiary, or roll over the funds from the old account into a new account.

Even if you've already done a tax-free rollover within the last 12 months or changed your investment strategy in an existing account, any rollover will be tax-free (provided it is completed within 60 days). The 12-month rule is suspended when a designated beneficiary dies. The IRS recognizes that you are not doing this through choice, but necessity.

Regardless of which direction you choose to go with the account — same account, different account, or new account — the new beneficiary needs to pass the family relationship test as discussed in Chapter 5.

Finally, should you choose to terminate the account and retrieve your savings, you'll have to pay income tax on the accumulated earnings in the account, but the 10 percent additional penalty will be waived.

Making choices if your child skips college

When little Joey grows up, he may no longer want to be a rocket scientist but would rather spend his life surfing. Or maybe Catherine's biggest desire has shifted from studying the law to living on a Katmandu commune. Life and differing expectations sometimes throw curveballs at you, and what may have been your desire doesn't fit into the game plan of your designated student.

When you save in a Section 529 plan, you're not saving for a certain event but one that has a reasonable probability. And sometimes your reasonable expectations are not realized, and the money that you saved specifically for that purpose won't be needed. That's when you can gnash your teeth, rip out your hair, and scream at the heavens because, had you known, you would have put all that money into a traditional investment account (see Chapter 12), paid the income tax on an ongoing basis, and never given any thought to how to deal with this unforeseen set of circumstances.

Section 529 does offer you some flexibility when you face the problem of money in your account but no qualifying student to spend it. Still, the day you first understand that you didn't need to do all this planning for this student is the day you have to begin calculating what to do with the funds you've saved.

Changing beneficiary designations

When you realize that your designated beneficiary isn't going to attend college, your first thought may be to change the designated beneficiary on the account. Good thought. If you have more than one student for whom you bear some financial responsibility, you can do one of three things:

- ✔ Change the beneficiary name on the existing account
- ✔ Open a completely new account for the new beneficiary
- ✔ Roll the value of the old account into an already existing account for the new beneficiary (provided, of course, that the total of the two accounts doesn't exceed the state limit on account size)

So long as you change the designated beneficiary to a new beneficiary who bears a family relationship to your previous designated beneficiary (as explained in Chapter 5), these maneuvers will have no adverse effects on you, your old beneficiary, or your new one.

You can change the designated beneficiary of an already existing Section 529 plan at any time, for any reason, so long as the new beneficiary passes the relationship test in Chapter 5. If you or your spouse can pass the relationship test, you can even choose yourself as the new designated beneficiary (isn't there some degree you've always wanted to pursue?). Unlike tax-free rollovers between plans with the same designated beneficiary, you aren't limited to making a beneficiary change only once in any calendar year.

You may also choose to terminate an existing account (suppose that your former beneficiary is a resident in one state, and your new one lives in another) and roll over the fund balance into a completely different account, tax free, provided the transfer is completed with 60 days. If you can't get the new fund up and running within that 60-day period, you're out of luck. You (not the designated beneficiary) will be taxed on the accumulated income in the fund, and then you can tack on an additional 10 percent penalty.

Whenever you're rolling over a plan, either to an already existing account or a new one, tell your current plan manager that you want to make a "trustee-to-trustee transfer." This prevents a check from being written to you and will keep you well within the 60-day limit. Many a rollover has come to grief because someone forgot to deposit a check in time.

Beware if you initially fund your 529 plan using your child's UGMA/UTMA money (see Chapter 12 for the rules regarding the Uniform Gifts to Minors Act/Uniform Transfer to Minors Act). You can't change the designated beneficiary on such an account, and when he or she turns the magic age when your custodianship of the money would've ended, it still ends. The no-longer-minor child becomes the plan owner and can make whatever decisions he wants concerning this money, including terminating the plan.

Terminating the plan

When your designated student clearly has no desire to continue his education, you may have no other prospective student waiting in the wings. In this case, the obvious choice is to terminate your plan.

Check the rules of your plan very, very carefully. A few prepaid tuition plans don't allow you to receive the money back when you terminate your plan but instead pay it to your designated beneficiary. At the time of termination, the designated beneficiary pays any income tax on the accumulated earnings and may also be hit with the 10 percent penalty for taking the money in a non-qualified distribution.

This whole scenario may work well for you if your designated beneficiary is an absolute wizard who is receiving a full-paid academic scholarship (in which case, the 10 percent penalty doesn't apply; see the next section). You may not feel as keen, however, about giving control over a lump sum of money to a child who's not living up to potential. If your plan will terminate only in favor of the designated beneficiary, you may want to consider making an intermediate tax-free rollover (as described in Chapter 5) to an account that will allow you to terminate in favor of yourself.

If you terminate a prepaid tuition plan, be prepared to receive a check for considerably less than the plan balance shown on your last statement. Once again, every state has its own rules, and you need to check out the ones specific to your plan. Very often, a plan will pay you back only your contribution amounts plus either a fixed interest rate (which may be much lower than what the money actually earned while in the plan) or a percentage of the contract earnings. In addition to the penalties you'll pay (which will show up on your Form 1040 in the year of termination), you'll also pay a cancellation fee to the plan.

In no case will the state confiscate your money if you choose to terminate a Section 529 plan; however, because the plans are designed for a specific purpose, you'll face consequences for not achieving that purpose. At the very least, the money you put into the plan should come back out to you (or your designated student); at the very worst, that's all you'll get back.

Limiting penalties for too much money

Your fondest dreams have been borne out, and your student is headed for a free ride. Or, more realistically, your student received a darn good scholarship and will need only a portion of the money you've saved to pay the difference. You have many options for using this extra money, and most of them revolve around your family circumstances and your thoughts about money. Here are a few of your options that will minimize the size of Uncle Sam's bite:

- ✔ **You may choose to make distributions to your student equal to or less than the scholarship amount without paying a penalty on the income portion.** Your student is responsible for any income tax on the income portion of the distribution that he's not using to pay for qualified educational expenses, but an additional 10 percent penalty will *not* be tacked on. Remember, lots of incidentals need to be paid for that don't fall under the category of "qualified educational expenses." Chapter 10 shows how this scenario works.

- ✔ **You may want to roll over part, or all, of the extra into a Section 529 plan for another child or a grandchild.** If you haven't already made a tax-free rollover in the previous 12 months, you're free to do this, and jump-start a new account or supercharge one that's been a bit anemic, as described in the section "Deciding what to do if your child doesn't attend college," earlier in this chapter.

- ✔ **You may want to hold off doing anything, at least for a while.** Many people continue on after college, and your student could be one of those. Although you may have thought that your ability to pay would stop after college, the fact that your child has received this additional assistance may enable her to continue on to graduate or professional school without taking loans. Remember, there is no age limitation on Section 529 plans — a student may be any age to qualify.

 As always, when you're facing a major financial decision, talk with a professional whom you trust (your accountant, attorney, or financial advisor). This person can help you see all the aspects of your situation and how your decision here may affect it.

Minimizing the blow for retrieving savings to weather hard times

Planning and plotting are part of the human condition, and after you have children, your propensity for doing more than going with the flow increases exponentially. That's why you've been investigating and, I hope, saving in a

529 plan in the first place. But sometimes your life may make a U-turn, and items that you may have thought were sacrosanct now need to be put on the table in order to deal with immediate family survival. Thinking of the distant future seems hard when the immediate present is looking grim.

In these cases, you may find it necessary to access the funds you've been so carefully saving in your Section 529 plan. Because 529s are designed for paying for college, you're not really supposed to use that money for something else — that's why the IRS charges you a penalty when you do. Still, the beauty of these plans is that they allow it, with some conditions.

Nonqualified distributions to yourself or your designated beneficiary that trigger additional tax

Uncertain world economies often lead to unstable family economies. Suppose that your income has dropped for any reason (loss of one salary, wage reductions, or investment income decline) or your expenses have increased significantly. You may find that you not only can't continue to fund your 529 plan but also need to liberate some money in order to pay your bills.

You could beat yourself up over this situation, because you put the money aside for your student. But there's a reason why 529 plans are regarded as the parents' (not the student's) assets when determining the financial need of a student, and this is it. You can take a distribution of some (or all) of the money you've saved from a prepaid tuition plan or a savings plan.

That said, it'll cost you. If your investments have appreciated in value, you'll pay the income tax on the accumulated earnings at your income tax rate, plus a 10 percent penalty for a nonqualified distribution. It's not a perfect solution, but in the right situation, it may be the only one that makes sense for you.

Don't think that you get off with only the federal tax and the federal penalty. If your state has an income tax, you also must pay a state income tax. And, if your state gave you an income tax deduction for your contributions into the plan, as you draw that money out, you may need to "recapture" the income that you didn't pay tax on in prior years and pay the tax now.

Nonqualified distributions to or for the benefit of the beneficiary, without penalty

Another benefit of Section 529 is the way it separates out your unforeseen circumstances from your designated student's. After all, even though you own the plan, you've put the money aside for the student's use, and you have received favorable gift tax treatment on that premise. Accordingly, although you may have to pay a penalty if you take back money from your student's Section 529 plan, if your student needs money and takes a distribution from the plan, it may be subject only to income tax on the earnings (paid at the student's tax rate, not yours), without the 10 percent penalty.

These exceptions, covered in detail in Chapter 5, include the following:

- ✔ Distributions that would have been qualified except for the fact that your student has received scholarship and/or grant money or other educational benefits from another source.

- ✔ Distributions used to pay enough educational expenses to qualify for the Hope or Lifetime Learning Education Credits. Remember, in this case, the student needs to claim the credit, so he can't be listed as a dependent on your income tax return, which may limit the value of this technique. Of course, if you (or your spouse) are the beneficiary as well as the owner of a 529 plan, using this becomes much more valuable to you.

- ✔ Distributions that are made on account of a severe disability or because of the impending death of the designated beneficiary.

In the first two cases, the distributions would have qualified except for the receipt of assistance from another source or because of the need to have some taxable income against which to use a tax credit; here, the lack of a penalty makes perfect sense. These are clearly situations where the student is a student, is attending a qualified educational institution, and is using any money he receives to forward his education. All that is happening here is that the income from the Section 529 plan is reverting back to pre-2002 treatment and is being taxed at the student's applicable tax rate.

In the third case, where the designated beneficiary faces a situation that will most likely preclude him from attending a postsecondary school, he is not being penalized for something that is far beyond his control. Much as distributions are allowable out of an IRA for medical expenses even though the payment is made before the beneficiary reaches the age of 59½, distributions from a Section 529 plan for grave medical cause are subject to income tax on the earnings portion, but no penalty.

Having money left over after graduation

Graduation day has come and gone, and your designated beneficiary is now confidently heading out into the workplace, credentials in hand, and with no immediate intention of continuing on for an advanced degree, which you may have no intention of paying for anyway. And you're feeling fairly good about yourself, knowing that your good planning and careful attention all the way through the process has helped your student to reach this point.

Now the only fly in the ointment seems to be that you planned too well, and you still have money left in your Section 529 savings kitty. If you used a prepaid tuition plan, while it's less likely that you'll have anything left, you may still have some unused tuition credits that you need to deal with. Oops!

Actually, good for you! You planned and then carried through. You had no way of knowing how much you would actually need, but you managed to save more than enough. So now on to the next phase — figuring out how to deal with the excess while minimizing, or even eliminating, any tax bite.

Remembering that you own the unused funds

When you funded this account for your prospective student, you may have filed a gift tax return, essentially giving this money to that designated beneficiary for the purpose of his future education. It would make sense, then, that now that the education is complete, she'd get what's left.

Wrong! You've been the owner of the account from Day 1, and nothing has changed here. The fact that your designated beneficiary has now graduated only means that she no longer needs the funds. You remain the plan owner.

If you can't decide what to do next, that's okay for a while, but be careful and check your particular plan. Many plans, especially prepaid tuition ones, have very specific time guidelines that you must meet. For example, your plan may require that all distributions are made and the plan is terminated no later than ten years after your designated beneficiary first begins his postsecondary education. Funds that remain could be either distributed to you at the mandatory distribution time (in which case you're looking at income tax and penalty on the earnings portion of the distribution) or even sent to unclaimed property at the state treasurer's office.

Changing beneficiaries

Even if your plan doesn't require that you take action immediately (or within a fixed time), all plans have provisions written in to prevent them from existing forever. Congress, the IRS, and all the state treasuries want to know that you're planning on spending that money on education. Although they'll grant you a bit of leeway in figuring out what to do with your excess, you need to make a decision. And that decision is a fairly basic choice: You need to terminate the account or change the beneficiary designation, either through a simple change of beneficiary on the current account or a tax-free rollover into a new or already existing account for the new designated beneficiary.

If you choose the rollover option, the rules are the same as for any rollover: Your new designated beneficiary must belong to the same family as your original designated beneficiary, in the allowed relationships listed in Chapter 5. You can roll the excess into a brand-new 529 plan for the new designated beneficiary (a younger child, perhaps) or into an already existing plan. Don't forget that you can also use this opportunity to change your investment strategy. For example, you may not want to be as conservative in your choices with a younger beneficiary as you may have been with the former beneficiary.

Tracking the basis in your Section 529 Plan

No matter what type of plan that you own and how much it might be growing, you always need to keep track of your *basis,* or how much money you or anyone else has put into the account. If you live in a state that gives you partial or full credit for contributions into a Section 529 plan, you'll need to keep two separate sets of records for this reason: Your federal contributions will be made after you've already paid income tax on the money, while your contributions for state purposes may be made before state income tax is paid. By knowing your basis, you can calculate just how much of any distribution from the plan represents taxable earnings.

For example, Melinda and Greg, who are Idaho residents, have a Section 529 plan for their son, and they put $2,000 a year into it for 17 years. After their son graduates from college (having taken $50,000 in qualified distributions on which the earnings were tax-exempt), $5,000 is still left in the plan. As they have no other children and no one whom they wish to name a designated beneficiary, they terminate the account and receive the final distribution. The following table shows how Melinda and Gregg calculate the taxable portion of their distribution:

Calculating Basis in Your Section 529 Plan

	Federal	*Idaho*
Contributions to plan	$34,000 (after tax)	$34,000 (before tax)
Total income earned	$21,000	$21,000
Distributions to son	$50,000 (of which $30,909 is allocated to contributions, and $19,091 to income earned)	$50,000 (of which $30,909 is allocated to contributions, and $19,091 to income earned)
Distribution to Melinda and Greg	$5,000 (of which $3,091 is allocated to contributions on which tax has already been paid, and $1,909 to income)	$5,000 (of which $3,091 is allocated to contributions on which tax has not been paid, and $1,909 to income)
Taxable amount to Melinda and Greg	$1,909 (income-only piece of $5,000 distribution)	$5,000 (income and contribution piece, since income tax was never paid on the original contribution)

Calculating taxes on unused funds

After you see all the members of your family through college and into the great working world beyond, you may finally reach a point where you still have excess funds in the very last Section 529 plan that you own, and no one is left for whom to fund a new account. (Remember, if your children have children of their own at this point, you can always roll over the remainder into new accounts for your grandchildren, as described in Chapter 5.) If you don't have anyone left to fund for, that's okay — you've really done a great job, and your students are all now well able to stand on their own two feet.

Still, now you really must terminate your last plan and get out of the 529 business. At this time, you need to request a distribution from your plan manager of the entire balance. This is clearly a nonqualified distribution, and you'll have to pay income tax on the earnings portion of the distribution and a 10 percent penalty. As you write your check to the United States Treasury (and to your state treasurer, if you live in a state with an income tax), focus on all the money you've saved over the years by deferring this tax and on all the benefits you and your students have reaped. Approaching the task with this attitude should make writing these checks a bit less painful.

Part III

Uncovering Coverdell Accounts

The 5th Wave   By Rich Tennant

"What 'ya need the money for this time, Frankie? Craps? The ponies? Coverdell ESA contribution?"

In this part . . .

Coverdell Education Savings Accounts (ESAs) are another entry in the tax-exempt/tax-deferred college savings plan arsenal available to you. Although you can't save as much moola in these accounts as in Section 529 plans, and you're limited in other significant ways, saving in a Coverdell account may prove to be a valuable addition to your overall ability to save for college.

In this part, I explain all the rules and regulations surrounding Coverdell ESAs and how to open, fund, and manage an account. I give you reasons why you may want to have one of these accounts, and discuss times when you may decide that ol' Coverdell isn't the best date for this particular dance. And I also give you some ideas of what you can do when your crystal ball proves to be unreliable and your great financial planning doesn't necessarily intersect with events in your student's life, leaving you with either too much or too little money saved in his Coverdell ESA.

Chapter 8

The Changing World of Coverdell Education Savings Accounts

In This Chapter

▶ Exploring the fundamentals of Coverdell accounts

▶ Contributing to the account

▶ Distributing the money

▶ Making changes to the account

*F*or people trying to save money for college, 2002 was a very good year. Not only were the rules regulating Section 529 plans (see Chapter 5) overhauled to make the plans more flexible and less taxable, but Congress also completely revamped and expanded the rules surrounding the old Education IRA's, going so far as to rename them Coverdell Education Savings Accounts (ESAs), after the late Senator Paul Coverdell (R-Georgia), who was the chief sponsor of the legislation regulating these accounts. The revamp has been monumental, both in size and in scope, completely changing the old Education IRA (which was fairly useless as a significant college savings device) into a mover and shaker in the field of educational savings.

In this chapter, you discover the ins and outs of the new Coverdell Education Savings Accounts, and you find out why so many people (your banker, your broker, you child's kindergarten teacher) all want you to start investing, and investing now. You also see how the improvements really do qualify as improvements, and you're alerted to red flags and warnings along the way.

Congress has put limits on who can contribute to Coverdell ESAs, based on annual income. If you make more than the phaseout limit allows, you can't contribute to an account. To find out whether your annual income falls within the limits, skip to the section "Making Account Contributions," later in this chapter. If you find that your annual income excludes you from making contributions, don't give up. If Coverdell is the way you want to save, a little careful planning can make it happen for you.

Covering the Basics

Coverdell ESAs are savings plans described in Section 530 of the Internal Revenue Code (IRC). They're accounts that Congress created to allow you to save now for future educational expenses, whether primary, secondary, or postsecondary, of a designated beneficiary.

You can invest money in Coverdell accounts in a variety of ways: stocks, bonds, money market accounts, certificates of deposit, and so on, although you may not invest in life insurance policies. And I really mean that you can invest; under the Coverdell rules (and unlike Section 529 rules), if you designate yourself the one responsible for all decisions on this particular account (also known as the *responsible adult,* who must be the parent or legal guardian of the minor child; see Chapter 9), you keep control of the money and make all the investment decisions for your child's account. Over the years, the investments will hopefully earn significant income through interest, dividends, and capital gains, until the time that the account is closed.

You pay no income tax on the income when it's earned, and as distributions are made from these accounts to your designated beneficiary for qualified educational expenses, the income portion of the distribution is not taxed, either to you or to your student.

A Coverdell ESA must be opened as such, in writing, and you need to designate a beneficiary when you create it; you aren't allowed to take an already existing account and decide that it's now the Coverdell account for your student. Money that you contribute into the account is held by a trustee or a custodian, which must be a bank, mutual fund company, or any other entity that's approved by the Internal Revenue Service (IRS).

Understanding Coverdell changes

When these accounts were first introduced in 1997 as Education IRA's, they were limited to $500 a year aggregate contribution per student, and distributions could be used to cover only postsecondary expenses. If you were thinking of making a contribution into any plan, you probably would've chosen a Section 529 plan, which had fewer restrictions and allowed you to maintain some contact with your money. Basically, the old Education IRA was a nonstarter for most people because contribution limits were fairly pathetic, and much better ways to save money for college were available.

In the new world of Coverdell (same code section, different name), the aggregate contribution limit has been raised to $2,000 per year, the definition of "qualifying student" has been hugely expanded, and you may now contribute to both a Coverdell account and a Section 529 plan for the same beneficiary in the same year. With all these factors, plus an increase in the income phase-out limitations present under Coverdells but not 529 plans, these accounts can become useful savings tools for many families.

Looking at the major differences between Coverdell accounts and 529 plans

On their faces, Coverdell ESAs and Section 529 plans seem to be two peas in a pod: Both are designed to encourage savings for higher education, and after passage of the Economic Growth and Tax Relief Reconciliation Act of 2001, both now allow tax-free distributions if they're used to pay for qualified educational expenses.

Still, Sections 529 and 530 (governing Coverdell ESAs) of the Internal Revenue Code are quite different, and the savings plans that they govern contain several crucial differences. Among them are the following:

✔ Coverdell accounts have strict limits on the amount of income any contributor (with the exception of a corporate or charitable one) may earn in a particular year in order to make contributions into the account; Section 529 plans carry no such restriction.

✔ Coverdell accounts have strict limits on the amount that may be given into any account for a specific designated beneficiary in each year, while Section 529 plans do not (only overall plan maximums). In addition, contributions may not be made after age 18 for the designated beneficiary of a Coverdell account. Section 529 plans have no beneficiary age limit. Accordingly, 529 plans have the capacity to transfer significant amounts of wealth, while Coverdell accounts are much more modest in size.

✔ Assets inside a Coverdell account are considered to be owned by the designated beneficiary and are therefore counted as the student's asset when calculating financial aid formulas (see Chapter 17), while asset ownership in a Section 529 plan is much more confusing, depending on how you look at it. For gift and Generation-Skipping Transfer tax purposes, the assets have transferred to your designated beneficiary, while for financial aid purposes, the assets are counted as the account owner's.

✔ If you live in a state that gives a deduction or credit for Section 529 contributions, no state gives the same benefit for Coverdell ESA contributions. All your contributions will be made "after tax" for both federal and state purposes.

✔ Qualifying students under Section 530 include everyone from kindergartners through college and graduate school students, and you may pay a wide variety of elementary and secondary educational expenses with distributions from Coverdell accounts (in addition to the qualified educational expenses of eligible postsecondary institutions). Under Section 529, only postsecondary students are qualified, and you may use plan distributions to pay only the qualified educational expenses of eligible postsecondary institutions.

Knowing who owns the account

No matter who makes contributions into a Coverdell ESA, the IRS considers the designated beneficiary to be the owner of the assets. If you structure the accounts for your children correctly, though, you can remain in control of the assets by naming yourself the responsible adult, or the person in control of the account, when you open the account.

If, when your children turn 18, your philosophy is to turn their finances over to them to help them establish their independence, or if you feel your child at that age is more savvy about money and investments than you'll ever be, you may put your child in control at that time, although you don't have to.

If your inclination is to give your child control of his Coverdell ESA account, think carefully before you do. As long as you remain the responsible adult, you make the decisions regarding distribution; your child may have other ideas about what constitutes appropriate use of the money in the account. Even though there are significant penalties for taking nonqualified distributions from a Coverdell ESA, 18-year-olds aren't known for making decisions based on sound financial reasoning; you have to understand that your child may decide to take the money you've saved for his college and run.

Identifying qualifying students

In a major departure from the Section 529 definition of "qualifying students," Coverdell qualifying students consist of almost anyone who's studying any-thing or who's likely to study anything at a later date. This means that, if your budding Picasso is taking up the fine art of finger painting at her local private kindergarten, you may choose to pay for the tuition there by using distribu-tions from your Coverdell ESA. You can do the same at each step along the way, all the way up to and through college and graduate school. There are some caveats, though, that you need to remember.

Age limitations at time of contribution

In general, you have 18 years in which you, or anyone else, for that matter, can fund a Coverdell ESA for your child, from his date of birth until the day before his 18th birthday. After that, you're done. No matter how much or how little you've managed to put away for that student, you can't add any more to the account. Any increases from now until the termination of the account will have to come from the earnings off your good investments.

Age limitations at time of distributions

Coverdell ESAs must be completely distributed by the time your designated beneficiary hits his or her 30th birthday. If money is still left in the account on that date, it must be distributed within 30 days, and any earnings on it will be taxed to the beneficiary, plus whacked with a 10 percent penalty.

If you're fast approaching your beneficiary's 30th birthday and substantial money that you may not want to be giving as a birthday gift remains in the account, you can change the designated beneficiary on the account to a member of the current beneficiary's family, provided, however, that the new beneficiary is under age 30.

Saving for disabled and special-needs students

While members of Congress have essentially stated that your children should have completed their educations by their 30th birthday, they do also recognize that some students will spend their lives in special schools. Accordingly, if you're the parent or grandparent of a special-needs student, there are no age limitations either on contributions or distributions on behalf of these students.

Regulations defining who exactly is a special-needs student haven't been released, and no one is sure where the line defining a disability will be drawn. For instance, total deafness may be included, but 50-percent hearing loss could fall outside the boundaries. If you feel that your student's disability or special need may not be severe enough to fit a narrow definition and if you're approaching the ordinary deadline for contributions, you may want to err on the side of caution and stop contributing at age 18 until clearer guidelines are available.

Recognizing qualified education expenses

Qualified education expenses under Code Section 530 are those expenses that you're required to pay (or figure out some other way of meeting) if your student is to enroll at an eligible school. Just as in Section 529, though, many other expenses may be qualified, depending on the requirements of the school and of the particular program your student may be enrolled in.

First, you need to know what constitutes an "eligible school." For the purposes of IRC Section 530 and Coverdell ESAs, eligible schools include all public, private, or religious schools that provide either primary or secondary education as determined under their applicable state laws. All postsecondary educational institutions that are qualified under Section 529 also qualify as eligible schools under Section 530.

The addition of primary and secondary schools to the list of eligible institutions is quite a bonus, as it assigns tax-exempt status to earnings used to pay for primary and secondary school expenses (this is the one and only place in the entire Internal Revenue Code where this happens). This provision is a part of the Economic Growth and Tax Relief Reconciliation Act of 2001 that changed the Education IRA to Coverdell. This legislation expires on December 31, 2010. If it isn't extended or made permanent by that date, the law sunsets back to its pre-2002 conditions, in which only postsecondary educational institutions will be qualified.

Qualified expenses for elementary and secondary education

In addition to tuition and mandatory fees, other elementary and secondary education expenses may be eligible for payment using Coverdell distributions. Some expenses may seem obvious; others may surprise you:

- ✓ **Books, supplies, and equipment related to enrollment:** In these days of shrinking school budgets, parents need to supply their children with more and more of what used to be considered necessary school supplies. Amounts that you spend for pens and pencils, notebooks, erasers, and the like are included here. You may also use a distribution from your Coverdell to pay for textbooks and any other required reading material that's not supplied by the school district.

- ✓ **Academic tutoring related to enrollment:** The math or science tutor (or even a dance instructor if your child is a dancer attending a school for the performing arts) is covered here, but your child's extracurricular piano or dance lessons are not.

- ✓ **Special-needs services for students with special needs or disabilities:** If your student needs a one-on-one aide with him and the school doesn't cover the expense, this service qualifies, as does special equipment necessary to accommodate him. However, when assessing what qualifies here, remember that the regulations regarding special needs haven't been issued yet.

- ✓ **Room and board, but only if a requirement of attending that particular school:** Clearly, if you send your child to a boarding school 300 miles from your home, room and board would be required; if, however, you live in the next town, this expense may be questionable.

- ✓ **Uniforms, when required by the school:** The cost of voluntary school uniform programs doesn't constitute a qualified educational expense, nor does the annual cost of buying your child school clothes.

- ✓ **Transportation, when required by the school:** The expense of driving your student to and from school every day doesn't qualify, but the price you're charged for the mandatory school bus does. As more and more communities begin to charge families for the cost of transportation to and from school, this expense will become an item that more people may choose to pay from their Coverdell accounts.

- ✓ **Supplementary items and services, including extended day programs:** If your child attends an after-school program or an extended day program at his or her school, you may choose to pay these costs from your Coverdell account. The payment must be made to the school, however, so once again, those extracurricular piano lessons probably aren't covered here.

- ✓ **Computers, printers, other peripherals, Internet access, software, and so on:** To the extent that you can document that the use of this equipment and programming is to benefit your student's education, even if you may be the primary user of this equipment, you may pay for it by using a qualified Coverdell distribution. Items that aren't used for educational purposes, though, don't count as qualified expenses, so the video games, the joystick you buy for your computer, and any gaming, sports, or hobby software don't qualify.

Qualified expenses for higher education

When your student reaches the halls of higher learning (or any other school after he's completed high school), the rules regarding what constitutes a qualified expense for the purposes of Coverdell distributions change. The higher education rules fall in line with those for Section 529 plans (see Chapter 5), which makes sense. The 2001 tax law changes focused on adding primary and secondary education; it pretty much left alone what was already in place regarding postsecondary education.

In general, the following lists constitutes qualifying educational expenses for postsecondary education payable by tax-free distributions from Coverdell accounts:

✔ **Tuition and mandatory fees at eligible educational institutions:** For a school to qualify, it needs to be able to participate (but doesn't have to if it chooses not to) in federal financial aid programs administered by the Department of Education.

✔ **Required books, supplies, and equipment:** The books on the lengthy list that every professor hands out on the first day of class, laboratory equipment, and any required computer equipment (including peripherals) qualify. Your child's cell phone, which you may require for your peace of mind, does not.

✔ **Room and board expenses:** These expenses are qualified only if

• They're paid directly to the school itself and your student is attending class at least half time or

• They don't exceed the amount the school budgets for these expenses, provided your designated beneficiary is at least a half-time student.

If the room and board fees that you pay directly to the school exceed the amount the school budgets for this expense, that's okay. You can still pay the full amount by using a qualified distribution from a Coverdell plan. It's only for that off-campus housing (including fraternities and sororities) that you need to be careful.

✔ **Contributions into Section 529 Plans:** The rules here are fairly straightforward and fairly stringent. If you take a distribution from a Coverdell ESA and contribute it into a 529 plan, the 529 plan needs to be for the same student. After this designation is made, you can't change it; the student was the owner of the funds under Coverdell, so the student needs to remain the beneficiary of the funds under Section 529.

✔ **Expenses for special-needs services that are required for special-needs students:** Once again, the regulations in this area haven't been finalized, so use your common sense. Don't include orthopedic shoes for your flat-footed student, or contact lenses. It's a safe bet that these aren't covered under the regulations.

The one rule that is apparent is that any services that are paid for by using a distribution from a Coverdell ESA needs to be required by an eligible educational institution.

Many qualified expenses for elementary or secondary school aren't qualified after your student graduates from high school. When you send your student off to college, don't try to pay for that new computer and peripherals from your Coverdell ESA unless the school requires it as a part of the course. You also won't be able to pay for any after-school programming, transportation, uniforms, or academic tutoring for your postsecondary beneficiary with Coverdell funds unless you also want your student to pay income tax and a penalty on the income portion of the distribution.

Following investing rules and regulations

Coverdell ESAs generally follow the same investment rules and regulations as both traditional and Roth IRA accounts. Unlike 529 plans, there's an awful lot that's allowed, and not much that's prohibited. Still, to keep everything kosher, you need to know what you can't do and ways you can't invest.

✔ **Your contributions need to be made in cash or cash equivalent.**

✔ **You may not purchase collectibles or life insurance with the money in your Coverdell ESA.** You're prohibited from buying insurance policies, artwork, household furnishings, antiques, metals, gems, stamps, or certain coins with that money, no matter how fine an investment it may appear to you. Specially minted U.S. gold and silver bullion coins and certain state-issued coins may be permitted. In addition, platinum coins and certain gold, silver, platinum, or palladium bullion are also allowed. If you're interested in making this sort of investment with Coverdell funds, check Internal Revenue Code Section. 408(m)(3) to make sure that the coins or bullion you have in mind qualify.

✔ **You may not commingle Coverdell account funds with any other funds.** Your Coverdell account needs to be set up and accounted for completely separately from any of your other assets. The custodian or trustee, however, has the ability to commingle the money in your Coverdell account with money in other Coverdell accounts, creating what's known as a "Common Trust Fund" or a "Common Investment Fund." These funds work to your advantage because they allow the custodian or trustee to buy investments in larger pieces (which is less costly overall) and then split the pieces among all the accounts that contributed to the purchase.

✔ **You may not pledge the value of a Coverdell ESA as collateral for any sort of loan.** Not only are loans to you and your designated beneficiary prohibited, but so too are margin accounts, or brokerage accounts that allow you to borrow against the value of your stocks in order to either buy more stocks or take cash out of the account.

✔ **You may not take a loan from a Coverdell ESA, nor may your designated beneficiary.** The money that's in the account stays in the account until it's time to make distributions to your beneficiary. Any money that comes out may only come out as a distribution. After it's removed from the account, it may not be returned or repaid later.

✔ **You may not pay yourself or anyone else for managing your student's Coverdell ESA by using funds from the account.** The only fees that may be charged against the account are the custodian's or trustee's. If you need to hire an investment advisor to help you select investments, you need to pay his fee out of your funds, not the account's.

✔ **You may not sell or lease your property or your beneficiary's property to a Coverdell account, nor may you make any other sort of asset exchange.** The only thing that goes into the account is cash, and the only thing that should ever come out is cash, in the form of distributions to your beneficiary. Any other transaction is prohibited.

The custodian or trustee you choose to manage your Coverdell ESA may have other prohibitions in place. You may not be allowed to invest in real estate, for example, or trade in anything more complicated than ordinary stocks and bonds (as opposed to options, puts, calls, or the like). The custodian may also limit you to a certain group of mutual funds or their own certificates of deposit. Investigate what limitations the custodian has in place before you open your account, and make sure that you can live within those rules.

If you goof and make a prohibited transaction under Section 530, you and your beneficiary are out of luck. The entire account will lose its tax exemption or deferral on the day of the prohibited transaction, and your designated beneficiary will be required to report 100 percent of the built-up earnings in the account from inception on his tax return for that year.

Making Account Contributions

You or anyone else in your family or circle of friends, including the student for whom the account has been established, may contribute to a Coverdell ESA, provided that you qualify under the income phaseout rules (see the section "Looking at income phaseouts for contributors," later in this chapter). Even your employer or a charitable organization may contribute (and in these cases, the $2,000 annual limit on contributions for the benefit of a specific beneficiary, which is explained in detail in the section "Spelling out contribution limits," doesn't apply).

Congress and, by extension, the IRS want you to set up these accounts, and they really want to encourage you to make contributions to save for your students' educational expenses. They do not, however, want to turn this program into a giveaway: Contributions into a Coverdell account are not income-tax deductible, either on your federal or state income tax returns.

When making a contribution into a Coverdell account, keep the following in mind:

- ✔ **Contributions must be made in cash.** Checks, money orders, and so forth are okay, too, but stocks, bonds, life insurance policies, real estate, and trading stamps are not.

- ✔ **Contributions can't be made into an account for the benefit of a beneficiary who's 18 years or older, except if that beneficiary falls under the special-needs category.** After your beneficiary hits that magic age, you must stop putting money into his Coverdell account unless you're absolutely certain that your student will qualify under the special-needs rules, in which case no age cutoff exists.

- ✔ **Contributions for a particular year must be made by the original filing deadline for your tax returns for that year.** Don't plan on making your contribution on October 15 of the following year because your income tax returns are on extension — original filing deadline means April 15 for calendar year taxpayers.

Spelling out contribution limits

Before 2002, contributions into the old Education IRA's were limited to $500 per student per year, subject to some phaseout rules (see the section "Looking at income phaseouts for contributors," later in this chapter, for more info). In addition, if you made a contribution to an Education IRA in a given year for a given student, you couldn't also make a contribution to a Section 529 plan. As a result of these low contribution limits, most people didn't bother to fund these accounts, and even if they did, it probably never amounted to much. The Economic Growth and Tax Relief Reconciliation Act of 2001, which changed Education IRA's to Coverdell ESAs, greatly expanded the number of people who were willing to contribute and the amount that could be given.

Today, although the amount that can be contributed is much greater, there are still contribution limits, and you have to keep track of them. You need to know not only how much you're putting into any one beneficiary's account but also how much other people may be putting into either that account, or other accounts, for the same beneficiary.

As always, the IRS expects you to know or to find out the answers here. Mistakes are your mistakes, and they'll be costly to your student.

Aggregate annual contributions, per beneficiary

Annual contributions into Coverdell ESAs for the benefit of any person may not currently exceed $2,000 per year. This means that you and everyone you know, all together, may not make contributions of more than $2,000 in any year for any beneficiary.

For example, Harvey and Cynthia have one child for whom they've set up a Coverdell ESA. In 2002, they contributed $2,000 to this account. They plan to do the same in 2003, but much to their surprise, they find that Harvey's brother has put his $500 birthday gift for his nephew into the account in 2003 (he's a pretty generous uncle). In 2003, then, Harvey and Cynthia may put only $1,500 into the Coverdell account they established, in order to not exceed the maximum contribution *per beneficiary* of $2,000 annually.

As this example shows, your contributions aren't limited only to plans that you set up; you may make payments into any plan established for a particular beneficiary.

Annual contributions per contributor

The $2,000 aggregate contribution limit refers only to the amount that may be given *per beneficiary.* Code Section 530 doesn't limit the number of beneficiaries into whose plans you may contribute.

For example, Harvey and Cynthia now have four children (they've added a set of triplets). They may establish Coverdell ESAs for each of their children. In each year in which they meet the income phaseout requirements, they may contribute up to $2,000 into an account for each of their children (as long as their children are under age 18), or a total of $8,000 annually ($2,000 x 4). Should Harvey's generous brother decide to contribute his birthday gifts into the kids' Coverdell accounts rather than giving the money to his nieces and nephews outright, the amount that Harvey and Cynthia may contribute will be reduced by the amount of that gift.

Gift tax and Generation-Skipping Transfer Tax consequences

Unlike gifts in Section 529 plans, which may be quite large and often trigger Gift and Generation-Skipping Transfer Tax (GSTT) consequences on their own, gifts into Coverdell ESAs will never, by themselves, create a situation where you need to fill out a Form 709. The limit on the size of the annual contribution per beneficiary prohibits this, as $2,000 will never begin to approach the $11,000 annual exclusion amount currently available to every donor for every donee.

However, if you use a Coverdell ESA as part of a savings plan and are taking advantage of other ways to push income and assets to your children, grandchildren, or any other friend or relative, you need to know that a contribution into a Coverdell account constitutes a *completed gift,* or a gift over which you've given up all right, title, and interest. As such, if your total contributions into a combination of a Coverdell account, a Section 529 plan or plans, trust account(s), and/or outright gifts to or for the benefit of a single person total more than $11,000 in any given year, then you have to file a Form 709, United States Gift (and Generation-Skipping Transfer) Tax return.

So suppose that Harvey and Cynthia add twins to their family (they're up to six children, and they may want to remember that they may need to put all these children through college). They can have a Coverdell ESA for each of the six, contribute the full $2,000 to each account every year, and never need to file a gift tax return even though they're gifting away a total of $12,000 every year. However, they also have a Section 529 plan for each child, into which they're putting $10,000 each year per child. Now, their total gift to or for the benefit of each child is $12,000 per year, and a gift tax return is required, as their annual exclusion amount per donee is only $11,000.

When you consider that gifts may come into any of your beneficiaries' accounts from a variety of sources, remember that, for gift tax purposes, the number you need to focus on is the amount you give to each person in any given year, not the total amount from all sources that is given to each person.

Looking at income phaseouts for contributors

Anyone can make a contribution into a Section 529 plan, regardless of how much income he or she earns. This isn't the case for Coverdell ESAs; income really matters here. If you earn too much, you may be dumb out of luck in any given year and may have to wait to make contributions into your students' accounts only in the years in which your income falls below the limits.

The income phaseout range for single taxpayers is $95,000 to $110,000, based on your modified adjusted gross income, described later in this section, and the range for married taxpayers is $190,000 to $220,000, or exactly double that of single taxpayers. Here's how the phaseout system works:

- ✔ If you're below the bottom of the phaseout range, you may contribute the full $2,000 per beneficiary.

- ✔ If you're within the phaseout range, your contribution will be limited according to a formula.

- ✔ If you're above the phaseout range, you may not make any contributions in the current year.

For the purpose of determining whether you may, or may not, contribute, you need to calculate your *modified adjusted gross income,* which adds the following items to your adjusted gross income from your tax return (from the line labeled "Adjusted Gross Income"):

✔ Your foreign earned income exclusion

✔ Your foreign housing exclusion

✔ If you're a bona fide resident of American Samoa, your excluded income

✔ Any excluded income from Puerto Rico

After you arrive at your modified adjusted gross income, you then can determine whether you can contribute at all or if your contribution will be limited. If you find that you fall within the phaseout range, you may calculate your limited contribution, using Figure 8-1 as an example.

If you complete the calculation in the worksheet and find that your ability to contribute into a Coverdell account for a given year is limited or not allowed at all, don't despair. Someone else with a lower income may be able to make the contribution instead of you. If that person doesn't have the spare cash lying around, you can make a gift to that person and trust that she'll then make a reciprocal gift right back to your designated beneficiary in his or her Coverdell account. Conversely, you may also decide to increase the amount you're putting into your student's Section 529 plan for that particular year.

Coverdell Education Savings Account Contribution Limit*

1. Maximum contribution . . . . 1. __$2,000__

2. Enter your modified adjusted gross income (MAGI) for purposes of figuring the contribution limit to a Coverdell account . . . . 2. _____

3. Enter $190,000 if married filing jointly; $95,000 for all other filers . . . . 3. _____

4. Subtract line 3 from line 2 and enter here. If zero or less, enter –0– on line 4, skip lines 5–7 and enter $2,000 on line 8 . . . . 4. _____

5. Enter $30,000 if married filing jointly; $15,000 for all others . . . . 5. _____

   Note: *If the amount on line 4 is greater than or equal to the amount on line 5, stop here. You are not allowed to contribute to a Coverdell Education Savings Account for the current year.*

6. Divide line 4 by line 5 and enter the result as a decimal. . . . . 6. _____

7. Multiply line 1 by line 6 . . . . 7. _____

8. Subtract line 7 from line 1 to determine the amount (per beneficiary) that you can contribute in the year . . . . 8. _____

*Adapted from IRS Publication 970, Tax Benefits for Education, page 33.

Figure 8-1: Worksheet to figure out limited contribution to a Coverdell account.

Getting rid of excess contributions

Because of the limits on contributions, you've probably already deduced that, when you give more than the maximum allowed, you're going to have your hand slapped. In fact, it's quite a hand slap — the penalty for making excess contributions is a 6 percent excise tax on the *overage* (contribution amounts plus any earnings attributable to those contributions) for each year that it remains in the account.

Despite your best planning and plotting, excess contributions do happen. You may have put money into your kids' accounts at the beginning of the year and then gone on to earn much more money than you anticipated. Or you could've contributed the maximum amount, unaware that Grandma was also funding an account she had set up for your student. Excess contributions happen for any number of reasons; the important fact to know is that they can be corrected.

Once your student receives his contribution information from the account custodian or trustee on Form 5498 each year, you can determine whether more than the maximum $2,000 has been contributed in a particular year for that child. If it has been, then you have three ways to deal with the problem:

- ✔ Withdraw the excess cash
- ✔ Pay the 6 percent excise tax
- ✔ Absorb the excess contributions in future years by not making additional contributions

Withdrawing the excess

When you discover that too much money has been put into a Coverdell account or accounts for your child, the easiest solution is to withdraw the excess contribution (plus any earnings that have accrued on that amount) before the due date of the student's tax return. There will be no excise tax on the excess, but the student is responsible for paying the income tax (but no 10 percent penalty) on the income earned for the period of time the extra money stays in his account.

If you've made excess contributions and you choose to withdraw money to fix the problem, the distribution that you take is not only taxed to your beneficiary (to the extent of any earnings) but also paid to the beneficiary. Depending on the size, this excess could represent a considerable chunk of money, money that you may not want to hand over to a child or a teen.

Paying the excise tax

Suppose that you fail to notice that you've put too much money into your student's account, or you don't manage to correct the problem in time (before your student's tax return filing deadline). As a result, for the year following the year of the excess contribution and for all subsequent years until the problem is resolved, your beneficiary will have to pay an additional 6 percent excise tax on all excess amounts each year that they remain in the account. At any time along the way, you can fix this by withdrawing the overage from the account; in the year the funds are withdrawn, your student will pay the income tax only on the income earned by the excess.

Absorbing excess contributions

Finally, you may find that the problem eventually disappears all by itself. If your designated beneficiary is under age 18, you may choose to stop making contributions into his account, and instead each year assign up to the maximum $2,000 contribution amount (depending on where your income falls in the phaseout rules) from the excess until the excess has disappeared. For example, Susan's Coverdell ESA currently has $6,000 in excess contributions. Because Susan is only 8 years old, her parents, whose combined income falls well below the phaseout amounts, choose to assign $2,000 from the excess in each of the following three years instead of making additional contributions into Susan's account. In the first year, Susan will pay a 6 percent excise tax on the full $6,000. In year two, she'll pay an excise tax only on $4,000; in year three, $2,000; and in year four, when Susan is 10 years old, she'll no longer pay any excise tax. Beginning in the following year, provided her parents continue to earn less than the phaseout amount, they may again begin to contribute a maximum of $2,000 per year.

Taking Distributions

The point of having a Coverdell ESA is to enable you to pay for some or all of your student's qualified educational expenses with a combination of money you've saved (on which you previously paid income tax) and the earnings on your savings, on which you've paid no tax.

What you may not realize is that *you* are not actually the one making the payments for these expenses; your student is when using distributions from a Coverdell ESA. When distributions are made from a Coverdell account, the IRS considers them made to the student (even if checks are written directly to an educational institution), and the student bears the financial consequences.

If distributions are made for qualified expenses before December 31, 2010 (and if Congress takes no action on extending or making the current provisions permanent), your student won't pay any tax. If a distribution is made for a nonqualified expense (for example, he used money to buy a computer for college, even though it wasn't a requirement of his course), then tax needs to be paid on the income portion only. A 10 percent penalty will probably also be applied, for good measure.

The amount of qualified educational expenses are always reduced when your student receives any tax-free form of educational assistance, including, but not limited to, tax-free scholarships, veterans' educational assistance, Pell Grants, and employer tuition reimbursement programs. Be aware of these other payments to or on behalf of your student when calculating how big a distribution to take from a Coverdell account; if you're too generous, your student will pay the price.

If your student takes a taxable distribution from a Coverdell account, the 10 percent penalty will be waived under the following circumstances:

✔ A taxable distribution is made on account of the death of the designated beneficiary, either to the beneficiary or to his or her estate.

✔ A taxable distribution is made when it's used for nonqualified expenses, but the expenses are incurred due to the disability of the designated beneficiary. You must attach a doctor's statement to your beneficiary's tax return, indicating the type of disability and the expected duration or whether it's expected to result in death.

✔ A taxable distribution is made in excess of qualified educational expenses because those expenses were reduced by the receipt of nontaxable educational assistance. For example, Joan has qualified educational expenses of $10,000, takes a $10,000 distribution from her Coverdell account to pay for those expenses, and then finds that she also is receiving a tax-free scholarship for $5,000 from her school. In this case, only $5,000 of the Coverdell distribution is being used to pay for qualified educational expenses. Because Joan's qualifying expenses were reduced by the $5,000 scholarship, the income portion of the remaining $5,000 Coverdell distribution is subject only to income tax, and not an additional 10 percent penalty.

✔ A taxable distribution occurs only because qualified educational expenses were used to enable the taxpayer to take the Hope or Lifetime Learning Credit.

✔ A taxable distribution occurs because excess contributions given in the current tax year are returned to the designated beneficiary before he files his tax return for that year.

Transferring Accounts and Changing Account Beneficiaries

Just as in a Section 529 plan, you save in a Coverdell ESA for a day in the future: the day your child attends an educational institution that has some real dollar costs attached to it. Of course, for some, this day never arrives, and the money languishes in the account until the magic mandatory distribution to the designated beneficiary at age 30. For some, this may not be such a bad thing — you may feel that you saved the money for this particular person, and by the time that person has reached age 30, she is mature enough to manage the funds herself.

If you don't belong to that specific group and the thought of handing over all that money to that particular beneficiary sticks in your craw, you may want to explore whether you can change to a new designated beneficiary, taking the old one right out of the equation.

The designated beneficiary of a Coverdell ESA is the deemed owner of the assets in the account; however, he or she may not be the person named in the initial account-opening documents as being responsible for making the decisions regarding the account. If you're the named responsible adult, you're in luck, and you can initiate the transfer.

You may change the designated beneficiary on the same account as often as you like without incurring any tax or penalty; however, if you choose to roll one account over to another Coverdell account, changing the beneficiary at the same time, you're limited to one such tax-free rollover of the funds in that particular account in any given 12-month period.

Qualifying relationships for successor-designated beneficiaries

In setting up a Coverdell account for your original beneficiary, you transfer all right, title, and interest in the money you gift into the account. Now, as the responsible adult named on the account, you're proposing taking that money away from your beneficiary. If you could do that without restriction, that would mean that you retained real control over the money. You don't, so you can't transfer to a new beneficiary without following the rules.

And the rules are quite simple. The new beneficiary must be related to the original beneficiary (not to you) in one of the following ways:

- ✔ A lineal descendent, such as a child, grandchild, or stepchild
- ✔ A lineal ancestor, including the beneficiary's mother, father, grandmother, grandfather, stepmother, or stepfather
- ✔ A brother, sister, stepbrother, or stepsister of the original beneficiary
- ✔ A niece or nephew (but no stepniece or stepnephew)
- ✔ An aunt, uncle, or first cousin of the original beneficiary (but no stepaunts, uncles, or cousins)

> ✔ A mother-in-law, father-in-law, sister-in-law, brother-in-law, daughter-in-law, or son-in-law
>
> ✔ The spouse of any of the people listed above, or of the original beneficiary

Maximum age of the successor beneficiary

All assets in Coverdell ESAs need to be totally distributed once the designated beneficiary reaches age 30. However, you do have the option of transferring the balance of the account to a new beneficiary just before that date, keeping the account open and operating well beyond the 30th birthday of the original designated beneficiary. So long as the new beneficiary is under 30 and falls within the acceptable range of family relationship to the original beneficiary, you can effect the transfer. If you choose a new beneficiary who is under age 18, you may even begin to make contributions into the account again.

Here's how it works: You begin to fund a Coverdell account for the first designated beneficiary, and continue making contributions until you're forced to stop when she reaches age 18. Suppose that this beneficiary then receives a full-paid scholarship and she doesn't need the funds, but you have another child, or even grandchild, who might benefit from the money you've saved. Instead of waiting and distributing the entire amount to the original designated beneficiary when she's 30, you choose to change beneficiaries and go with the younger child. Until that child reaches 18, you may make contributions into the account to the extent allowable by the governing rules.

Additional transfers of this nature can continue to be made using the same account, so long as the new beneficiary always is under 30 years old and is related to the original beneficiary in the manner described in the section "Qualifying relationships for successor-designated beneficiaries," earlier in this chapter. Whoever is the beneficiary when the account makes distributions is the person who pays income tax on the earnings, if any tax needs to be paid. Whoever is the beneficiary when excess contributions are inside the account is the one who must pay the excise tax on the excess contributions. And whoever is the beneficiary when the account finally terminates is the one who receives the final distribution and pays income tax on whatever income remains inside the account.

Rolling over Coverdell accounts

In addition to changing the designated beneficiary on an account, if you're the responsible adult on an account, you may also choose to move from one Coverdell account to another, either for the same beneficiary or for a new one (but one who fulfills all the requirements listed in the section "Qualifying relationships for successor-designated beneficiaries," earlier in this chapter).

You may make an account rollover by withdrawing funds from your current account, and then, within 60 days, depositing them into a new Coverdell account. You need to keep track of the dates; if you wait until the 61st day, you make a nonqualified distribution, and the designated beneficiary on your first account is responsible for income tax on the earnings plus a 10 percent penalty. In addition (and not to scare you), you're also handing the control over that money to that beneficiary — good luck trying to retrieve it.

Transferring into a Section 529 plan

Although you're limited by beneficiary age within a Coverdell account, Section 529 plans have no age limitations. Accordingly, you may want to make a tax-free transfer from the Coverdell account into a Section 529 plan for the same designated beneficiary before that beneficiary turns age 30. Transferring from a Coverdell account to a Section 529 plan gives rise to some interesting consequences, though, so you want to be careful.

When you initiate a transfer from a Coverdell account, the account trustee or custodian will write a check to your designated beneficiary, not to the new account. If you choose to have those exact funds go into the Section 529 plan, the 529 plan it goes into needs to have your designated beneficiary listed as the account owner. When you contribute to a Coverdell account, you make a completed gift to your student; you may not take it back.

If giving Baby Alex control over a Section 529 plan gives you the heebie-jeebies, consider making a contribution directly into a 529 plan, using an equivalent amount of your funds rather than the proceeds from the Coverdell account. You must deposit your funds within 60 days after making the withdrawal from the Coverdell account. By funding the 529 plan with your own funds, you retain control over the 529 plan as the account owner; you've also fulfilled the rollover requirement of completing the transfer within 60 days. The proceeds from the Coverdell withdrawal now belong to your designated beneficiary (over whose assets you still have control until he or she reaches age 18), and the new 529 assets remain under your control.

If you choose to fund a Section 529 plan with your own funds but you're not able to put the full amount that was in the old Coverdell ESA into the new 529 plan, your designated beneficiary pays income tax and penalties on the income earned on the amount of the distribution that isn't being rolled over.

Neither scenario is perfect, in that they allow control over money to pass to your designated beneficiary, either by making her the account owner on a Section 529 plan or by actually handing her the cash. Still, if the amounts are not huge or if your designated beneficiary is incredibly mature for her age, it may work for you.

Transferring due to divorce

When planning for your student's education, you're probably not imagining a time when your designated beneficiary will be old enough to think about any marital issues, especially a marital dissolution. After all, you probably set up this account when your child was just a kid, and the first thought that crosses your mind when you check on him asleep in his bed is not how he's going to divide his assets when he gets a divorce.

Still, a Coverdell ESA can live on well into adulthood, and it may still be an asset owned by your designated beneficiary after he marries, and even at the time of a divorce. If this happens to your student, there are some things you both should know:

- ✓ **Coverdell ESAs aren't counted as community property in community property states.** Funds are gifted directly to the owner of the account (even if the gifts occur after marriage through a tax-free rollover from a different Coverdell ESA) and are maintained solely for the benefit of the account owner.

- ✓ **The owner of the account may include a Coverdell ESA as part of the divorce or separation agreement, transferring ownership to his or her spouse or former spouse.** In this case, provided the new owner is under age 30, this is a tax-free transfer, even if another tax-free transfer or rollover occurred within the last 12 months.

Chapter 9

The Mechanics of Coverdells

*A*lthough Section 529 plans suit many people (or maybe even you), Coverdell Education Savings Accounts (ESAs) are far more flexible in some ways, and they may fill a specific need in your educational funding plans that 529 plans can't. Provided that you meet the requirements in order to contribute to an account, you may be able to make this type of savings vehicle really work for you. (Chapter 8 tells you about the rules and regulations surrounding Coverdell accounts, so if you haven't read that chapter, you may want to flip back there first.)

This chapter gets you cooking on the practical stuff — the hows and whats you need to know to get started, and keep going, with a Coverdell ESA.

In this chapter, you find out the nitty-gritty of Coverdell accounts, from how and where you may open an account to what you need to do after that account is open in order to make it a success. You look at what you should and shouldn't do over the lifetime of the account, and discover pitfalls to avoid as you make your contributions and as your student takes his or her withdrawals. Finally, you see how Coverdell accounts dovetail with Section 529 and other college savings plans, creating a patchwork of education savings options that will eventually provide for all your student's needs.

Getting a Handle on What You Want

Before you ever start putting money into a Coverdell account, you need to know what you want to do and where you want to go with that money, some of which you may already have saved in a more traditional bank or brokerage account. None of these education savings options are as technically simple a savings technique as opening a bank account and making regular deposits into it. There are consequences to funding any of these accounts, and you need to understand not only what those consequences are but also how they fit into your and your student's future plans.

You need to be able to supply answers to all the following questions before making your initial deposit:

- ✔ **What are you saving for?** You may already be saving in another sort of plan, such as a Section 529 plan, for the major expenses, such as tuition and room and board. If so, picture this smaller plan as the place where the funds for some of your student's more personal expenses, such as books and supplies (and his computer, so long as he's still in high school or below, or if it's required by your child's college), can come from. Or, you may picture your student attending a private or parochial school long before he ever begins college, and you want this account to help pay for that. Have a clear idea in your head of how you plan for this money to be spent.

- ✔ **Who will be your designated beneficiary, and whom do you have waiting in the wings as a backup?** Saving money in a Coverdell account for the sake of saving money in a Coverdell account just doesn't cut it. You have to be saving for a specific person, and you have to have a reasonable expectation that the person you're saving for is going to need this money to pay for educational expenses at some point before her 30th birthday (or longer, if she's a special-needs student). What if you have any doubts whatsoever that you're not going to use up all the money you've saved over the years on that student? In that case, you may want to consider who can step into shoes vacated by your original beneficiary, either through choice or by necessity, whether it's another child of yours, a grandchild, or any other allowed relation of your original beneficiary who's included on the list in Chapter 8.

- ✔ **Who is actually going to contribute to your child's plan?** You may not be the obvious choice here. All your good intentions and the practicality of this particular type of account may not amount to a hill of beans if you're prohibited from making contributions because you earn too much money (see Chapter 8). If you'll meet the requirements in some years but not in others, you may want to line up an alternate contributor who'll meet the income limitation requirements in years that you don't (even if you have to make gifts to that person in order for him to make gifts into the Coverdell account).

✔ **What educational costs are you planning to pay for with the money in this account?** Coverdell accounts are far more limited in terms of total size than Section 529 plans. (You're just not going to be able to put as much money into an account where the maximum annual contribution is $2,000 as you are in an account that basically has no maximum annual contribution.) These plans, however, are much more flexible in the type of expenses that you can pay for.

You may want to consider just how much of your money you'll need in this account to pay for some of the expenses that your Section 529 isn't able to cover and try to limit the size of your Coverdell ESA to that amount and no more. For example, if you've invested in a Section 529 prepaid tuition plan, you may want to use distributions from your child's Coverdell account to pay for room and board, books, and other supplies. Or your secondary school child may be sooo close to achieving that perfect academic record and may need just a little extra tutoring in calculus in order to make the grade. In this case, paying for tutoring while in high school with Coverdell distributions may actually be a very savvy investment, as that extra edge may now qualify him or her for lucrative academic scholarships. In Chapter 10, I discuss more ways that Coverdell accounts can complement other savings plans.

After you know for whom and how much you're saving, you're ready to jump in.

Opening a Plan

After you figure out the answers to all the questions in the previous section's list, you need to fill out the forms, write a check, and get this account rolling.

First, though, you need to decide where, exactly, you want to open your account. Unlike Section 529 plans, states don't get involved in Coverdell accounts; accordingly, you have many more options to choose from, and you need to make many more decisions.

While you're in the process of choosing a bank, savings and loan company, or other institution, you need to focus on two essential items:

✔ The range and variety of investments that the account will offer

✔ The cost to you annually, upfront, or both to set up and administer the account

Keep in mind that none of these companies is in the business of paying for your child's education, but they're all in the business of making money. Your account represents nothing more than a moneymaking opportunity for them; make sure that it will also be one for you.

You also need to decide whether to invest in a *self-directed account* (one in which you decide on individual issues, both stocks and bonds, to invest in) or one in which you have a choice of mutual funds, bank certificates of deposit, and/or money market funds. Clearly, in the self-directed account, you bear more of the risk personally because you're making all the investment decisions by yourself (unless you hire, at your own cost, an advisor to select what you should buy and when to buy). If you choose to go the mutual fund route, even if your investments do poorly, you can still lay some of the blame on the fund manager. Still, a bad investment is a bad investment; your account loses money regardless of who made the decisions of what, and what not, to buy.

If this is your first venture into the world of investing, you may want to initially open your account in an institution that limits your investment options, or hire someone to make these decisions for you in a self-directed account. If you don't want to go to the expense of hiring an investment advisor, leaving the actual investing of your money in the hands of the mutual fund managers may give you a greater comfort level than choosing your own issues, especially when you're just beginning. A wise approach may be to ease yourself in and make safer (although maybe not as lucrative) choices at first. As you gain confidence in your own abilities, you always have the option to change to other options, such as investing in individual stocks and bonds. On the other hand, if you're making money and happy with how your investments are doing, don't feel that it's a requirement to always be searching for a better mousetrap.

Shopping for a place to open your account

When you begin shopping for a home for your Coverdell account, you may be surprised to find out who does — and who doesn't — offer these accounts. Not every bank, savings and loan company, and mutual fund company does. Check around and ask questions. Financial institutions must apply to, and be approved by, the IRS in order to offer Coverdell accounts. A good place to start your search and gather information about available custodians and trustees is IRS Announcement 2002-12 (www.irs.gov).

IRS Announcement 2002-12 clearly sets out the rules that govern which companies may act as a non-bank trustee or custodian of Coverdell ESAs. This announcement also contains a list of the non-bank trustees and custodians who were in place as of December 31, 2001. The list hasn't been formally updated since that time, but new financial entities can be added at any time, if the IRS commissioner approves them before they begin accepting Coverdell deposits. When you investigate non-bank custodians or trustees, you need to know that they must provide you with a copy of the IRS notice of approval before they can accept your account.

Announcement 2002-12 provides names and addresses of approved non-bank trustees and custodians, and some of the names on the list may surprise you. The list includes not only credit unions, mutual fund companies, and brokerage firms but also financial advisors and insurance companies (but remember, you can't invest in life insurance products inside these accounts). Some foreign banks are also on the list, as are a few truly unexpected entries — the Berklee College of Music, the Christian and Missionary Alliance, and the El Paso Electric Company. Clearly, one doesn't need to be purely in the business of financial services to apply for and be approved as a non-bank trustee or custodian of Coverdell ESAs.

Since December 31, 2001, the IRS has approved other non-bank trustees and custodians to offer Coverdell accounts. If, in your investigations, you find a plan that looks good and that you want to participate in, just make sure that you receive a copy of the necessary notice of approval from the IRS before you open an account and hand over your money.

Regardless of whether the plan you choose is sponsored by a bank, an institution listed on Announcement 2002-12, or a more recent entry into the Coverdell game, your custodian or trustee must provide you with a copy of the trust or custody agreement governing your account before you ever open the account. Very frequently, it's attached to the actual application; keep this agreement as part of your permanent records.

Just because your current bank or savings and loan company or your favorite mutual fund company offers these accounts doesn't mean that's the best place for you to park your account. Although your bank may seem like the obvious place to open this account, it may allow you to invest your money only in certificates of deposit or money market funds, neither of which will generate much income from earnings. Likewise, mutual fund companies may limit investments in Coverdell accounts to only certain mutual funds. Shop around for something that best suits your needs.

Meeting the initial requirements (besides money)

After you decide where to open your Coverdell account, you need to begin completing the necessary paperwork. And there should be no surprise here — nothing is ever as simple as filling out and signing a signature card any more. You'll most likely have to complete an account setup form (which is often the same form that you use to open a traditional IRA or a Roth IRA account — make sure to check the correct box) and a Form W-9, which certifies the Social Security number for the account owner (the designated beneficiary) and prevents back-up income tax withholding. You may also have to fill out a separate form to choose your investments or a form that certifies that your designated beneficiary falls under the "special-needs student" category.

The USA Patriot Act of 2001 has substantially increased the amount of information you must provide to open any account, and banks and other financial institutions no longer allow you to leave blanks in their paperwork to fill in later. If you can't provide this information when you want to open the account, the account won't be opened until you can.

Every company has its own forms, but they all require the following information:

> ✔ **Name, address, date of birth, and Social Security number of your designated beneficiary:** You may also be required to provide proof of citizenship and, if a non-U.S. citizen, proof of resident alien or valid visa information. Be prepared with photocopies of birth certificates, Social Security cards, passports, green cards, and the like.
>
> ✔ **Name, address, date of birth, Social Security number, and relationship to your designated beneficiary of the parent or legal guardian in charge of the account:** This is where the terms for the responsible adult/individual on the account are defined. While your child is a minor, the responsible adult on the account needs to be a parent or legal guardian, even if that person is not the source of the account's funds or the person who opened the account in the first place. In addition to the biographical information, you may need to supply proof of your citizenship or resident alien or visa information. If you are the minor's legal guardian, you need to provide copies of the relevant documents.
>
> ✔ **Answers to the following questions:**
>
>> • Will responsibility for the account remain with you after your beneficiary reaches the age of majority, or will it revert to the beneficiary at that time?
>>
>> • During the time that you're the responsible individual, will you retain the ability to change the designated beneficiary on the account to another family member?

In addition to the items listed, you may also be required to disclose who's actually contributing the funds into the account, including that person's Social Security number, or the federal tax identification number of a corporate or charitable entity.

Finally, although not all account setups require this information, you need to be prepared to disclose not only an alternate beneficiary but also the person who will take over responsibility for this account should you die or become incompetent. As always, you'll need full names, addresses, Social Security numbers, and dates of birth for any alternate names you list on these forms.

Save yourself some trouble by lining up ahead of time all the information you need to open a Coverdell account.

Devising an Effective Investment Strategy

After your account is open and you've actually placed money into it, you need to create an investment strategy you feel comfortable with. If your student is very young, you may choose to begin with a more aggressive approach, putting most of your money into stocks rather than bonds, certificates of deposit, or money market funds. If your student is older and closer to needing the money in the account, you may select a less risky approach, leaving only a small amount of money in the stock market and placing most of your funds into safer investments. Limiting your risk also limits the amount of money you're likely to make; however, the trade-off is in knowing how much money will be in the account when you need it.

You also need to create a set of rules under which you feel comfortable operating. Maybe you're the type of person who begins to sweat when your investment appreciates by 20 percent. Or perhaps you're someone who won't be satisfied until it approaches 50 percent or 100 percent appreciation. And when will you sell if an investment doesn't perform the way you thought it would? Do you begin to bite your nails once it drops 10 percent below its purchase price, and proceed to chew on your knuckles, elbows, and toes as it continues to decline by 20 percent, or more, below the amount that you bought it for? Maybe your blood pressure can only survive a drop of 20 percent below its absolute high point, and that next penny of loss has you reaching for the telephone at the same moment that you eat a bottle of antacid tablets. Just like in most other areas of life, establishing guidelines in investing gives you a structure within which to work.

Rules and guidelines are meant to be broken and changed. After you devise a strategy, don't set it in stone. As your student ages, you need to reassess your investments. He'll be needing the money soon, and you may want to preserve at least some of the money you've managed to accumulate to date.

Creating a set of investing guidelines gives you a valuable tool when determining what's going right and what's going wrong inside your student's account. If you have no specific strategy, you'll have a hard time knowing what to change if you're not achieving your hoped-for results. With guidelines in place, you can better understand what's not working quite the way you want, and then change it.

Understanding your investments

You've heard all the cautionary tales since you were a kid: Look before you leap, test the waters with your big toe before you stick your whole foot in, read the fine print, and don't let yourself be blindsided. So why is it that most people, when faced with an investment decision, close their eyes and point or buy whatever Great-Uncle Al tells them to buy?

If you're going to have any success at all in investing, you need to understand what you're buying, and you need to be comfortable with that knowledge. You gain absolutely nothing by being able to explain how a covered option works if the idea of putting your hard-earned money to work for you in that manner makes you sweat.

Understanding your investments and how they work makes devising an appropriate investment strategy easier for you. Terms such as risk, high-growth, low-yield, and so on, which trip effortlessly off the tongue of your financial advisor, may be completely meaningless to you. And your financial advisor is pretty much counting on that fact (he looks good, you feel not-so-smart, and he can then peddle his expertise to you). Understanding investment terminology helps you to figure out where your comfort level lies and allows you to stay there.

Your goal is to create a balanced portfolio, one in which the risk level is tolerable to you and which includes a variety of different types of investments. This approach is also the most effective long-term way to invest. Any portfolio that relies too much on one particular investment or one sort of investment adds unnecessary risk. Spread your money over as wide a range as possible to maximize your opportunities while minimizing your risk.

Although what follows focuses on stocks and bonds (because that's where most people need the most help), remember to keep all money invested at all times. Every Coverdell ESA has some sort of money market option; make sure that any cash sitting in your account is swept daily into the money market funds. Even though the interest that you earn on this money won't pay for much on its own, over time, it will help to improve your overall investment result.

Regarding risk

Whether you're investing in *stocks* (shares in companies that you own) or *bonds* (loans that you make to companies in exchange for interest payments), an element of risk is involved. It's up to you to determine how big an element of risk you're talking about and how much risk you're willing to assume. Here are some points to keep in mind when pondering the level or risk to take:

- ✔ **Never put all your eggs in one basket.** No matter how confident you are that something will take off, invest part of your money in other ventures just in case. There is no denying that the opportunity exists for you to make a killing in the market — any number of people did during the technology and dot.com boom of the late 1990s — but the opportunity to lose it all is just as great (if not greater).

- ✔ **Most people assume that buying stocks is riskier than buying bonds, and to some degree, that's true.** In a worst-case scenario, where a company goes bankrupt, a bondholder has some opportunity to recoup his investment, because he's a creditor of the company. A shareholder in that bankrupt company, however, knows to kiss the value of his investment goodbye; as a partial owner in the company, he'll receive money only after all creditors have been paid in full.

However, understand that some companies' financial situations are so solid as to represent an almost sure thing, not insofar as the variations in its stock price go, but as to whether they're still going to be around tomorrow or next year. In this regard, they may represent a less risky investment than investing in *junk bonds*, or bonds that are rated lower than investment grade by bond rating companies such as Moody's or Standard & Poor's (S&P). Junk bonds (which is anything that Moody's grades as Ba or lower, and that S&P rates as BB or lower) present the potential of a very high interest rate on your money; the bond ratings companies also recognize that the companies issuing these bonds have a higher than average chance of defaulting on their loans. Once again, risk raises its head — you've invested in something that has the very real potential of significantly raising the value of your investment account, but it also carries with it the possibility of sucking that amount of value, and more, out.

✔ **Doing some research helps you to assess the risk of a particular investment.** Check the history of a stock price. If you see wild fluctuations and you don't have a strong stomach, you may want to pass on that particular issue. Look to see whether dividends have been paid and whether they've been paid regularly and over a long period of time. A company's ability to pay dividends to its shareholders shows a tendency for financial health, although it's not a sure indicator. And look at a company's balance sheet before you ever hand over a single dollar into its care. The balance sheets of all publicly owned companies are matters of public record and are available either from the company itself or on the Internet.

Bonds and mutual funds carry creditworthiness ratings; check the ratings. Moody's Investors Service and Standard & Poor's are the best-known bond rating organizations. They judge bonds from highest quality (S&P = AAA, Moody's = Aaa) to those in default, with recovery unlikely (S&P = D, Moody's = C). The higher the quality of the bond, the lower the stated interest rate is likely to be, but the higher your chance is of actually collecting that interest. Generally, any bond that's rated B and below is increasingly speculative; although some may represent the debt of genuinely solid companies, you need to begin to do your research a bit more carefully to identify these gems.

✔ **No investment is absolutely risk-free.** Your bank may go belly up (although your bank deposits, but not your investment accounts, are protected by deposit insurance). The United States Treasury may start defaulting on its loans (in which case, we're all in much bigger trouble than the fact that we've lost the value of our treasury bills, notes, or bonds). Your house may float away, taking all the savings you've stitched into the mattress down the river with it. There is no such thing as a sure thing.

Choosing growth stocks versus value stocks

Any discussion about stocks and the stock market inevitably includes the terms "growth" and "value." Here's what those terms mean.

- **Growth stocks:** Very simply, *growth stocks* are shares in companies that still are experiencing, or anticipate experiencing, significant earnings growth. They may be pharmaceutical, high-tech, or biotech companies, all busy inventing the next great magic pill, miracle cure, or computer application that will completely change your life. And it may, but not in the way they think. There is great potential for a significant increase in the value of your investment when you put some of your money in a growth company.

- **Value stocks:** On the other hand, *value stocks* are shares in companies who already have an established product line or service, a product or service that generates steady income for the company. Usually, the current share price of the company is well below the actual value of the company if it were sold or otherwise liquidated.

  Value companies often include utility companies (but not the telecom companies) and consumer and durable goods companies. Somehow, even though a breakfast cereal company may seem to constantly be bringing new cereals on to the market, it's still basically making breakfast cereal and still generating roughly the same amount of net income from that cereal.

Value stocks are often viewed as being stodgy, but their stodginess can reap real rewards for you. Because of their low valuations against share price, their prices often creep up, increasing the worth of your investment. At the same time, you're still receiving those quarterly dividends. It's a win-win situation, especially during periods when the overall stock market tends to be in the doldrums. Historically, value stocks have outperformed the overall market during market downturns. For more about value stocks, check out *Value Investing For Dummies,* by Peter Sander and Janet Haley (published by Wiley).

Comparing high-cap, mid-cap, and low-cap stocks

This section is not a comparison of top hats, stocking caps, and flat caps. What it does refer to is the size, or market capitalization, of a company selling shares in itself. *Market capitalization* is the value the market has put on a company (as opposed to the company's actual value, as determined by its assets and balance sheet).

For example, if a company has 1 million shares issued and outstanding and the shares sell for $10 per share, the market capitalization of the company is $10 million. But because this company may only be worth the value of one bright employee's new idea (which is still being developed and so hasn't earned the company a red cent yet), the market clearly values the company far higher than the total value of the underlying assets. And maybe the market is right; the new idea may just pay off, and those people who gambled $10 per share when it was nothing more than an idea will turn around in a few years and sell those same shares for $100. Such is the magic of the stock market.

Large capitalization (large-cap), middle capitalization (mid-cap), and low capitalization (low-cap) companies comprise the entire stock market. Here's how they break down:

- ✔ Generally, large-cap companies are those whose market capitalization ranges from $5 billion and up.

- ✔ Mid-caps cover those companies with market capitalization between $1 billion and $5 billion.

- ✔ Small-cap companies are everyone else.

Generally speaking (and there are no hard and fast rules here), large-cap corporations (which include the so-called blue-chip stocks and all the issues on the Dow Jones Industrial Average) tend to be more stable in price than their smaller counterparts. Just as a semitrailer takes a while to get up to speed after starting up when the traffic signal turns green, a large-cap corporation is a behemoth that isn't going to do anything quickly. Share prices can rise and fall, but you won't often see spectacular leaps or plummets. Instead, the price changes tend to be slow and gradual (although you should never forget the lessons of Enron, Tyco, and WorldCom, to name but a few large-cap corporations that hit the skids and failed spectacularly).

Overall, large caps tend to hit lower on the risk scale than mid caps or small caps. As market capitalization decreases, risk, with both its upside and its downside, generally increases.

Looking at your bond options

Bonds are loans that you make to government entities or corporations. In exchange for the use of your money, whoever you've lent the money to is supposed to pay you interest. During the lifetime of the bond, you'll receive interest payments, probably twice each year. When the bond matures, or the issuing body chooses to pay it off early, you receive back the full-face amount of the bond, plus any interest still owed to you. (An issuing body often chooses to pay off the bond early, especially as interest rates drop and it can borrow the same money for less interest.) In theory, bond investment is pretty simple, and overall, it seems like a fairly safe, essentially unexciting sort of investment. Here are your options when it comes to bonds:

- ✔ **U.S. Treasuries:** There may be nothing duller than U. S. Treasury bills (which exist for no more than one year), notes (the period from issue to maturity from one year and a day to ten years after issue), and bonds (maturities begin more than ten years after their issue). These debt instruments represent pieces of the *national debt,* or the cumulative amount of money the U.S. government has spent in excess of the total tax revenues collected since the beginning of the U.S. government. And, because the U.S. government needs to be able to finance its debt at the lowest possible interest rate it can afford, U.S. Treasury bills, notes, and bonds are guaranteed by the full faith and credit of the United States. In other words, they're about as safe and risk-free as you can get, probably even beating the money-under-the-mattress scenario. To make them even more attractive, interest from U.S. Treasuries is income-tax-free in all states. U.S. Treasury obligations may be purchased through brokers, directly from any branch of the Federal Reserve Bank, or online through the Bureau of the Public Debt Online at `www.publicdebt.treas.gov`.

✔ **Government bonds and certificates:** Moving up the risk and excitement scale for bonds, you next reach so-called government bonds and certificates, such as those issued by the Government National Mortgage Association (GNMAs, or Ginnie Maes) and the Federal National Mortgage Association (FNMAs), to name two. These are very similar to Treasuries in that the federal government and its agencies issue them, but they're not exactly Treasury-like, either in risk or in state income tax exemptness. There's no "full faith and credit of the U.S. government" standing behind these investments. Still, it's highly unlikely that any federal agency will go belly up and stop its debt repayment. Because these investments are marginally riskier than U.S. Treasury issues, they do pay higher interest rates. Unlike U.S. Treasuries, government bonds and certificates may not be purchased directly from the U.S. government, but only from financial services firms (such as brokerages) that trade in government securities. If you want to purchase one of these securities, ask your broker whether he can purchase it for you; if your broker can't help you, he'll direct you to a firm that can.

✔ **Municipal bonds:** Municipal bonds are debt instruments issued by state and local governments (including issues from Puerto Rico, the District of Columbia, the U.S. Virgin Islands, American Samoa, and Guam) to finance things such as hospitals, higher education, or the construction of roads and sports stadiums. They're only as solid as the governments and agencies issuing them. Here is where you need to begin checking either with Standard & Poor's (`www.standardandpoors.com`) or with Moody's Investors Service (`www.moodys.com`) regarding the reliability of any particular bond or its issuing body. States and municipalities sometimes have difficulties in paying their bills, a situation that does reflect negatively on their creditworthiness and their rating.

As ratings drop, interest rates and yields increase. Most interest on municipal bonds is federally tax-free (and therefore, not the best investment for your tax-deferred or exempt Coverdell account). However, municipal bonds could make sense for you in some situations.

✔ **Corporate bonds:** Finally, corporate bonds represent the debt that corporations take on in order to continue doing business. And the quality of that debt corresponds to the financial health of the corporation issuing the bond. A financially healthy company, one that has no problems now or in the foreseeable future, issues investment-grade bonds (above B grade) that pay higher rates of interest than you get from any sort of government bond, whether federal, state, or local, but still not so high that it blows your socks off. The lower that rating drops, though, the higher the interest you'll receive; the company issuing the bond needs to entice investors with inflated rates of return to attract their money.

Taking advantage of dollar cost averaging

Even the pros have a difficult time knowing exactly when to buy and figuring out what's really the bottom of the market (on the theory of buy low, sell high). And you're not an investment professional, staring at the ticker tape, poised to jump in with your buy or sell order. So what?

You can use a technique called *dollar cost averaging* to provide almost the exact same result as those pros are getting, with a lot less effort and time. Simply, dollar cost averaging is the technique where you purchase the same dollar amount of a security at periodic intervals, either over an indefinite term or for a specific number of weeks or months.

Here's how it works: When you set up your account, you outline a portfolio that you want. You tell the account custodian that you want this percentage of your monthly contribution to buy this investment and that percentage to buy the other. Every month when you make a contribution to the account, and until you give the custodian instructions to stop, you'll be buying these same investments in those percentages. In addition, if you make contributions only once a year, then the custodian can divide that money into however many periodic purchases you want to make. You may decide that you want to spread your purchases out over the entire year or maybe just a few months. For as long as you participate in this program buying, you benefit from all the fluctuations in that particular investment. Although you won't be buying all your shares at the absolute low, neither do you run any danger of buying all of them as they hit their peak.

Doing your research

It's all well and good to read a column and follow someone's advice; the only problem is that the person giving the advice isn't investing his own money in your account. You are, and although advice from the experts may seem like a good thing, you'll never get two experts who completely agree on anything. In the end, *you* are going to make the decisions regarding your student's account, and your choices will determine how well the account will perform. There's nothing like a little pressure to make you sit up a bit straighter, is there?

Don't ever rely on someone's stock tip, whether friend or stranger; do your own homework and assess the positives and negatives yourself. Every investment has its good points, but it also has bad points. It's up to you to decide whether the upside outweighs the downside. If you can't discover the short-comings, you'd better run quickly in the opposite direction. There's no such creature as a sure thing, and the person offering advice may have an ulterior motive. That motive may be as mundane as being paid by a newspaper to come up with a column idea or as sinister as trying to artificially crank up the price of a stock to make a personal killing in the market. Never assume that someone is giving you stock market advice for your health.

I'm not saying that you should ignore everything written in the paper or talked about on television or that you should walk away from the advice of people whom you know and trust. You do need to understand, though, the biases of the people giving advice and factor those into your own decision. Many people have their fathers' portfolio because Dad has always told them what to buy. The only problem with that approach is that Dad's investment criteria aren't necessarily your own, and a portfolio that suits Dad's needs to a T may be completely inappropriate for you.

Never rely on investment advice that you receive through unsolicited e-mails or faxes. These are generally scams that you should avoid at all costs. If you follow this type of advice, it'll likely cost you plenty. Remember, what seems too good to be true usually is. Run, don't walk, away from these offers.

Selecting Investments and Placing Buy Orders

After you choose what type of account to open and determine your strategy and rules, you need to sit down and do your research. You may already have devised a reasonable plan to put a certain percentage of your money into stocks and another percentage into bonds. You may even have thought about how much you want to invest in chemical companies and how much in high-tech corporations. Now you must select the actual investments and place your initial buy orders.

Depending on which custodian you're using for your Coverdell account, placing a buy (or sell) order may require you to contact the custodian with your instructions (the custodian will actually make the transaction), or you may be able to initiate the transaction over the Internet. Many brokerages are valid Coverdell custodians. When your Coverdell account is with one of them, you can usually buy and sell securities within your account just the same as you would in any other brokerage account — by calling your broker or placing the trade online.

Paying Into a Coverdell Education Savings Account

You can put money into your student's account in a variety of ways. Just like with Section 529 plans, you have the option of writing a check, making an automatic fund transfer from your bank account, or even having funds deducted through a payroll deduction program. If you use a bank's Coverdell account, you may even have the choice of paying in cash (although this won't work with any brokerage firm or any institution that deals primarily through electronic means).

However you choose to fund your student's account, you may not use stocks, bonds, real estate, or built-up value in an insurance policy as a contribution. If the money that you plan to put into a Coverdell account is currently in one of those forms, you need to liquidate your nonqualified investment and then deposit the cash.

You may contribute to a Coverdell account at any point throughout the year. There are no limits on when or how often you may make a deposit, provided, of course, that you don't exceed the limitations on how much you can deposit, which I describe in detail in Chapter 8.

Just like with either traditional and Roth IRA's, you have the option of making a contribution into a Coverdell account for a particular year after the year has ended but before you file your income tax return for that year. Indicate on your deposit slip that you're making a so-called *carryback contribution* and that you want it applied to the preceding calendar year. The ability to make a contribution for a year just ended in the first part of the following year may provide you with a valuable planning opportunity. Very often, because of year-end bonuses and late-in-the-year stock sales (with capital gains) and distributions from mutual fund companies, you won't know how great your income for a particular year will be until well into January of the following year. If you have the opportunity to defer your bonus (or any other item of income) into the following year, you may not know whether you're even eligible to make a contribution for a particular year until after December 31.

Managing Your Account

You maintain total control over the investments in any Coverdell account for which you're the responsible individual, even though your designated beneficiary is actually the account owner. This seems to be a complete turnaround from Section 529 plans (where you're the plan owner but don't really own the plan assets and have very limited control over the actual investments).

And the investment choices you have are amazingly varied and can be quite complex. You can invest in a wide variety of investments, both through mutual funds and individual investments (known as self-directed accounts). This variety may enable you to reap huge rewards if you're savvy in your investments, but you don't have any safety net to catch you when they fall.

Watching your investments with respect to the overall markets

You rely on outside input to judge your performance in so many ways — from receiving merit increases (and well-deserved pats on the back) at work to cheers from your family for a job well done. Unfortunately, performance measurements on your student's Coverdell account won't come from the outside; you have to provide your own. Whether you choose a self-directed approach to your student's Coverdell account, place your funds in the hands of a mutual fund manager, or hire your own investment advisor to choose investments for you, it's up to you to make sure that your portfolio lives up to the standards of the rest of the market. Although you don't need to perform this sort of assessment every day, you do need to look closely at your investments at least monthly or quarterly to make sure that you stay on track and out of trouble.

If you invest in a more restrictive account, one where your choices are limited to a fixed number of mutual funds or certificates of deposit, assessing the account's performance against similar investments outside of your account is fairly simple. Remember that making apples-to-oranges comparisons isn't fair — you always need to compare your investments to those that are roughly the same as what you own. So if you own an index fund in your Coverdell account, place it against other index funds and then grade its performance. Likewise, you can compare a foreign fund only to other foreign funds (preferably with the same foreign mix), and you can compare money market funds only to other money market funds.

Individual stocks and bonds are more difficult to compare, as no two are exactly alike; you can, however, get a rough idea of where your choices stand by looking at the various industries you're invested in and seeing how you stack up against the industry average.

Not only do you need to compare the percentage improvement (or devaluation) of your investments against other, similar investments, but you also need to check the overall risk of your investments against other like issues. If you own a particular stock and/or bond that's hopscotching all over the map in price while the rest of that particular industry stays fairly stable, you may want to switch to another company within that overall industry. Likewise, if news sources report that your company is verging on the edge of bankruptcy, now may be the time to switch to something that may maintain its value a little better. Yes, you can often make a killing in the market by buying a stock teetering on the edge. More often than not, however, such a stock falls off and takes you with it.

Even though you don't need to check your entire portfolio every day, if you're self-directing the investments in your student's Coverdell account, you do need to stay current on your riskier investments (and that does mean checking those stocks every day). The Internet is a good place to start — you can easily create your portfolio on a personalized search engine page and then monitor your individual investments. Especially in the case of companies that may be poised for a breakthrough that suddenly doesn't happen, keeping on top of the breaking news regarding that stock can give you a quick heads up to sell something before the price sinks to nothing. Remember that the object is to earn money overall in your account; losses are allowed, but do your best to limit their size.

Making the most of investment flexibility

When you're the responsible individual for a Coverdell account, you fully control your strategy and your specific investments. You may change them at any time without penalty as long as you stay within the boundaries of that particular account. You may buy and sell stocks, bonds, mutual funds, and most other sorts of investments. You can play it safe and keep all the money in a money market fund, or you may choose to crank up the risk and invest in high-growth stocks and junk bonds.

Not every bank, savings and loan company, or other qualified financial institution offers you a full variety of investment options. If you're interested in a more variable approach to investing your student's funds, you may want to search out a custodian or trustee who will. Many banks now have wholly-owned subsidiary investment divisions that can provide you with some or all of the same financial products as a mutual fund company or a brokerage.

When setting up a Coverdell ESA, you also need to keep in mind that, although you can roll over your account to a new custodian, you must complete the rollover within 60 days of the withdrawal from the old account, and you may not roll over an account more than once in a 12-month period (see Chapter 8). You can avoid this problem by making sure that the account you initially choose gives you a wide variety of investment options and that any account that you move to does the same. You have infinite opportunities to change your investments within an account; you're limited only when moving from account to account.

Timing your contributions and withdrawals to gain maximum benefit

Many people liken investing to gambling, and one similarity is that both have winners and losers. Although your chances of winning depend to a certain extent on factors beyond your control, you can do some things to increase the odds in your favor. Remember, in this particular game, timing is key; two people who make all the same investments with exactly the same amount of money may still achieve very different results on the basis of timing issues alone. Here are some ways to improve your odds in the investing game:

- **Start saving early.** The sooner you begin to put money inside a Coverdell ESA, the more you'll be able to save overall. You also extend the period of time your investments have to ride through the ups and downs of the investment markets. Remember that unless your designated beneficiary is a special-needs student, you'll have to stop making contributions when she turns 18.

- **Make your contributions as soon as you can, instead of waiting until the last minute.** If you're sure that you'll be contributing to your student's Coverdell account in any given year, make that contribution as early in the year as you can — remember, the longer the money stays inside the account, the longer it has to earn tax-free or tax deferred income. If you think that you may be prohibited from making a contribution in a particular year because you earn too much, make a gift of that money to someone who can, and then make sure that person makes the contribution to your student's account.

- **When you sell investments in order to make distributions, don't limit yourself to the sale of one or two specific investments.** When you have highly appreciated stocks in your Coverdell account, pare down your positions gradually instead of selling them all at once. If your stock continues to climb after that initial sale, you've then ensured that you'll reap even more profits from that particular company. At the same time, if you need to raise cash in order to make a distribution and you have one or two losers sitting in your account, now may be the time to bite the bullet and get rid of your underperformers.

- **Keep an eye on your proportional investment strategy.** If you decide that you want to keep a certain percentage of your account in various areas of the market, you need to keep an eye on how each investment is doing. One or two companies whose stock either soars or sours will throw off your entire strategy. You may need to periodically buy and sell in your portfolio to achieve the proportionate mix that you want.

- **Don't wait until the last minute to sell investments in order to have the cash to make a distribution.** Everyone else who has students waiting for tuition and other payments is also selling at these times; historically, the stock market dips and prices for securities fall when everyone needs cash in a hurry. Check your portfolio and your student's anticipated expenses and then sell when you can realize a reasonable profit. Remember, no one can absolutely tell you when a particular stock or bond has reached its absolute top price.

Making Distributions

Your account is now in place, and you've been making contributions to it for a while. You've made some great investment decisions, and even though you may have much more money sitting in your student's Section 529 plan, his Coverdell account isn't looking too shabby either. As a matter of fact, as you prepare to make distributions from it to pay for qualified educational expenses, you're feeling pretty good about managing to save so much money.

As you request checks from your student's Coverdell ESA, keep in mind just how much you actually need. You're responsible for keeping track of what is and isn't a qualified expense (see Chapter 8). Your trustee or custodian doesn't care and can't be bothered. If you request a check for more than your qualified expenses, your student will bear the burden of income tax on the earnings portion of any excess distribution, plus the 10 percent penalty.

Keeping track of distributions and qualified expenses

Whenever your student takes a distribution from his Coverdell account, he'll receive a Form 1099-Q from the custodian/trustee of the account, showing the total distribution, the amount of the distribution that is attributable to contributions (remember, you've already paid the tax on this piece so your beneficiary doesn't have pay again), and the balance of the distribution, which represents earnings on your contributions. The earnings piece has never been taxed, and if you use the entire contribution to pay qualifying expenses, the earnings portion will not currently be taxed (although this provision is set to expire on December 31, 2010, if Congress doesn't extend it).

You and your student — not the school that he attends or your Coverdell custodian — decide how much of his expenses are qualifying. Your student's school may provide you with a form at the end of the year, showing all money that you (or he) paid. This is only one piece of the qualified educational expense pie, however, and it's up to you to decide if all, or only part of those payments, qualify (remember, things like health insurance don't). Keep track of all receipts for qualifying educational expenses as you receive them. The occasional book or notebook may not seem like a big ticket item, but over the course of a year, such items can add up to a substantial amount.

If, at the end of the year, the amount of your student's Coverdell distribution is equal to or less than the total amount of qualified educational expenses, and if your student didn't receive any money from either a Section 529 plan, a scholarship, a grant, or any other tax-free distribution, or if you've decided that you're not going to use either the Hope or Lifetime Learning Credit discussed in Chapter 16, you're home free. None of the earnings shown on the Form 1099-Q will be taxed to your student.

Computer equipment is a qualified expense only for primary and secondary students, not for postsecondary students unless the postsecondary educational institution requires that computer. Don't forget, though, that the tax year that your student begins as a college freshman may also be the tax year that he completes his secondary education. When you buy that computer before high school graduation, it qualifies as a valid expense for Coverdell distribution purposes; if you wait until the summer or the fall, you may be out of luck.

Using distributions for nonqualified expenses

A Coverdell account doesn't provide a completely tax-free ride for all the expenses your student will incur over the course of his education, although it does cover a whole lot of them. Sometimes, though, there's just no way around it, and your student needs to access money for expenses that don't qualify for tax-free treatment under Section 530. Face it, the kid may need to put gas in the car or pay bus fare, and if he's living off-campus or he's less than a half-time student, all or part of his food and rent may not qualify (not to mention utilities). And did I mention clothes, vacations, and health insurance? They may be necessary for the health and well-being of your child, but they don't make the list of qualified educational expenses.

If you're making distributions to your student and you suspect that some of the money being handed over to him may be taxable to him, collecting receipts becomes even more important. Chapter 8 tells you exactly what expenses qualify. You want to be able to exclude as much as possible from the tax man, but you need to substantiate your numbers in case you're asked.

Determining income for tax purposes

Clearly, when your student takes a distribution from his Coverdell account and uses it to buy a car, she's going to have to pay income tax on the earnings portion of that distribution. Likewise, if she reaches her 30th birthday and a balance remains in her account, she receives the balance and pays income tax on the earnings.

The situation becomes a bit more complicated when only a part of your student's distribution pays for nonqualified expenses. When trying to figure out how much of an annual distribution qualifies for tax exemption and how much is taxable, the rules for Coverdell accounts are exactly the same as they are for Section 529 plans. Both the contribution piece and the deferred earnings piece of all distributions are allocated between qualifying and nonqualifying distributions. The earnings on the qualifying piece will not be taxed to the student; the earnings on the nonqualifying piece will.

Chapter 6 shows how to calculate the taxable piece of a combination qualifying/nonqualifying distribution for a Section 529 plan; you do the calculation in exactly the same manner for a Coverdell distribution.

If your student is the designated beneficiary on both a Coverdell account and a Section 529 plan and she plans on paying for qualified educational expenses by using money from these plans, she may end up taking distributions from both plans in a single year. If the total amount of both distributions exceeds her qualifying educational expenses, a portion of both distributions (Coverdell and Section 529) will be taxable to her based not only on the proportion of nonqualifying distributions to total distributions but also on the proportion of each plan distribution to the total annual distribution. The IRS suggests that you can use any reasonable method to determine the proportion of taxable earnings from both accounts; however, in Publication 970, Tax Benefits for Education, the IRS highlights the method illustrated in Figure 9-1.

Keep in mind that distributions qualifying for tax-exempt treatment from both Coverdell accounts and from Section 529 plans are reduced by any tuition scholarships or grants that your student may receive.

For example, Lydia attends college, and her annual qualifying expenses were $20,000 for the tax year just ended, although her actual expenses were $25,000. She received a partial tuition scholarship of $5,000 and used a $15,000 distribution from her Section 529 plan (of which $5,000 is accumulated earnings) and $5,000 from her Coverdell account (of which $2,000 represents earnings) to pay the balance of her expenses. In January, she received a 1099-Q from both plans. Check out Figure 9-1 to see Lydia's calculation to determine the taxable amounts from her Coverdell account and from her Section 529 plan.

As you can clearly see from Figure 9-1, even though Lydia's annual education cost is really $25,000, only $20,000 of it is considered qualifying educational expenses on which both Section 529 and Section 530 are built. Although she receives a scholarship to fill the gap, it first goes towards reducing the amount of her qualifying educational expenses, leaving poor Lydia in a bind: She needs the full $20,000 distribution from her plans, but now she has to pay tax on a portion of the earnings.

Adding insult to injury: The 10 percent penalty

Fortunately for Lydia, as Figure 9-1 shows, the gap between her actual costs and her total qualified educational expenses was made up by a scholarship. If Lydia had to take distributions from her Coverdell and/or Section 529 plan for the full $25,000, she would have had to pay not only the tax, calculated as shown in the example, but also an additional 10 percent penalty on the income portion only of the nonqualified distribution. Because the $5,000 shortfall between the amount of total expenses and qualified expenses is made up with a scholarship, it falls under one of the allowable exceptions to the penalty rules described in Chapter 5.

	FROM COVERDELL	FROM SECTION 529
Lydia's total qualifying expenses	$20,000	
SUBTRACT: Lydia's partial tuition scholarship	− 5,000	
Lydia's net qualifying expenses	$15,000	
	FROM COVERDELL	**FROM SECTION 529**
Total plan distributions	$5,000	$15,000
SUBTRACT: Net qualifying expenses (allocated between both plans)	− $3,750	− $11,250
Total nonqualifying distribution (allocated proportionately between both plans)	$1,250	$3,750
Ratio of nonqualifying to total distribution	$1,250/$5,000 = 25%	$3,750/$15,000 = 25%
Calculation of nonqualifying earnings portion of distribution	$2,000 × 25% = $500	$5,000 × 25% = $1,250

Figure 9-1: Calculating the tax on multiple plan withdrawals.

Dealing with death and taxes

When you open a Coverdell ESA for your student, you're clearly focusing on the day when he completes his education and joins the world of productive adults. And that's as it should be — planning for your children's future is a focal point of many people's lives. Still, sometimes the unforeseen happens, and either you or your student doesn't live to that magic day. And although your first thoughts probably won't be centered on what happens to your Coverdell account, you need to know the consequences.

When you first set up your account, the initial form may have a place for you to insert the name, address, and Social Security number of a successor responsible adult, a topic that I discuss in the section "Meeting the initial requirements (besides money)," earlier in this chapter.

If you completed that section at that time and none of the information has changed, great! If you die, your named successor assumes control as the responsible adult, and that person now is in charge of making all the investment and withdrawal decisions. If your designated beneficiary is still under 18, the new responsible adult can even continue contributing to this account, provided his income falls under the phaseout amounts.

The death of a designated beneficiary triggers two sorts of tax events — income and estate. You have to deal with these taxes in completely different ways, and you can't ignore either one. Cover all the bases in both areas; failure to do so will only cause you further grief.

When you first set up a Coverdell ESA for your student, you name one or more additional people who'll receive the proceeds from that account if the named designated beneficiary dies. After you complete that task, you probably think that you're done dealing with that matter — if the truly awful happens, your death designations will take effect, and the account will do whatever the account is supposed to do.

Well, nothing to do with finance and taxes is ever quite as simple as that. By naming death beneficiaries, all you're doing is assuming that your student, should he die, will die without a last will and testament (if he's a minor, that's a safe bet) and determining who you want to receive the money. Still, there are definite tax consequences when the named beneficiary of a Coverdell account dies. Keep the following in mind:

✔ The total value of a Coverdell account is included in the estate of the deceased designated beneficiary.

✔ If you've named a successor-designated beneficiary who qualifies under the family relationship rules in Chapter 8 and he's under 30 years old when he succeeds to the account, you may make an income-tax-free rollover from the existing account into a new Coverdell account for the new beneficiary.

✔ If your successor-designated beneficiary is over age 30, you have to completely distribute the account to that person within 30 days after the death of the original beneficiary.

✔ If you fail to name a successor beneficiary and the account remains in the original beneficiary's estate, it must be completely distributed within 30 days after the beneficiary's death to his estate.

Because nothing to do with death and taxes is ever as straightforward as you'd like (which is to say you'd like to have nothing at all to do with either), if your designated beneficiary should die, you should not attempt to tackle these tax issues on your own. Seek the advice of a competent attorney who specializes in estates to help you prepare the necessary filings. When looking for professional advice, ask for referrals from friends and family or find a lawyer through the Martindale-Hubbell database (www.martindale.com).

Chapter 10

Figuring the Pluses and Minuses of Coverdell Accounts

. . . .

In This Chapter

▶ Looking at the benefits of Coverdell accounts

▶ Recognizing the drawbacks of Coverdells and working around them

. . . .

*A*lmost everyone agrees (which is unusual) that higher ed is where it's at if you want your children to get the best start in their adult lives. And in a rare instance of unanimity, almost all the same people agree that you should save something to pay those eventual higher education costs. Where perfect agreement falls apart is when people discuss their "perfect" savings plan.

The truth is that there's no one perfect savings plan. What works for one person may be totally wrong for another, and rules governing one type of account may fit perfectly into one person's saving strategy while strangling another's attempts. Coverdell Education Savings Accounts (ESAs) are a perfect example. Although they may be real players in your strategy to save for your student's education, they're not the perfect solution for everyone. To use a Coverdell account effectively, you need to understand your financial situation now and consider where you think you'll be in the future to see if, and how, a Coverdell plan makes sense for you and your family.

In this chapter, you explore what's really great, and what's really not, about Coverdell ESAs. You also find out how to magnify what's good about Coverdell while minimizing what's bad.

Knowing the Pluses of Coverdells

Before you bog down in the minutiae of all the rules and regulations that go along with Coverdell accounts, take a couple minutes to reflect on some reasons why they can potentially be really good for you and your family.

Having total control

One of the great advantages of Coverdell ESAs (and the one that most banks and financial institutions spend a great deal of time telling you about) is that you, the responsible adult listed on the account, have total control over how the money is invested. If you want to be socially responsible and not buy into tobacco companies or companies that do business in countries that have repressive regimes, you can do that. If you only want to buy bonds, you can do that, too. You can also completely change your investment strategy on a dime. When the investments markets start to soar upwards, or conversely, begin to plunge, if you're paying attention, you can move your investments to take advantage of a perceived benefit or limit an impending loss faster than any institutional investor can.

Keep in mind, though, that with you in control, you not only take full credit for your successes, but you also bear the responsibility for your failures. And as anyone who's spent any time at all studying the stock and bond markets knows, some of the overall market failures have been spectacular.

To exercise that control to your best advantage, educate yourself about investing and read Chapters 8 and 9 to find out how Coverdell accounts work and what you need to do to make your student's account a viable entity.

Comparing Coverdell tax savings to 529 plans

Although the tax-deferred/tax-exempt provisions of Coverdell Education Savings Accounts are almost identical to those of Section 529 plans, the total tax savings in a Coverdell account may not be as great for two reasons:

✔ **No current income tax deduction:** Depending on where you live, you may receive a current income tax deduction for contributions into a Section 529 plan; these don't exist for contributions into Coverdell accounts.

✔ **Less time for money to grow:** Coverdell accounts usually exist for a much shorter period of time and so have less time to earn money. Remember, there is no federally mandated final distribution date for a Section 529 plan, although individual states

and plans may impose one. However, Coverdell accounts must be fully distributed by the designated beneficiary's 30th birthday. Thirty days after that date, the money is distributed to that person, whether or not the person has any expenses for which to use that money.

Still, despite the limitations present in Coverdell accounts, they can help your money grow faster than saving that money in an ordinary investment account. The fact that all tax is, at the very least, deferred until distribution gives you a consistently larger pot of money to use in your investment strategy, which should increase your overall return on your initial investment, all other things being equal.

Benefiting from tax-deferred and tax-exempt growth

One great benefit of any tax-deferred account is that the money in it grows every time you receive interest, dividends (generally, corporate profits that are distributed to shareholders, usually in cash, but sometimes in additional shares), and capital gains (when you sell an investment for a higher price than you purchased it for, the difference between those two amounts is your *capital gain*) on your investments, and no tax issues arise until the money is taken out.

In a Coverdell ESA, if the money comes out and pays for a qualified educational expense, you pay no income tax on the earnings included in that distribution. If, on the other hand, you use the money to pay a nonqualified expense, your designated beneficiary must pay income tax on the earnings portion of the distribution (using the formula shown in Chapter 6), and then, depending on the circumstances of the distribution (see Chapter 5), an additional 10 percent penalty may be tacked on to your beneficiary's tax bill.

Paying for primary and secondary school expenses

You may have absolutely no intention of sending your child to private or parochial school (although you can pay for private and parochial school fees by using distributions from your child's Coverdell account), and certainly many fine public school systems out there can provide your child with the very best education your tax dollars can buy. But still, there are always those extra expenses, the little things that come up year after year, such as tutoring, after-school programs, school busing costs (which are becoming more and more prevalent around the country), student athletic fees, and so on. The list seems endless, and as school budgets become tighter and tighter, this list will only continue to grow.

Until at least December 31, 2010 (and longer, if this provision of the law is extended), you may pay for all these big and little primary and secondary school expenses (including school uniforms, computers and peripherals, and any software for which you could conceivably find an educational purpose) by using tax-free distributions from your child's Coverdell ESA.

Dealing with Coverdell Snags

Now that you've looked at what's really, really good about Coverdell ESAs, you also need to be aware of stuff that may make you think twice about investing here. Coverdell accounts don't make sense for a lot of parents because of these negatives. Conversely, you may decide that a Coverdell account makes sense, but only in a very limited way, if you keep the amounts invested small, or if you use them only for the short term.

Whether your overall savings come up short (so you'll need to apply for financial aid), your student actually wins some outright scholarship aid (so you have more money in your child's Coverdell account than you need), or your child decides against any education beyond high school, you need to stay on top of how having a Coverdell account for that child will play into these scenarios, and figure out ways to minimize any negative consequences.

Minimizing a Coverdell account's impact on financial aid awards

Hopefully, you won't even need to read this part, because you've been successful in your savings ventures and you have all the money you and your student need to see him through college or any other postsecondary educational endeavor. If, however, your savings are a little short and you're not earning quite enough to make up the gap every year, you need to pay attention. Coverdell accounts can become negative in this type of scenario. You need to carefully monitor your particular situation to avoid the minefield.

There's just no good way to say this: A Coverdell ESA may pose a dilemma if its designated student needs to apply for financial aid. Basically, if you choose to save only in a Coverdell account and those savings are insufficient for your student's needs, your student will be penalized for having such a conscientious parent. The value of assets in a Coverdell account are considered to belong to the student, and federal financial aid rules will include 35 percent of the value of the student's assets as part of the *expected family contribution* (or EFC, which is the amount that the Department of Education calculates you should be able to pay for one child's educational costs in any given year; see Chapter 17) available to pay college expenses.

When your student applies for any financial aid, the existence of a Coverdell ESA in his name will only hurt him. Coverdells are unlike Section 529 plans, which are considered to be an asset of the account owner (and if the owner is a grandparent, relative, or family friend who's not a part of your immediate family, it's not reported on the Free Application for Federal Student Aid, or FAFSA, form at all). Coverdell accounts are counted entirely as the student's assets and included at a far higher rate than so-called parent assets. A maximum of 5.6 percent of the value of a Section 529 plan and just about any other nonretirement parent asset other than home equity and life insurance are included in the formula used to arrive at the EFC because you're considered to be the plan owner, even if your student is the designated beneficiary (see Chapter 7). With a Coverdell, however, because the student is considered the owner of the plan, a whopping 35 percent of the total value of the Coverdell account is included in that formula.

And it just gets worse. In addition to counting 35 percent of the value of the account as available to pay current expenses, the total amount of any distributions your student received in the prior year is also included on his current year financial aid application, even if none of the distribution was taxable. Because the folks at the Department of Education assume that the parents are responsible for supporting their child and that all the child's income is then available for education expenses, 50 percent of that child's income (adjusted for a small income protection allowance), whether taxable or not, is counted as available to pay educational expenses.

If you have a small Coverdell account for your student, the asset and income inclusions probably won't impact his financial aid award too adversely. If you're successful in making contributions and even more successful in your investments, however, the existence of that Coverdell plan may effectively prevent your student from receiving certain forms of financial aid. In addition, he may well be saddled with paying back full-cost, unsubsidized Stafford Loans at the end of his college career (see Chapter 17). Of course, if your student isn't likely to ever qualify for need-based financial aid, you don't need to worry about this consideration.

There are, of course, ways around this dilemma. If you choose to save inside one of these accounts for your student and your student still needs additional funds, it doesn't mean that your saving was in vain, your student is doomed to a ten-year payback of high-cost loans, and you're a failure. This problem has some possible solutions, but you need to be on top of the fact that you have a problem well before you ever complete that first financial aid application.

Spending down your student's Coverdell account early

First, you may choose to use up your student's Coverdell account before he reaches college and starts applying for financial aid. Remember, you may use Coverdell distributions to pay for all qualifying educational expenses for both primary and secondary school, as well as for postsecondary school, and the rules concerning what qualifies are far more lax for K–12 expenses than for college ones.

Even if your child doesn't attend private school, many expenses that qualify during his primary and secondary years don't qualify for postsecondary education (see Chapter 8). If you can manage to make the final distribution from your Coverdell plan before your child applies for financial aid (ideally, a year or two before filing the FAFSA), perhaps by buying that new computer that you know he'll need for school or by paying for some extra tutoring, the fact that a Coverdell account once existed for this student won't make one whit of difference in your child's aid award.

Rolling over your student's Coverdell account into a Section 529 plan

If you can't completely exhaust your student's Coverdell account before he's likely to start applying for financial aid, you may consider rolling the account over into a 529 plan for your student. The rollover is tax-free if you complete it within 60 days of the initial withdrawal from the Coverdell account.

In a rollover to a Section 529 plan, you need to keep in mind the following:

- ✔ **If you take the check you receive as a distribution from your student's Coverdell account and use it to fund the new Section 529 plan, your student (not you) is the plan owner of the Section 529 plan.** And, of course, if your student is now the plan owner, he gets to include the total amount of that Section 529 plan as a personal asset, included in the financial aid formula at a generous 35 percent. Distributions, however, are currently not includable as taxable income, so long as any deferred income inside that distribution is used to pay for qualified higher education expenses.

- ✔ **If you choose to distribute the funds from the Coverdell account directly to your student and then you contribute that exact amount into a Section 529 plan, you retain control over the new Section 529 account.** The Section 529 plan is counted as your asset (included at only 5.6 percent in the financial aid formula), and you have the ability to change the designated beneficiary (according to the relationship test described in Chapter 5).

If you choose the rollover option, you've just made a new gift to your student (the original Coverdell contributions, which you've just distributed, were gifts to that child when you made them; the new Section 529 contribution is a completely new gift). You may have some gift tax consequences here.

Transferring the money to another beneficiary

The assets in the Coverdell account belong to the designated beneficiary; so when you change that beneficiary to another child or other related person (using the familial relationships stated in Chapter 8), you take these assets away from the first beneficiary, and he no longer has to count them on his financial aid application. You have, however, just made a new gift to the new beneficiary, and there may be gift tax consequences. In addition, you now need to pay careful attention to the financial aid needs of the new student.

If you see financial aid applications in that child's future, you may want to consider paying down the remaining balance in the Coverdell account as quickly as possible by making qualified withdrawals covering primary and secondary educational expenses.

Do not transfer a Coverdell account to your original designated beneficiary's spouse if you want to maximize the amount of financial aid your original student will qualify for; spousal assets are included at the same rate as the student's own assets. Although married students are no longer treated as their parents' dependents for the purpose of financial aid calculations (so parental information is no longer included in the FAFSA), it doesn't matter whether it's your student or your student's spouse who actually owns the assets. Transferring an account to a spouse gives you more paperwork, but it doesn't change the final outcome on the student's financial aid application.

Closing the account and completely distributing the proceeds to your student

Finally, you may choose to close the Coverdell account and hand the distribution check over to your student. Your student will owe income tax on any accumulated income in the account and also a 10 percent penalty for the privilege of receiving a nonqualified distribution. Still, if the amount of income isn't great and your student has little or no other income to report on his tax return, the overall tax burden may be slight, and this option may be your best way out of this particular jam.

When choosing this option, though, you need to be aware of a couple points:

- ✔ You're handing a chunk of change to a kid, who may not have the best money management skills. Actually, though, this is what you're hoping for in this scenario, because you really want that money to be spent.

- ✔ If your student has wonderful money management skills and promptly stashes that cash away in a savings or investment account, he still has an asset that will be subject to a 35 percent inclusion rate on his FAFSA, which was the treatment you were trying to avoid in the first place. The only income that is counted in calculating his aid award, though, is the current income earned on that money, not the amount of any withdrawals that he takes. It's not much relief from the initial Coverdell/financial aid dilemma, but it's something.

Taking the best strategy if your student receives educational assistance

I'm planning on my son receiving a four-year football scholarship (although he's not particularly athletic). If that fails, he will, of course, be a National Merit Scholar (did I mention he's brilliant?) and receive a four-year free ride to the college of his choice. So much for my fantasy life, and I have a rich one In real life, I'm saving for his education because I figure I'll have to start paying tuition bills approximately ten years from now. Now, he may hit the jackpot and actually receive one of these scholarships, and if he does, I'll be prepared.

When your student receives any form of tax-free educational assistance, whether it be through veterans' benefits, employer tuition reimbursement plans, or outright scholarships and grants, any income from a Coverdell withdrawal originally distributed to cover those higher education expenses is taxable to that student, but no 10 percent penalty is assessed. Be careful, though — this exemption from the penalty exists only in the year or years in which your student actually receives the tax-free educational assistance and incurred higher education expenses. You can't save up your withdrawals until the account needs to terminate and then tell the IRS that there's still money in this account because your student received all this tax-free aid in prior years. To limit the amount of taxes your student will pay, go ahead and make withdrawals from the Coverdell account in years in which he receives the aid.

Keep in mind that tax brackets are incremental based on total income and that a student is usually in a lower bracket because he doesn't have much income. For example, if Nathan receives a full scholarship and his parents have established a Coverdell ESA for him that has $60,000 in it on his 18th birthday ($36,000 of contributions and $24,000 of accumulated income), they may want to consider making an equal distribution of $15,000 for four years, so that an equal amount of their original contribution ($9,000 x 4 = $36,000) is paid to him in each of his four years of college.

Because Nathan is receiving all this extra money, he's not going to have to get a summer job (probably) or do anything else to earn money for these years. If his parents are willing to make these withdrawals from his Coverdell account for nonqualified expenses, Nathan's tax situation will look like Table 10-1 (assuming that the money left in the account continues to earn income at the rate of 5 percent per year).

Table 10-1	Nathan's Federal Income Tax Situation when Nonqualifying Distributions Are Made in the Same Years that He Receives a Full-Tuition Scholarship			
College Year	*Total Annual Coverdell Withdrawal*	*Coverdell Contribution Amount*	*Coverdell Accumulated Earnings*	*Federal Income Tax on Accumulated Earnings @ 10%*
Year 1	$15,000.00	$9,000.00	$6,000.00	$600.00
Year 2	$15,750.00	$9,000.00	$6,750.00	$675.00

College Year	Total Annual Coverdell Withdrawal	Coverdell Contribution Amount	Coverdell Accumulated Earnings	Federal Income Tax on Accumulated Earnings @ 10%
Year 3	$16,537.50	$9,000.00	$7,537.50	$753.75
Year 4	$17,364.38	$9,000.00	$8,364.38	$836.44
Totals	$64,651.88	$36,000.00	$28,651.88	$2,865.19

Now, suppose that Nathan's parents wait until his 30th birthday to make that distribution (at which point he is hopefully earning a reasonable sum of money), and assume that he hasn't gone to graduate school and completely depleted the account. In this situation, his parents risk increasing the percentage that he may pay in tax. Remember, the $60,000 that was sitting in his Coverdell account on his 18th birthday has now increased significantly (using the 5 percent per year assumption, the cash in the account has grown to over $107,750), and all that money will be coming out at one time, in a lump-sum distribution. Of the $107,750 total distribution, $71,750 represents accumulated earnings on which Nathan must pay income tax. If you assume that he's now paying in a 25 percent federal income tax bracket, his income tax on the lump sum distribution at his 30th birthday will be a princely $17,977.50. Added to that, he'll also pay an additional $7,175 penalty, for a total federal tax liability of $25,112.50, or more than $22,000 more than he would've paid in taxes had his parents made distributions to him in the same tax years that he was receiving his scholarship.

If your designated beneficiary also lives in a state with a so-called piggybacked income tax (where your state income tax is calculated by using a percentage of your federal income tax), he will pay a higher percentage of the total accumulated income in his Coverdell account not only in federal income tax but also in his state income tax. You should note, though, that state income tax numbers are piggybacked only on the actual federal income tax piece; if a penalty is applied, there should be no additional tax on the penalty portion. If you have another kid you're going to sending to college, you may also consider transferring the account to that beneficiary (see Chapter 8).

Limiting the blow if your beneficiary decides against going to college

Despite your high hopes and careful planning, you may be paying into a Coverdell account that your student will never use. What can you do then with all that money?

Probably your best bet is to transfer the account to a new beneficiary (see Chapter 8). But if you have no one who can step up to the plate and replace him as beneficiary or if you feel like that money belongs to the person, you can just hand it over. The tax consequences of doing so can be fairly dramatic, as shown by Nathan's example when his plan is distributed to him at his 30th birthday in one lump sum, but they don't have to be quite as drastic. Some careful planning and the ability to remove the rose-colored glasses can minimize the tax bite for your designated beneficiary.

You always minimize a tax bill when you spread it out over a number of years, and there are no limitations on the number of years you may make nonqualified distributions from a Coverdell account as long as the designated beneficiary is under age 30. It's as simple as that. When you realize that your beneficiary is not going to further his education, you may want to begin making nonqualified withdrawals immediately.

Although putting money into the hands of someone who's failed to live up to your expectations may cause you to grind your teeth, you really don't have a choice. That money belongs to that beneficiary, and your only control over the matter is when he actually receives it. You need to remember, though, that the longer you keep it in the account, the more income will accumulate there, and the higher the eventual tax bill. The sooner you start paying and the more payments that you make, the lower the total tax bill will be over time.

If, for example, Nathan doesn't receive that full scholarship but instead attends a three-week bartending school (which isn't an eligible educational institution) when he turns 21, the money that his parents have saved in his Coverdell account will need to be distributed to him at some point either before or immediately after his 30th birthday. If all the other factors in the earlier example remain the same, the damage incurred by the lump sum distribution at his 30th birthday remains the same. Suppose, however, that his parents choose to distribute the account to him beginning when he's 18 and make equal distributions of their contributions over the 12 remaining years the account may remain open. In that situation, Nathan's overall tax liability is decreased, even if he pays federal income tax on the accumulated earnings at a 25 percent marginal rate (remember, Nathan is now a bartender and earning reasonable money).

Table 10-2 shows how spreading the account distributions out over time minimize the income taxes and penalties Nathan will pay.

Table 10-2		Nathan's Federal Income Tax Situation When He Takes Nonqualifying Distributions over 12 Years				
Age	Total Nonqualified Distribution	Contribution Amount	Accumulated Earnings	Federal Income Tax on at Earnings 25%	10% Penalty on Earnings	Total Tax Paid
18	$5,000.00	$3,000.00	$2,000.00	$500.00	$200.00	$700.00
19	$5,250.00	$3,000.00	$2,250.00	$562.50	$225.00	$787.50
20	$5,512.50	$3,000.00	$2,512.50	$628.13	$251.25	$879.38
21	$5,788.13	$3,000.00	$2,788.13	$697.03	$278.81	$975.84
22	$6,077.53	$3,000.00	$3,077.53	$769.38	$307.75	$1,077.14
23	$6,381.41	$3,000.00	$3,381.41	$845.35	$338.14	$1,183.49
24	$6,700.48	$3,000.00	$3,700.48	$925.12	$370.05	$1,295.17
25	$7,035.50	$3,000.00	$4,035.50	$1,008.88	$403.55	$1,412.43
26	$7,387.28	$3,000.00	$4,387.28	$1,096.82	$438.73	$1,535.55
27	$7,756.64	$3,000.00	$4,756.64	$1,189.16	$475.66	$1,664.82
28	$8,144.47	$3,000.00	$5,144.47	$1,286.12	$514.45	$1,800.57
29	$8,551.70	$3,000.00	$5,551.70	$1,387.92	$555.17	$1,943.09
Totals	$79,585.63	$36,000.00	$43,585.63	$10,896.41	$4,358.56	$15,254.97

Because Nathan's parents have chosen to pay down his Coverdell account over the period of time from when they first realize that Nathan won't need this money for qualified educational expenses until the time that the account needs to be completely distributed, they help him save almost $10,000 in taxes. Paying tax and penalties on the earnings accumulated in a Coverdell account is never the outcome your dreams when you first open the account. If that does happen, however, careful planning can help you minimize the damage, as Table 10-2 shows.

Investing in tax-deferred accounts as tax rates drop

A great deal of hoopla accompanied the passage of the Jobs and Growth Tax Relief Reconciliation Act of 2003, which lowers the tax rate on corporate dividends and long-term capital gains (on investments held for longer than one year) to a maximum of 15 percent and which also lowers income tax brackets for all taxpayers. Not so much has been written about how these tax changes will affect your tax-deferred accounts, probably because they're not pretty, and no one really wants you to think about them.

Although the Jobs and Growth Tax Relief Reconciliation Act of 2003 never set out to gut the tax-deferred savings markets, it has, in essence, done just that. The huge reduction in tax rates on dividends and capital gains affects only dividends and capital gains earned and taxed currently, not those earned now and taxed later. When you take a taxable distribution from a tax-deferred account, you receive the income portion of that withdrawal as so-called ordinary income, and you're taxed at "ordinary income" rates, regardless of how that income was earned. By comparison, if you earn that money by buying, keeping, and then selling stocks (thus earning dividends and capital gains), and paying the tax in the year in which

your money was earned, you'd pay a maximum income tax of 15 percent on that money. Now that the tax rates on ordinary income are considerably higher than those on corporate dividends and long-term capital gains, saving in a tax-deferred account isn't quite as sweet as it once was.

Tax-deferred accounts still have benefits, though. Remember, the longer your money isn't taxed within the account, the longer it has to grow. In addition, you have every reason to believe that the income earned in your Coverdell account or Section 529 plan will eventually be distributed to your student tax-free to pay for qualified educational expenses. And even if your student takes nonqualified distributions from these accounts, the odds are in his favor that he'll be in a lower tax bracket than you are currently (even with the reduced rates on these forms of income).

Note that the reductions in income tax rates on long-term capital gains and corporate dividends are only temporary and are due to expire in 2009. If budget deficits and the national debt continue to grow, you have every reason to believe that they won't be extended.

Part IV

Filling In the Gaps: More Ways to Save for College

The 5th Wave

By Rich Tennant

@RICHTENNANT

$(a+5)^9 =$

$\int x dx = \frac{\partial^2}{2}$

$\downarrow / Y$

$x \rightarrow$

$:= xe(\dot{-}x)$

" It's part of my employer tuition assistance agreement with the 'Pizza Bob' corporation. "

In this part . . .

*V*ery often, life is way too uncertain to be able to set aside a given amount of savings and say, "This is for college, this is for retirement, and this is for my new-furnace savings account." Even if you're able to have a specific account for every one of life's future events, how can you possibly know that you have enough in each account to cover the full cost of each event? And when you look at college savings, in particular, you need to cover many college-related expenses that aren't the so-called "qualified educational expenses" to which Section 529 plans and Coverdell accounts restrict your spending. You need a way to pay for these additional costs, too.

In this part, I explain other savings options available to you — options that don't require that you use your savings for future college expenses, but that don't prohibit you from doing so. In some cases, taking savings from these places to cover college expenses will make perfect sense; in others, you may want to liberate money from these accounts only in an emergency.

Finally, I also use this part to look at the options available to you if you haven't been able to save enough to pay your student's full educational costs — scholarships, grants, and loans.

Chapter 11

Saving for College with Qualified U.S. Savings Bonds

*W*hen members of Congress first dabbled with the idea of giving taxpayers incentives to save for college expenses, they didn't roll out some fancy new plan or program, creating unnecessary complexity (they saved that for much later). And they also didn't want to target the upper and upper-middle classes — they figured that those folks could pay for college expenses on their own. Instead, they looked to the solidly middle class, checked out the ever dropping savings rate, and built a new savings perk into an already existing savings option that people viewed as generally stodgy and unexciting: U.S. Savings Bonds.

U.S. Savings Bonds, specifically Series EE and the new Series I bonds, remain a stodgy and unexciting way to save. Which is why you may be surprised to find out that these small pieces of the national debt can often provide you with a great tax-saving option: When you use them to pay for qualified higher education expenses, you're allowed to exclude from your taxable income all the interest you've earned on them over the years.

In this chapter, you take a fresh look at Series EE and Series I savings bonds and find out how they work, what they do, and how you can use them to save for all or a part of what you later will need to pay to cover your own, your spouse's, or your child's postsecondary educational expenses. You see how easy savings bonds are to buy, own, and redeem. You find out how interest rates are set and when interest is posted. And finally, you discover what to do when you redeem your bonds and use them to pay for college expenses.

Choosing Savings Bonds that Work

You may use any sort of U.S. Treasury obligation, from bonds, notes, and T-bills all the way to Series EE, Series H, and Series I savings bonds to pay for anything at all that you'd like, including college expenses. Every one of them is backed by the "full faith and credit" of the U. S. Treasury, and all of them represent safe, if somewhat uninspired, investments. You may use only two of them, though, Series EE and Series I savings bonds, to pay postsecondary education costs without having to pay federal income tax on the interest that you earn on your investment.

Regardless of whether you manage to avoid paying federal income tax on the interest earned on your savings bonds, you won't pay any state income tax; all interest earned on U.S. Treasury obligations is free from your state income tax.

Series EE savings bonds

Series EE savings bonds are your old-fashioned, garden-variety sort of savings bond, the kind your grandmother used to give you for high school graduation or your wedding. If you meet all the requirements (see the "Rating the Usefulness of Saving Bonds for You" section later in the chapter), you may redeem them to pay for some college expenses without paying any federal income tax. In addition, they have the following features:

- **They're issued at 50 percent of their face value.** This means that a $100 bond costs you $50 to purchase.

- **They're offered in a variety of face amounts.** They range in face value from $50 to $10,000.

- **They're guaranteed to reach their face value within 20 years.** But they'll continue to earn interest after they've reached that value until the bond is 30 years old.

- **Their issue date is always the first of a month, no matter what day of the month you actually purchase the bond.**

- **Interest is compounded semiannually and is paid only when the bond is redeemed.** Interest rates are announced every May 1 and November 1 for the following 6-month period.

- **You may cash the bond at any time, provided it is at least 6 months after the issue date for a bond issued prior to February 1, 2003, or 12 months after the issue date for a bond issued after that date.** If you cash a bond that you purchased after April 30, 1997, that you've owned for less then 5 years, you'll also forfeit 3 months' worth of interest. For example, if you hold a bond for 2 years and then cash it in, you'll only receive interest for 21 months.

> ✔ **You may exchange a Series EE bond for a Series HH bond at any time.** You can defer the income tax on the accumulated interest in the EE until the HH reaches maturity. This can extend your tax deferral up to 20 years.
>
> ✔ **You may not purchase more than $30,000 face value ($15,000 cash value) of Series EE bonds in any calendar year.**

Not every Series EE bond is eligible for the educational expenses tax exemption. If you purchased any of these bonds before January 1, 1990, you have to pay tax on the interest even if you, and your expenses, are qualified in every other respect. Congress didn't grandfather older bonds when it enacted the new rules.

Series I savings bonds

Series I bonds are the new kid on the U.S. Treasury block, and they represent a major departure for the Treasury in that they offer you some inflation protection. Although Series EE bond interest rates are calculated using a fixed formula (the interest rate is adjusted every six months), the Series I bond interest rate is calculated to give you a fixed rate of return *plus* an inflation adjustment based on the Consumer Price Index.

Like Series EE bonds, Series I bonds may be used to pay some college fees if you can meet all the requirements (see the "Rating the Usefulness of Saving Bonds for You" section later in the chapter). Although they're very similar to Series EE bonds in many ways, following the same rules regarding issue dates, how long you must hold a bond before you can cash it in, and how much interest you forfeit if you redeem a bond that you've owned for less than five years (three months), Series I savings bonds have the following differences:

> ✔ **Series I savings bonds are offered at face value.** You may purchase them in denominations ranging from $50 to $10,000, but you have to cough up the full face amount when you buy the bond.
>
> ✔ **They have no guaranteed return.** Because you already paid $100 for that $100 face bond, the government doesn't need to guarantee that you'll receive $100 when you redeem the bond. What you will receive on redemption, though, is your original $100 investment *plus* the interest on that $100, calculated monthly and compounded semiannually, making the value of your bond grow and grow.
>
> ✔ **You may not purchase more than $30,000 face value ($30,000 cash value) of Series I bonds in any calendar year.**
>
> ✔ **The only thing you may exchange this bond for is cash.** You can't turn it into a Series EE or a Series HH bond.

Determining Who's Eligible

There are no limitations on who may own a U.S. Savings Bond. These bonds existed long before Congress ever attempted to mold them into a preferred college savings option, and they're far too imbedded in the savings psyches of a wide group of people for Congress ever to try to limit who can own them or how many may be owned.

On the other hand, when the regulations surrounding the use of these bonds as a tax-free way to pay for college were created, Congress was in a position to place limitations on who could use this method of saving and how much could be saved. If you've already read the chapters on Section 529 plans (Part II) and/or Coverdell Education Savings Accounts (Part III), you may find the restrictions surrounding the use of U.S. Savings Bonds to be particularly burdensome. Keep in mind, though, that without this first foray into the world of tax-exempt saving for college, Section 529 plans and Coverdell accounts probably wouldn't exist today.

Age requirements

To save for college tax-free using either Series EE or Series I savings bonds, the owner needs to be at least 24 years old on the first day of the month when the bond is issued. There are no exceptions here. If you turn 24 on June 18, 2003, and you purchase a bond on June 19, 2003 (so you really and truly are 24 years old), the issue date is regarded as June 1, 2003, when you weren't yet 24 years old. Tough luck, but you'll have to pay tax on the interest that you earn on that particular bond. You should have waited until July.

Ownership

To exclude the income earned from a Series EE or Series I savings bond from your income, you must be the owner of the bond. You may not buy bonds as a gift for someone (perhaps you're 24, and the person you want to buy for is not) and retain the tax benefit for yourself. Additionally, if you do buy bonds as gifts for your children or grandchildren who are under 24 at the time the bonds are purchased, they'll have to pay any income tax that is due on the earnings, regardless of how old you were when you purchased the bonds.

If you want to give these bonds as gifts to be used for your child or grand-child's post-secondary education, register them in your name and Social Security number (for your child) or your child's name and Social Security number (for your grandchild) in order to take full advantage of the tax-exemption for educational use these bonds provide. When the time comes to pay those tuition bills, the person who is redeeming the bond will also be the person who is paying the bill. But don't forget: In order to qualify for this treatment, the person to whom you register the bond must be at least 24 years old in the month before the bond is issued.

Relationship test

Education savings schemes such as Section 529 plans and Coverdell Education Savings Accounts allow you almost unlimited scope when choosing a potential student to save for. Series EE or Series I savings bonds, however, are much more restrictive. You may pay for qualified educational expenses for only the following students without paying income tax on the interest you've earned:

- ✔ **Yourself:** Provided the bonds were issued after your 24th birthday, you can use them for your own qualified educational expenses and not pay any income tax at all.

- ✔ **Your spouse:** A spouse qualifies provided that you're filing a joint income tax return.

- ✔ **Your children:** Children are eligible as long as you still claim them as dependents on your income tax return. After they claim their own per-sonal exemption, you're out of luck.

Annual income

Congress always intended that this particular tax break be reserved for those people who, despite limited income, were doing their best to see their chil-dren through college. Because of that, it seriously restricted who could partic-ipate in these tax-free redemptions by putting very strict income requirements in place. Fortunately, these amounts are adjusted annually for inflation. Unfortunately, the amounts were never overly generous to begin with, and they don't improve much even with the inflation adjustment. Figure 11-1 shows the 2002 and 2003 limitations for both married and single taxpayers.

If you file your tax returns using the "Married filing separately" filing status, you can't redeem any of your bonds tax-free, even if you meet all the other criteria. It just isn't allowed.

Tax-Exempt Interest Status	2002 Modified Adjusted Gross Income		2003 Modified Adjusted Gross Income	
	Single and Head of Household	Married Filing Jointly and Qualified Widow(er)	Single and Head of Household	Married Filing Jointly and Qualified Widow(er)
Fully tax exempt	$57,600 and below	$86,400 and below	$58,500 and below	$87,750 and below
Phaseout of tax-free redemptions	Between $57,600 and $72,599	Between $86,400 and $116,399	Between $58,500 and $73,499	Between $87,750 and $117,749
No tax-free redemptions	$72,600 and above	$116,400 and above	$73,500 and above	$117,750 and above

Figure 11-1: 2002 and 2003 income phaseouts for tax-free Series EE and Series I savings bond redemptions.

Paying for Qualified Expenses

If you're planning on using savings bonds to pay for college, you need to know what expenses are qualified for the purpose of redeeming these bonds tax-free. Remember that although U.S. Savings Bonds are safe and reliable, they're not particularly exciting when you look at how much money you can make with them. They become players when you can make that money not pay any income tax.

In comparison to the definition of qualified educational expenses for Section 529 plans (Chapter 5) and Coverdell Education Savings Accounts (Chapter 8), the expenses you may pay using tax-free redemptions of Series EE and/or Series I savings bonds are quite restrictive. Only postsecondary expenses qualify, and of those expenses, only the following are allowed:

✔ **Tuition and fees to an eligible postsecondary educational institution:** The school's ability to participate in federal financial aid programs administered by the U.S. Department of Education is the test here. Although you're not required to provide anyone with proof of what you include as qualified educational expenses, be sure that you can substantiate your claims. If the IRS comes calling and asks for your records, be certain that you can gently place those canceled checks or receipted tuition bills under the agent's nose.

✔ **Payments into Section 529 plans or Coverdell Education Savings Accounts:** You may already have purchased one or two or more Series EE or Series I savings bonds with the idea of using them for educational expenses, but you're watching your salary rise, and think that you may soon be earning more than is allowed in order to take advantage of tax-free redemptions (see the "Annual income" section later in this chapter). Before this window closes, you may want to redeem those bonds, and invest all of your redemption funds into a Section 529 plan, a Coverdell account, or both.

You can't pay for room and board, books, supplies, and all the other great things that you're allowed to pay for by using distributions from Section 529 plans or from Coverdell accounts with tax-free savings bond redemptions.

Keep in mind, though, that whenever you redeem a bond, even if some of what you use it for is a nonqualified expense, you pay only the federal income tax on the income portion — no state tax, and no 10 percent penalty for a nonqualified withdrawal. So even if you don't get the tax exemption, you're still getting a pretty good deal.

You may not double dip. You may claim any qualified expenses that you have only in one place. If you make a qualified withdrawal from a Coverdell account or from a Section 529 plan to pay for certain expenses, you aren't allowed to also have a tax-free savings bond redemption to cover those same charges. You may, however, choose to pay some educational expenses from one savings plan, and others from another.

To further complicate matters, if you're planning on taking the Hope Credit or the Lifetime Learning Credit (see Chapter 16), you must pay for the qualified expenses that you assign to these credits with money you've paid tax on. If you're paying for expenses using Series EE or Series I savings bonds, you have to pay the income tax on the interest to be eligible for the credits.

Just as with Coverdell and Section 529, you must have actually paid these expenses to be able to exempt the income earned on these bonds from tax. If you received scholarships, veteran's educational assistance benefits, or qualified tuition reductions, you need to reduce the otherwise qualifying amounts by the tax-free assistance you receive.

Buying and Redeeming Savings Bonds

You may have decided that Series EE and/or Series I savings bonds sound good to you. You want to start implementing a savings program using them, but you're not quite sure how you go about buying them. Actually, they're quite easy to buy through a variety of means, and they require a lot less paperwork than Section 529 plans or Coverdell accounts. And, after you actually buy a bond, you don't need to do anything further until you redeem it. You don't have to read any statements or make any investment decisions.

You may purchase Series EE and Series I Savings Bonds in several ways:

- ✔ At your local bank.

- ✔ Through payroll deduction plans at your workplace.

- ✔ From your local Federal Reserve Bank (in Atlanta, Boston, Chicago, Cleveland, Dallas, Kansas City, Minneapolis, New York, Philadelphia, Richmond, San Francisco, and St. Louis).

- ✔ Directly from the Bureau of the Public Debt through the mail or over the Internet. You can use the EasySaver Plan (which makes automatic transfers from your bank) or Savings Bonds Direct (which uses a major credit card).

However you buy your bonds, you must provide your name, address, and Social Security number to complete the transaction. And that's it. If you buy a bond as a gift for someone else, you need to provide their name, address, and Social Security number.

If you buy bonds with the intention of using them to pay for qualified educational expenses, and you're sure that you won't have any difficulty falling under the income phaseouts, don't pay income tax yearly on each year's interest income. You always have the option of paying income tax on U.S. Savings Bond interest each year or waiting until you redeem the bond. If you pay as you go and then choose to use the bond redemption to pay educational expenses, you lose the tax benefit that you could have had.

You may redeem your bonds at any institution where you can buy them; you don't need to redeem them at the same place where you first purchased them. When you make that redemption, you receive a Form 1099-INT for the interest you haven't reported. If you use the total amount of the proceeds (the amount you first paid to buy the bond plus all the interest) to pay for qualified expenses, no problem. You'll exclude that interest by using Form 8815 on your income tax return. Form 8815 also walks you through the calculations if you fall into the income phaseout gray area or if you use only part of the bond proceeds to pay for qualified expenses.

Rating the Usefulness of Saving Bonds for You

On their face, U.S. Series EE and Series I savings bonds may not seem the swiftest way to stash a substantial amount of money away for college. However, they have a lot of good points, especially for the small investor, including the following:

✔ **Your money is safe with Uncle Sam.** No ifs, ands, or buts about it — U.S. Treasury issues are the safest investment around. If you're worried about the ups and downs of the stock market or you just watched yet another bank close its doors, that safety may appeal to you.

✔ **You may save in very small amounts.** As in any investment scheme, you must pay a minimum amount to start playing. With U.S. Series EE savings bonds, that amount is a princely $25. If you're concerned about paying the rent but still want to be putting something aside, this may be just the ticket for you.

✔ **You'll never pay any initiation or annual fees to maintain a savings bond account.** Even if your bonds exist only on the records of the Bureau of Public Debt (which cuts down on the chances that you may lose the little slips of cardboard that pass for savings bonds these days), it doesn't charge you for the privilege of looking after your money.

✔ **Interest rates are competitive and actually exceed most bank and money market interest rates, and you won't ever pay any state income tax on your interest.** The interest rates for Series EE bonds are calculated at between 85 and 90 percent of the current five-year U.S. Treasury Note, depending on the issue date of the bond. For Series I bonds, the rate is calculated by adding a fixed rate of return to an inflation component that is calculated semi-annually.

✔ **If your student ends up not going to college or another eligible school, you don't have to pay any penalty to get your money out.** When you redeem your bonds, you'll pay the federal income tax on the interest, but you don't have a mandatory deadline for cashing in your bonds.

On the flip side (and there's always a flip side), you won't ever get rich putting all your money into U.S. Savings Bonds. The interest rates are very low and will probably stay that way for quite some time. To add to that, interest is compounded only semiannually, which further lowers your potential earnings. If you're looking to make a lot of money fast, Series EE and Series I savings bonds aren't for you.

If, however, you've started saving early and have another college savings plan in place, savings bonds are a great addition.

Chapter 12

Setting Up Personal Investment Accounts for Yourself and Your Kids

· ·

In This Chapter

▶ Saving for educational expenses in traditional investment accounts

▶ Deciding how to register your account

▶ Taking care of the account

· ·

Section 529 plans, Coverdell Education Savings Accounts, and even good old U.S. Savings Bonds are wonderful ways to save money for those (hopefully) inevitable college expenses looming on your horizon. They all, to some extent, allow you to put away money for later use, deferring, and even exempting, income you earn on that money from the income tax monster. And, given that everyone can invest in at least one of these savings plans and reap the tax benefits, why would you even consider putting money into more traditional investment accounts for yourself, your spouse, or your children and/or grandchildren with an eye toward using the cash for college expenses?

The answer is simple: Funds from tax-advantaged college savings accounts may only be used to pay certain qualified educational expenses. All other college expenses, such as health insurance, transportation costs, and excess living expenses, don't fall into this category, and you may be looking at income tax and a penalty if you use funds from your Section 529 plan or Coverdell account to pay for them.

In this chapter, you discover how to save enough to pay for those nonqualified (but necessary) expenses that the other plans just can't cover. You find out how total flexibility and absolute control may sometimes be worth the price of admission (the loss of income tax breaks). You explore the most advantageous ways to register for and invest in personal investment accounts in order to maximize their potential while minimizing your tax burden. You look at how new tax legislation may affect your investment choices. And finally, you see the pitfalls to avoid at all costs.

Pondering Personal Investment Accounts

Basically, a *personal investment account* is any financial account, whether a savings account, a stock or bond account, or a mutual fund account, into which you deposit money and on which you should receive some sort of investment return — either interest, dividends, or capital gains. These accounts are all *taxed currently* (you pay the tax in the year in which you earn the income), and you have absolute freedom to add money, subtract money, or leave the whole thing alone.

Freedom is what a personal investment account is all about. Other than following the rules that apply to all people dealing with investments (for example, no insider trading is allowed), you have absolutely no limits on what you may, and may not, do with the money going into or out of these accounts.

That's why personal investment accounts can be so valuable when you're planning for a future event that may or may not happen. The flexibility of a personal investment account registered in your name, your spouse's, or jointly, also allows you to concentrate on your investments rather than trying to allocate resources between your children before you determine their needs. If you think you're saving for one child's college education, that's fine; if that child then has no need of the money, you're free to use it to pay for another child's expenses, for your retirement, or to buy a sailboat and sail around the world. You have no limits on what you may use the money in the account for.

By lumping the available funds for all your children's excess needs in one place, you minimize fees, and can therefore maximize results. And, if it turns out that your children's financial needs aren't exactly equal (one child is happy at a community college; another heads off to a private college), you can allocate your resources as needed without having to deal with complicated roll-over rules, and without any fear of tax penalties.

In addition to flexibility, you maintain complete and total control over your money. When you take distributions from an account registered to you, the check is made payable to you, and you get to cash it. You may even register an account in the name of your minor child, which then becomes his when he reaches the age of majority (either 18 or 21, depending on what state you live in). You direct your investments, unless you hire someone like a broker or an investment advisor to give you advice (see the "Choosing to hire an advisor or go it alone" section later in the chapter). You may move from investment to investment, or between accounts, as often as you like and for any reason.

You get the benefits of flexibility and freedom for the low, low price of . . . paying taxes on any income earned. As your money grows, so does your annual tax bill. Because income taxes aren't deferred in this type of account, the amount that you pay in income tax will probably increase each year (the larger the account becomes, the more income is earned on those investments).

Still, when invested appropriately, personal investment accounts can be a valuable addition to your overall college savings program, and it's up to you to know how to make the best choices for your money.

Looking at Your Investment Options

No matter what you're looking for, there's a type of account that will fit you perfectly. You may choose to go the staid and sedate root, sticking with a savings account at your local bank or savings and loan. You could give a broker a call, and set up an appointment. You can go online and see what's being offered there. Or you can walk into the local office of your friendly mutual fund company and check out its offerings.

Interest-bearing bank accounts — "Ol' Faithful"

Bank accounts are the most common type of personal investment account, and they may not be something that you typically associate with the term *investment.* Still, interest-bearing bank accounts have been around for a long time, and they represent a very safe, not-too-exciting place to keep your money. Savings and loan companies, commercial banks, and credit unions (which aren't strictly banks, but which operate so similarly to a savings and loan that the difference, for this discussion, is moot) offer these accounts.

When you put your money in a savings account (including passbook, regular savings, bank money market, or even certificates of deposit), you give your money to the bank, which in turn lends it to someone else. That person pays interest to the bank on the money he borrows, and the bank pays you interest (lower than the amount it charges the borrower) on your deposit. For handling this transaction, the bank keeps the difference between the amount it charges the borrower and the amount you receive. Everyone's happy; at least while bank interest rates offer a reasonable return on your investment.

If you like the idea (and the perceived safety) of a bank account, shop around for the one with the highest interest rate and lowest fees. And, if your high rates vanish overnight (which often happens when certificates of deposit come due), don't be afraid to go shopping again.

Interest-bearing savings accounts at commercial banks and savings and loan companies are insured by the Federal Deposit Insurance Corporation (FDIC) up to $100,000 for your total deposits inside one particular institution. Credit union accounts are usually federally insured by the National Credit Union Administration for the same amount, but check with your credit union.

The $100,000 maximum insured amount isn't per account; it's per depositor per institution. If you have several accounts at one bank all registered the same way (John Jones, for example), be certain that your combined balance doesn't exceed that figure. If it does and the bank goes bust, you can recover only the $100,000. You lose the rest. If you have multiple accounts at the same bank, but they are registered differently (one is John Jones, for example, and the second is to John Jones and Mary Jones, jointly), each account is insured for the maximum $100,000 in case the bank fails.

Brokerage accounts

The days are long gone when only the rich had stockbrokers and brokerage accounts. In these times of easy access to stocks via discount and Internet brokers, anyone with a minimal amount to stake can play the stock market. And, because you need to have a brokerage account to buy or sell any stocks, bonds, or other type of marketable security, many people find themselves with one or more accounts in their names.

A *brokerage account* is one of the most flexible investment vehicles: You may buy, sell, and hold stocks and bonds, mutual funds, and any other sort of investment, including cash. If the brokerage lets you, you may borrow against the value of your stocks inside the account (a so-called *margin account*). You can place shares of stocks that you already own into this account. In fact, there's not much that you can't invest in a brokerage account.

When you do this, the brokerage transfers the registration (how the company that issues the security records the name of the owner) of any stocks, bonds, or mutual funds of the account to its name, as nominee for you. At this point, the physical stock certificates you're familiar with disappear, and are now accounted for electronically. Regardless of whether you have physical certificates with your name typed on the front, or your shares are registered in the brokerage's nominee name, you remain the owner of the shares.

These accounts are widely available from the following sources:

- ✔ **Full-service brokers:** They may charge you a fee to manage your account (but not always).

- ✔ **Discount brokers:** They offer you no advice but provide you with *statements* showing transactions for the period covered, lists of your securities at the end of the month, and the beginning and ending values in your account.

- ✔ **Internet brokers:** They operate almost entirely online. Discount brokers charge you a fee only when you actually buy or sell anything in the account; an Internet broker may also hit you with a monthly fee, or a statement fee, if you don't keep a certain value in the account or if you don't place any trades, and they'll charge you a higher fee if you call them to buy or sell rather than placing that trade over the Internet.

✔ **Commercial banks:** Many of them now own subsidiary brokerages.

Although brokerages do have insurance on the securities they hold, that's insurance in case someone in their operation decides to walk off with the contents of the company vault. You're not insured if the investments in your account do poorly or completely lose their value.

For more details on investing, check out *Investing For Dummies,* by Eric Tyson, and *Stock Investing For Dummies,* by Paul Mladjenovic (both published by Wiley).

Mutual fund accounts

Last, but not least, are *mutual fund accounts,* which you open any time you purchase a mutual fund directly from a mutual fund company. These accounts often function more like a bank account than a brokerage account (many accounts offer check-writing privileges and give you deposit tickets to add new money to an existing account), yet the investments inside the account more closely resemble those in the brokerage account.

Mutual fund accounts offer you the ability to hold one or more of a fund company's funds inside the same account. After you purchase a fund, you can redeem it for cash at a later date or transfer it to any of the company's other funds if you decide to change your investment strategy.

Unlike a brokerage account, a mutual fund account permits you to invest in the funds of only one particular mutual fund company, and that is its biggest limitation. If you want to change to another company's funds, you have to open an account with that company or purchase that fund through your brokerage account (if that is allowed by the fund company — many only sell their products themselves and don't allow brokers to become involved).

Mutual fund accounts, like brokerage accounts, aren't insured against market downturns and loss in value. Invest carefully — there are no safety nets.

Registering Your Account

Whether you open a bank account, a brokerage account, or a mutual fund account, you have to provide the financial institution with some bare-bones information about yourself, namely your name, your address, and your Social

Security number. You may also have to provide employment information and your date of birth. With this information, the institution can report your annual taxable earnings to you and the government for income tax purposes.

When you open that account, though, you'll have a variety of options as to how you want that account owned, or registered. The two most popular choices are individual ownership and joint tenants with the right of survivorship. You may also choose to register an account in the name of your minor child, either as a custodial account (which may accept only cash), or as an account opened under the Uniform Gift (or Transfer) to Minors Act, discussed below. What you choose may have a staggering difference in what happens to that account down the road.

Owning the account all by yourself

When you open an individual account (and you must be at least 18 years old to do so), only your name will appear on the account registration. You are the sole owner, and you're responsible for paying income tax on all the taxable earnings from the account.

Whenever you take money out of the account, you don't become subject to income tax on that withdrawal; however, should you take the money and give it to someone else, you may have to deal with Gift Tax and/or Generation-Skipping Transfer Tax issues, depending on the amount of the gift. Check out Chapter 3 for the Gift and Generation-Skipping Transfer Tax rules.

Be prepared with a plan in case you die. With an individual account, if you die without a valid last will and testament, the value in the account is divided according to the laws in your state. If you assume that the money will automatically go entirely to your spouse or kids, think again. Living parents or siblings may also get a cut. If you don't have a last will when you die, you may be able to avoid this scenario by setting up a so-called living trust or grantor trust and registering the account in the name of the trust.

Sharing ownership

Joint tenants with right of survivorship (JTWRS) is typically what people think of when they refer to *joint ownership,* and for most people who use it, it works well. *Joint tenants with right of survivorship* means that two owners are listed on a particular account; in the event of the death of one of the owners, the other becomes the owner of all of the property inside the account.

When you open a JTWRS account, both account holders must supply all the required information. At tax reporting time, you are each responsible for half of the total tax due. If you hold the account jointly with your spouse and you file a joint income tax return, there's no problem. You report the full amount of your taxable income on the return. If, however, you hold the account jointly and you each file your own income tax returns, you need to split the income between the two of you so that you each pay tax on your half.

If you make a gift using funds from the account, there is no income tax conse-quence to you; however, the IRS considers that half of the gift comes from you, and the other half from your joint tenant, and you may both be required to file a Form 709, U.S. Gift (and Generation-Skipping Transfer) Tax return, depending on the size of the gift (see Chapter 3).

Finally, if you die, it doesn't matter at all what your last will says — the joint owner inherits your share of the account.

Gifting your money to a minor

If ever there was a place where good tax planning ran completely counter to parental common-sense, gifting money or securities to your minor children qualifies. When you deposit cash into a *custodial bank account* (which may only accept cash), you transfer those funds into your child's name and Social Security number. The taxes earned on income generated by that cash is now your child's responsibility, and when your child turns 18, you no longer even have the nominal control over that account that you had as a parent.

If you want to make a gift of something other than cash, you may opt, instead, to fund an account for your child that is regulated by the Uniform Gifts to Minors Act (UGMA), also sometimes called the Uniform Transfers to Minors Act (UTMA) in some states. Under this provision, you can open an invest-ment account for a minor child (even if it's not your own child), gift it with money or securities, and operate it for the benefit of that child until the kid reaches either 18 or 21, depending on what state you live in and the age of majority. At that point, the account (which has always belonged to the minor child anyway) ceases to be your responsibility, and whatever is in it on that date reverts to the tender mercies of your formerly minor person.

Tax avoidance

What a great idea! When Congress first came up with the UGMA/UTMA marvel, it was touted as a great tax-planning device. Subsequent legislation has closed up most of this particular loophole, and whatever income tax benefit you (and your child) may still have will largely be eaten up trying to figure out how to calculate your child's income tax. What's more, the recent Jobs and Growth Tax Relief Reconciliation Act of 2003 has lowered income tax rates for long-term capital gains and dividends for everyone (see the section "Talking taxes" towards the end of this chapter).

When your child reaches majority

If UGMA/UTMA and custodial accounts no longer pack much punch as an income tax avoidance scheme, these fare even worse when you think about some of the real-life consequences of gifting large amounts of cash and securities to a child with no real-world experience. When your minor child is no longer a minor, she succeeds to the property, to save or spend as she will. If she opts to trek the Amazon instead of paying tuition, well, she can, and you have no recourse. The same holds true if she becomes the target of some unscrupulous scum, who sees a chicken ripe for the plucking.

Financial aid impact

And then there's the financial aid angle. Actually, with an UGMA or UTMA account in your child's life, or with a large custodial account, there is not much of a financial aid angle, if any; if you can't find all the money to pay your child's full expenses, you'll probably end up taking unsubsidized Stafford Loans and/or PLUS Loans to pay the balance (see Chapter 17 for more info on Stafford loans and other forms of financial aid).

When your child files his FAFSA (Free Application for Federal Student Aid), the full value of any account held in your child's name, even if you are still listed as the custodian or trustee, is counted as an asset of the child, and 35 percent of the value of that account (plus any other assets your child has) will be counted as available to pay college costs for the next year. Your child may have other ideas, though, and between the time you fill out the form in the spring and he attends in the fall, he may spend all that money on a car.

Registering and administering an UGMA/UTMA account

Still, if you're absolutely bound and determined to set up one of these accounts for your child, you need to provide the financial institution where you set up the account with your kid's name, address, date of birth, and Social Security number. The registration on the account will actually show your name as custodian for your child under the Uniform Gifts (or Transfers) to Minors Act. Generally speaking, to make sure that you're giving up all right, title, and interest in the property you're gifting, it usually makes sense for one parent (or grandparent) to make the gift, while the other parent acts as the account custodian.

Each state has specific rules under which the account may operate. Regardless of where you live, you're acting only as a *fiduciary* (a person responsible for someone else's assets), so you must act prudently and make every effort to maintain the value of the account. Here's what you can do with the account:

✔ Buy and sell securities inside the account

✔ Transfer the account from one financial institution to another

✔ Make any other reasonable financial decision concerning account assets

Managing Your Personal Investment Account

After you open a personal investment account, you need to figure out what to do with it. Obviously, you'll have to decide for what purpose you're saving and how much you want to save on a regular basis. And then you need to follow through, making sure that money is deposited in the amounts and with the frequency you've determined.

You clearly have other matters to consider here. You must decide what types of investments you're comfortable with and understand how those investments will help you achieve your goals. (Chapter 9 explains many terms you'll run across as you begin your life as an investor, and many of the different sorts of investments available to you.)

Your personal investment accounts and your tax-deferred or tax-exempt accounts differ in two important ways: the level of control you have over your assets and how (and when) the income you earn on your investments is taxed.

Choosing to hire an advisor or go it alone

When you place money into a personal investment account, whether it's a savings account, a mutual fund account, or a brokerage account, you retain absolute control over the money and over your investments. You may add or subtract money at any time in the account, and you may completely change investment strategies whenever and wherever you want. You may choose to wing it and invest solely on the basis of your own research, or you can hire someone to do it for you. Literally, all options are open to you.

Because you have almost no limitations, creating an investment strategy, as outlined in Chapter 10, is an important step. An investor who flails about and never clearly identifies any sort of direction is a gambler who almost always loses money.

Do-it-yourself research

When I was growing up, my father checked his stocks every morning in the newspaper, crowing when they inched up and turning stony-faced when they lost money. Now, of course, you can go through that exercise as many times in the day as you want, thanks to the Internet. Stock and bond quotes are available, at no cost, on a variety of search engines and Web sites. If you already have an Internet brokerage account, you can research an offering and buy some shares on the spot, all in the matter of a few seconds. Snagging a few shares of some hot stock can be incredibly gratifying, especially if you never have to pick up a phone or talk to another breathing body.

The ease with which you can trade in the stock and bond markets doesn't mean that making money in these markets is easy. Take advantage of all the literature available on the Internet, through libraries, and in newspapers; find out how to read the detailed quote pages for various types of investments. Before you ever click on the "buy" icon, check out the earnings reports that are available and make sure that you'll still want to own a piece of this company tomorrow. When you buy on a whim, you generally live to regret it. Do your research first!

Hiring (and firing) an investment advisor

Should you feel uncomfortable investing in anything more exciting than a bank certificate of deposit without first checking with someone else, you may be a prime candidate for the services of a professional investment advisor. An investment advisor can be anyone — your accountant, your lawyer, an insurance agent, a financial planner, or any other person who claims to know how to make money in investments. Remember, however, that because there is no such thing as Investment Advisor School, and because advisors don't need any specific credentials, finding someone to work with can be tricky.

Still, it is possible to find a person who can help you choose and manage your investments. Here's how to shop for an advisor:

- ✔ **Check credentials.** Not everyone in the investment world has the same credentials, but find out whether the person has some professional standing, financially speaking. If the advisor is an accountant, tax professional, attorney, Certified Financial Advisor, Certified Financial Planner, or something along those lines, take some comfort in knowing that the person actually has some knowledge of what he's doing.

- ✔ **Check references.** Anyone who wants your business should be willing to provide you with some references, both business and personal. You want to trust not only your advisor's business acumen but also his personal integrity. You're considering handing control of your money over to a relative stranger; make sure that you trust him.

- ✔ **Find out how he makes his money.** An advisor who makes his money selling a financial services product will generally steer you to the benefits of that product instead of looking at all available investments. You're better off paying an hourly rate or a percentage of your asset base as your advisor's fee — without the need to sell you a specific product, your advisor can then help you select what's truly best for you.

- ✔ **Trust your personal instincts.** If an advisor you're thinking of hiring makes you in the least bit uncomfortable, walk away. He may be a terrific analyst, but if you can't get past your feelings of unease about him personally, he's not the person to handle your money.

After you choose an advisor, you're not honor-bound to stick by him through thick and thin. If you give that person a reasonable amount of time to manage your account and he doesn't do as well as you'd have liked, or you find someone you think you like better, you can move your account and change your advisor. Even if you sign an agreement with an advisor, it's generally not set in stone, and an escape clause is usually built in. An ethical advisor never wants an unhappy client.

Talking taxes

When you invest in a personal investment account like those described in this chapter, you pay income tax each year on the income your account earns on your investments annually. This means that when you take money out to pay for education expenses, for example, you don't pay any tax at the time you withdraw the money because you've been paying the tax on an as-you-go basis. And, because the tax is already paid, you don't need to worry about whether your withdrawal is used to pay for qualified or nonqualified expenses.

The Jobs and Growth Tax Relief Reconciliation Act of 2003 has made investing outside of tax-deferred and tax-exempt savings accounts more attractive. The reduction of income tax rates on *corporate dividends* (the slice of profits that a corporation may choose to pay its shareholders) and *long-term capital gains* (the profit you make when you sell a security that you've owned for longer than one year for more money than you purchased it for) means that, even without the tax deferrals, your money may grow faster, and cost you less in income tax, than it would within a tax-deferred account. All bets are off with a tax-exempt account, though, because paying no tax is always better than paying just a little tax.

The investment portions of this new bill, which covers only the years 2003 through 2008, include the following provisions:

- ✔ **A top income tax rate on corporate dividends of 15 percent:** If you are a lower-bracket taxpayer, this new tax rate on dividends may be as low as 5 percent.

- ✔ **A top income tax rate on long-term capital gains of 15 percent:** You must own an asset for over one year to qualify for this rate. Once again, lower-bracket taxpayers could pay as little as 5 percent if their income tax rate is only 10 or 15 percent.

- ✔ **An immediate reduction in overall income tax rates:** In 2003, the income tax rates run from 10 percent for low income taxpayers to 35 percent for extremely high income taxpayers, lowered from a range of 15 to 38.6 percent prior to the 2003 act. (People who earn less money pay a smaller percentage in tax than people who earn more money — at least that's how it's supposed to work.)

To make the best use of these rate reductions, you may want to consider using your investment account to buy securities that pay corporate dividends or that have a real chance of appreciation, enabling you to realize a capital gain when you sell. Interest-bearing bonds that you own may be better placed in tax-deferred or tax-exempt accounts, such as Section 529 plans or Coverdell ESAs, as the interest earned on these securities is taxed at the ordinary income tax rates of between 10 percent and 35 percent.

The Jobs and Growth Tax Relief Reconciliation Act of 2003 is set to expire on December 31, 2008, and all these provisions will disappear in a puff of smoke unless Congress makes them permanent. Don't count on it happening; many of the provisions in the overall bill are viewed as regressive, and as national budget deficits continue to explode, the wisdom of these cuts may be questioned. Still, while they're in effect, take advantage of this gift.

Investing in real life

Almost everything that is written about investing and investments is tackled from a purely theoretical standpoint — how to achieve the best result given a certain set of circumstances. In real life, your circumstances almost never absolutely conform to the model, so your proper choices may not be the same as those of the so-called experts.

No place is this truer than when looking at tax benefits and ways to avoid tax. Paying tax is, to some extent, inevitable and necessary. And while trying to minimize the amount that you pay is natural, using the tax card to trump every other consideration is short-sighted and foolish. You may actually save some tax by gifting securities to your child in an Uniform Gifts to Minors Act account; however, you may have also just given control over a substantial sum of money to someone who, at age 18 or 21, will probably not be equipped to handle it. The amount of money that you save in income tax during the time your child is a minor could be far exceeded by the amount that your minor could lose when he takes possession of the account.

When you invest, first identify your savings goal, whether it's college expenses, retirement money, or just the security of knowing that you have a healthy nest egg stashed away. Then you should arrive at a plan for how you think you'll get there — through careful saving and cautious investing, perhaps, or through a more aggressive investment approach, if you're comfortable with that. Only after you've outlined your plan should you attempt to mold it more by using the various tax considerations.

Remember, an investment plan that makes perfect tax sense but that doesn't serve your needs is a plan doomed to failure. Use your common sense.

Chapter 13

Saving for College in Trust Accounts

....

In This Chapter

▶ Understanding the basics of trusts

▶ Using different types of trusts

▶ Figuring out taxes on trusts

▶ Looking at how well trusts work for college savings

....

*I*f you're like most people, you may immediately associate the word *trusts* with a picture of great wealth and privilege. After all, the only people who set up trusts are those who can afford to fund them, and the only people who have trust funds set up for them do things like play polo and wear blazers with little crests on the pockets. Right?

Wrong. Trusts come in all sizes and shapes, and they may serve your needs. Because of their amazing flexibility, the protections they offer you and your family, and the fact that you determine how the trust will operate, saving for all or a part of future college expenses inside of a trust may suit you better than relying totally on other forms of college saving, including a Section 529 plan or a Coverdell Education Savings Account (ESA). You may also discover that augmenting other savings you have with those in a trust gives you the control and the safeguards you're looking for.

In this chapter, you find out what trusts are and what they can do for you. You see how they can provide you with the assurance that the money you save today will be used only for purposes that you approve of down the road. You discover ways to be certain that your children or grandchildren receive the education they deserve (and you want to pay for) even if you're not around to see it happen. And you find out how to structure your trust(s) so that you pay the least tax possible while gaining the greatest advantage.

Getting the Definitive Word on Trusts

A *trust* is a legal entity that is able to hold assets of one person for the benefit of any other person or people (including the person whose assets the trust holds).

You may put as much money into a trust as you want, know that the money is always invested, and then have the trustee make distributions when the time comes for whatever expenses, educational or otherwise, you want. You have no limitations on contributions if you make over a certain amount of money, and no restrictions (other than the ones you impose) on the size of the distributions when they are made. None of the rules that govern what expenses you may pay using tax-free or tax-deferred distributions from Section 529 plans, Coverdell Education Savings Accounts, or Series EE or Series I savings bonds apply to trusts. Depending on the rules contained in the trust instrument (which you create when you create the trust), the trustee may make distributions to the beneficiary, or on the beneficiary's behalf, to pay for any of that beneficiary's expenses, whether directly for educational expenses or for any other purpose.

In exchange for the freedom a trust offers, you pay a price. The income earned inside a trust is taxed in the year in which it is earned; there are no deferrals.

When you hear people talking about trusts, they generally throw around a lot of terms that sound impressive but that really only define clear roles and relationships within this legal entity. Here are a few of those terms:

- ✔ **The grantor (or the donor):** This person (or people) actually creates and funds a trust.

- ✔ **The beneficiary:** This is the person (or other being) who is entitled to receive payments from the trust. You're not at all limited here. When you create a trust instrument, you must define who the beneficiary is (either by name or by class of people, such as your children or your grandchildren), as well as a whole slew of contingencies if that beneficiary can't or doesn't use up all the money. Your contingent beneficiaries, however, don't have to be related to the original beneficiary in any way. Not only do you not need to name specific names, but beneficiaries (and contingent beneficiaries) don't even need to be alive yet when you set up your trust. You choose.

- ✔ **The trustee (or fiduciary):** This person or institution (accountants, attorneys, banks, and trust companies are very popular choices here) is responsible for the assets in the trust and for making sure that the assets are used in the manner you indicate when you set up the trust.

✔ **The trust instrument:** This legal document governs how your trust works. Have an attorney who is very knowledgeable about trusts and how they function draft this document for you, and be certain you understand its provisions before you sign it.

No two trusts are identical, and there is no one, perfect trust that will solve everyone's needs. When creating your trust, be as specific as you can about what you're trying to achieve. Only then will the attorney drafting your trust instrument be certain to include all the provisions you feel are important.

Never, never, never use a fill-in-the-blank trust form. Having the right trust can make all the difference in your savings; having the wrong one usually spells disaster. Take the time, pay for good advice, and get it done right the first time. Fixing mistakes after they've happened is far costlier. When engaging an attorney to draft a trust for you, ask for recommendations from people you trust. If you're the first person on your block to explore this option, you may obtain names and specialties of attorneys in your area by checking the Martindale-Hubbell nationwide directory of attorneys on the Internet at www.martindale.com or at your local library.

Trusts are among the costliest ways to save money. Not only will you pay for an attorney to draft the instrument, but you may also pay yearly trustee and tax preparation fees in addition to the normal investment fees associated with an investment account. However, as in so many things, you get what you pay for: A well-drafted, well-invested trust account *may,* in some circumstances, serve to fill the gaps in your college savings better than personal investments accounts or any other assets that you own outright.

Because the trust is its own entity, it enjoys its own set of legal protections. Depending on what type of trust you create, you may be able to completely separate the affairs of the trust from your own, providing your student with adequate funding for those important college years even if your personal affairs suffer from declines and setbacks. When you look at the initial sticker price to create a trust and the costs associated with running it, think of this as a way in which you can protect your children from the financial fall-out of a major family disruption such as death, divorce, or remarriage.

Looking at Types of Trusts and How They Work

No two trusts are alike in every respect. Different grantors, beneficiaries, and fiduciaries make sure this is the case. Individual provisions make the variations even more pronounced. And that doesn't even begin to touch the wide variety of types of trusts that are available: living trusts, grantor-type trusts, irrevocable inter vivos trusts, testamentary trusts, and so on. The list is lengthy, and each serves a particular purpose. Still, some basic types of trusts may be particularly appropriate for you when saving for your children's college education.

Investigating inter vivos trusts

If you're so fortunate as to remember some of the Latin you learned in school, you know that "inter vivos" refers to a period during life. In the case of these trusts, it's during *your* life. *Inter vivos trusts* are created by you (the grantor) during your lifetime, to hold assets for another person. These trusts can be *revocable* (you can change your mind at any time and do away with it, taking back all the assets that you've placed in it) or *irrevocable.*

Living and other grantor-type trusts

A so-called living trust is probably the most talked-about trust variety in the media these days. Everyone and his brother is touting these trusts as a way to avoid probate and even estate taxes, and they're generally being sold as the greatest thing since sliced bread. In reality, a *living trust* is an entity that you set up, fund, and then retain total control over. You have the right to revoke the trust at any time as long as you're still alive — once you die, all bets are off. All trusts become irrevocable at the death of the grantor. Because you retain control over the assets, you're taxed on any income earned by this trust just as if you never put it into the trust.

As a college savings vehicle, a living trust really doesn't make much sense. Here are a few reasons why:

✔ When the financial aid folks come around counting your assets, whatever is in this trust is counted as your asset and a maximum of 5.6 percent of the value will be included in the federal formula for the expected family contribution outlined in Chapter 17. You haven't successfully removed it from the mix.

✔ Even if you make a distribution to your child to pay for his college expenses, you still have to pay the annual income tax bill on the income you've earned in the current year (just like you've been paying every year since you set up the trust).

✔ If you're the type of parent that wants your child to really understand how much this education is costing, and you hand your child a check and tell him to use it to pay his expenses (fortunately for you, he's a good kid and does what he's told), you've just made a gift to him that may have gift tax consequences (see Chapter 3).

Irrevocable inter vivos trusts

Although many financial planners use the term *inter vivos trust* interchangeably with *living trust* or *grantor trust*, you can create an inter vivos trust that is irrevocable. And it's with irrevocable trusts that you begin to see some benefits of using trusts to save for future events.

With an inter vivos irrevocable trust, any assets that you put into the trust represent a gift to the person for whose benefit you've created the trust, even though that person may not receive any benefit from the money either now, or ever. And here begins the tricky legal waltz you'll dance, because, in order to receive annual exclusion treatment for the gifts you're making (see Chapter 3), you have to make a completed gift of a present interest.

A *completed gift of a present interest* contains two essential aspects: First, it consists of property over which you've given up all dominion and control, and second, the person to whom you've given the property must receive immediate benefit from that property (a present interest). Because, in the case of a trust, you're not actually putting the money into the beneficiary's hands, most contributions to ordinary irrevocable inter vivos trusts don't qualify as annual exclusion gifts (see Chapter 3) and become subject to gift tax (and Generation-Skipping Transfer Tax for gifts to grandchildren) rules and regulations. Even though your control over the gift is severed, your beneficiary doesn't receive any current benefit from it.

Although making taxable gifts into an inter vivos trust isn't necessarily a bad tax move, if you're in the position to be able to gift money away, you really want to be able to benefit from the annual gift exclusion. Three types of trusts allow you to take advantage of this particular tax break.

Crummey trusts

The name of this particular type of trust isn't a reflection on whether it's a good trust or a bad trust. It's actually named after the poor soul who invented it who was blessed with an awkward last name.

Crummey trusts are irrevocable and must contain so-called *Crummey powers,* or specific instructions regarding what must happen every time you make a contribution to the trust. And what must happen, in order for the gift to be deemed completed and a present interest, is that your trustee must notify all the beneficiaries that a gift has been made. The trust must then give them the opportunity to withdraw the value of the gift (within a specific period of time, usually 30 or 45 days from the date the gift is made) from the trust and take the cash or other property. The beneficiary's ability to cash out the gift to the trust is what makes it a gift of a present interest and therefore eligible for annual exclusion treatment.

Here's how it works. Aunt Jane decides to set up a Crummey trust for her nieces and nephew (she has three), and names her sister as trustee. Each year, Aunt Jane makes a gift of $33,000 (3 x $11,000 — the current annual exclusion gift per child) into the trust. After her sister receives the check, she sends letters (certified mail and with return receipts, so she can prove to the Internal Revenue Service (IRS) that the notices went out should they decide to ask) to each of the children (or their parents, in the case of minor children), notifying them that a gift has been made into the trust and that they each have the right to withdraw $11,000 within the next 45 days.

Not surprisingly, no one decides to withdraw their share of the money, and their right to ask for the money expires with all the money still sitting in the trustee's possession. Now the trustee is free to invest the money, and Aunt Jane is perfectly within her rights to show she made three annual exclusion gifts on her gift tax return. Meanwhile, the money remains invested in the trust, growing until that time when the beneficiaries need distributions to pay for college expenses (or to buy that first house, pay for a wedding, or whatever other good reason the beneficiary needs the money for).

Even though Crummey trusts are irrevocable, remember that it's very easy to inadvertently turn them into grantor-type trusts (where the grantor pays all the tax each and every year). To avoid this treatment, don't make yourself or your spouse a beneficiary of the trust, and don't name yourself or your spouse as trustee of the trust, because the IRS views a husband and wife as essentially the same person (in case you wondered). To have this trust treated as its own entity, you really need to keep all the roles very distinct.

Section 2053(c) and 2053(b) trusts for minors

The only way a minor child can own securities outright is through a Uniform Gift to Minors Act (UGMA) account (see Chapter 12). One of the great drawbacks of this account, however, is that, at age 18 (or 21, depending on the state), the no-longer minor child now controls the account and everything in it to use as he or she determines.

To give parents and grandparents more control over the situation, you may also create trusts under Internal Revenue Code Section 2053(c) or (b), which allows you to save for that child until he or she reaches the age of 21. Unlike the Crummey trust, this trust doesn't require that you maintain the rather elaborate fiction of providing an opportunity for that child to take money out every time you put money in.

Instead, Section 2053(c) and (b) trusts to minors allow the grantor to create the premise of making annual exclusion gifts (as described in Chapter 3) in the following ways:

- ✔ Section 2053 (c) requires that the trust (all contributions plus all accumulated income) become completely payable to the beneficiary on his or her 21st birthday.

- ✔ Section 2053 (b) requires that all income earned (but none of the contributions received from the grantor) is paid to the minor child every year that the trust is in effect.

You may wonder where the benefit lies in creating trusts of this type when you can achieve much the same result by using a UGMA/UTMA account. Well, when drafting the trust instrument, you can include language in it that allows you to change the trust to a Crummey trust when the beneficiary reaches age 21. Because staying away from grantor-trust rules when dealing with a minor child is especially difficult, formulating the trust as a Section 2053(c) or (b) trust during your child's minority and then changing it over after he or she becomes an adult allow you to neatly sidestep some unfavorable tax treatments.

Tackling testamentary trusts

As the name suggests, these trusts are created under, and through, your last will and testament. Because these trusts are governed by terms contained in your last will, and because your last will doesn't become truly effective until you die, a testamentary trust comes into being and is administered after your death. Beyond that, it functions in all ways exactly the same as an irrevocable inter vivos trust does. You may include the same provisions in your testamentary trust as you might in any other, especially regarding how, when, and to whom distributions are made.

For obvious reasons, funding a testamentary trust has no gift tax consequences; however, you may have estate tax consequences. To ensure that all your desires for your children and/or grandchildren are carried out after your death, make sure that a competent trust and estate attorney draws up your last will.

If your priority during life is being sure you have adequate resources for your own needs, and you haven't made lifetime gifts of significant pieces of wealth to your family, a testamentary trust may be the ticket. Rather than making specific bequests of money to your children, grandchildren, or other relatives, the terms of the trust govern how your money will be used, preventing your descendents from frittering away their legacies. Because you define what that money may be used for (education is always a nice choice) before you die, you ensure that your money is actually used for those purposes.

Paying Tax on Your Trust

As you've no doubt figured out by now, putting money into a trust doesn't mean that you don't pay any tax on the income. Quite the contrary — all taxable income earned by a trust, in whatever form, is subject to applicable federal, state, and local income taxes. What you have to figure out is who pays the tax, how much has to be paid, and what you can do to make the taxes as minimal as possible.

Figuring out who foots the bill

What makes trust taxation interesting is figuring out who gets to pay the tax. If the trust is a revocable trust, or otherwise falls within the grantor rules (where the grantor retains at least some of the benefit of the assets inside the trust), the grantor includes the income on his income tax return and pays the tax. In certain situations, the trust may need to file its own income tax return, but in such cases, it shows only that the income will be reported on the grantor's return.

For all other trusts, the rules are more complex. Irrevocable trusts, such as Crummey trusts, Section 2053 (c) or (b) trusts for minors, and testamentary trusts, must file their own income tax returns. For trusts that make no distributions to beneficiaries, the tax return preparation is roughly the same as it is for an individual.

If a trust makes distributions to a beneficiary during the year, though, things change. A trust is an entity that the IRS refers to as *flow-through* or *pass-through.* Just as the income comes into the trust (in the form of interest, dividends, rents, business earnings) and then flows out of the trust to the beneficiary in the same form, the income tax liability that travels with the income flows into the trust and out to the beneficiary, who then has the responsibility to pay the tax. In every year in which a distribution is made, the trustee must provide to the trust beneficiary a copy of Schedule K-1 from the trust's income tax return, which provides the beneficiary with the breakdown into the various types of income he received during the year.

Running through the trust tax brackets

Although most trust tax laws do follow the individual tax rules very closely, there is one place with a huge discrepancy: where the tax bracket changes occur. Trusts aren't a very popular area with the IRS, and Congress generally considers trusts fair game when trying to balance its checkbook — after all, trusts don't vote.

Kiddie tax: Making the children pay

If you fund a trust for a minor child and you determine that he should receive a distribution from the trust, if he is under age 14, the trust distribution may trigger the *kiddie tax.*

The *kiddie tax* was inaugurated in 1986 as a way to prevent high-income taxpayers from shifting their income to their children, who were presumably in a lower tax bracket. The rules and forms are somewhat complicated, but the net result is this: In any year, a child under age 14 who has investment income in excess of a pathetically low base amount, which is looked at annually and adjusted periodically ($1,500 in 2003) will pay tax on the excess amount at his parents' highest bracket. In other words, if in 2003 you paid in a 35 percent tax bracket, your child also paid at that rate for all investment income over $1,500.

Unless you're making trust distributions to a young child, the "kiddie tax" shouldn't be a cause for concern for you. Because you've probably created the trust to deal with future college expenses, you probably don't need to fret over this particular provision unless you're living with Einstein reincarnated, who'll be starting college when he's twelve.

Accordingly, the amount of income you need to go from the lowest income tax rate to the highest (the *bracket ride*) for non-grantor trusts is short, not-so-sweet, and very much to the point. For example, in 2003, a trust begins to pay income tax at the highest rate with only $9,350 of income (as compared to $311,950 for single individuals and married couples filing jointly). There is some relief, though — the new 15 percent top dividend and long-term capital gains rates created by the Jobs and Growth Tax Relief Reconciliation Act of 2003 and explained in Chapter 12 apply to trusts as well as to individuals.

Obviously, when investing the assets in a trust, you want to make the most of the dividends and long-term capital gains tax rates (see Chapter 12), and rely less on other investments that produce income taxed at a higher rate. Municipal bonds are also very popular trust investments due to the tax-exempt nature of the interest. A great trust investment strategy is to buy investments that you expect will appreciate in value but that don't produce much income. When you finally sell, you'll pay the tax at the lower long-term capital gain tax rate rather than the rate on ordinary investment income.

Identifying the Pros and Cons of Trusts in Relation to College Savings

Clearly, funding trust accounts has some very real benefits when saving for your kids' future education expenses. Trusts also have a very strong downside.

You have to decide whether the balance tips positive or negative for your own financial and family situation.

Trusts have these benefits:

- ✔ You have absolute flexibility in funding, choosing beneficiaries, investing, and deciding how much, when, and for what distributions may be made.

- ✔ These accounts keep control out of the hands of your kids but give them the benefit of your savings.

- ✔ A properly drafted trust protects you, and your family, from personal catastrophes and financial disruptions. Funds that are segregated in an irrevocable inter vivos trust (and your intentions when you put that money there) will survive your death, a divorce (either your own or one of your beneficiary's) or a remarriage, to name a few issues.

- ✔ You pay no penalties for failing to use the money for its intended purpose, and you can use what you don't use for education expenses to help purchase that first home, pay for your kid's wedding, or even start funding his retirement. You really have no limitations.

On the downside, if you plan to fund a trust for your child's education, depending on the eventual value of the trust, you may want to consider not even filling out the financial aid forms discussed in Chapter 17 (which may actually be a positive, because these forms are bears). An irrevocable trust that you create for your child's benefit is counted as an asset of your child and is included at that nightmarish 35 percent rate when calculating the expected family contribution. When you add to that the costs, both administratively and in lost tax deferrals and exemptions, you may decide that other ways of saving better serve your purposes.

Chapter 14

Saving in Your Retirement Plans: The IRA Dilemma

*A*s you begin the run-up to college, you may be patting yourself on the back, sure in the knowledge that you've saved every penny you're likely to need to pay for your child's college education. If so, fantastic! You've overcome a huge obstacle, and now all your child needs to do is be accepted to the college of his or her choice.

If, on the other hand, you've left saving for college until late in the day, and are now sweating because you don't have enough funds in your Section 529 plan, Coverdell Education Savings Account, or Series EE or Series I savings bonds, all is not lost. If you're like many people, especially those who had children later but who started saving for retirement early on in their careers, you may actually have adequate money saved to not only fund your retirement but also to make up the difference between college costs and college savings.

In this chapter, you find out how to access some of the money in your retirement accounts (if you absolutely, positively must) to pay for qualified educational expenses. You see how best to liberate that money so that you minimize the amount of tax you'll pay on it. You explore how to strategically move savings around in order to actually take distributions from the most tax-advantageous account. And finally, you take a look at how using these funds will affect your own retirement down the road, and why you may want to view using any part of your retirement savings to fill college savings gaps as a last resort.

Although using some or all the money in your traditional IRA may make perfect sense when you're still relatively young and retirement seems distant and unreal, you need to remember that, while you can borrow for college, you can't borrow for retirement. Use retirement funds of any variety for college expenses only if you're certain that you'll have enough for retirement without that money. If you're far from retirement age, you still have the opportunity to increase your contributions into retirement plans. If, however, you're paying for college expenses only shortly before you'll be needing these funds yourself, be certain that you're not condemning yourself to a lifetime of limited opportunities and beans-on-toast dinners. Retirement now lasts longer, on average, than it ever has, and raiding your retirement savings now could sentence you to 20 to 30 years of subsistence living without adequate funds.

Using Your Traditional IRA to Cover College Expenses

If you've been contributing and saving every year in your traditional *Individual Retirement Account* (IRA), you may already have a tidy sum socked away and earmarked for your retirement. That money may beckon to you when the bills for your child's tuition and other educational expenses begin to roll in and your savings in other areas just aren't enough to cover them all. Clearly, the temptation is great — that money is just sitting there, you don't need any of it yet for retirement purposes, and your only option may be to either take a distribution from your IRA or take a loan to pay for those pesky college expenses.

What's more, you can do it and not pay an early distribution penalty (if you plan things right). The IRS allows you to take penalty-free distributions from your traditional IRA before you turn 59½ years old if that distribution is used to pay qualified educational expenses, although you do, of course, have to pay the income tax on the distribution.

Before you jump in and cash out your traditional IRA, consider these questions:

- **How much money will you need in order to retire and maintain your current lifestyle?** Calculators that allow you to make this estimate are available on the Internet and in most money management software packages. In addition, any good financial planner should be able to help you make this calculation.

- **How much money do you currently have saved in your (and your spouse's) various retirement funds, investment accounts, and so on?**

- **If you use part, or all, of your current retirement savings to pay for college expenses for your kids, will you still be able to save enough to adequately pay for your retirement after doing so?**

Figuring out qualified expenses

Maybe you're quite certain that you have more than you'll ever need and that it makes perfect sense for you to pay at least some of your student's expenses from your traditional IRA. If so, here's what you need to know to avoid paying a 10 percent penalty on your distribution:

✔ **You may pay only for qualified higher educational expenses.** Once again, these expenses include tuition, fees, books, supplies, and equipment required for enrollment at a qualified educational institution (schools qualified to participate in federal financial aid programs administered by the U.S. Department of Education). In addition, if the student attends school at least half-time, room and board paid to the school itself or as determined by the school also qualifies.

✔ **You may only pay qualified expenses for yourself, your spouse, your children (and your spouse's children, if they are different), and your and your spouse's grandchildren.**

✔ **If your beneficiary is a special-needs student, services incurred by him or for his benefit qualify.** Of course, regulations defining who is a special-needs student and what services are covered by this designation haven't been issued yet — use your best judgment when making a determination of what you think will be covered.

Calculating the amount of the distribution not subject to the 10 percent penalty

If you're under age 59½ when you take a distribution from your traditional IRA, remember that the general rule is that you will pay income tax on one of the following:

✔ The full amount of the distribution if you were able to make pre-tax contributions to the account

✔ The income earned in the account over its lifetime if you made after-tax contributions

✔ An amount somewhere in the middle if some of your contributions were made pre-tax and others were made after-tax

In addition to the income tax piece, you're also liable for a 10 percent penalty because you've taken an early distribution. However, when you use all, or a part, of that distribution to pay for qualified educational expenses, you're creating an exception to this rule. And if you use a distribution from your traditional IRA to pay for only qualified expenses, the result is clear. You'll need to calculate the portion of your distribution that's taxable to you and then pay the income tax on it, but you'll escape the penalty entirely.

Calculating the income tax and penalties on an early traditional IRA distribution becomes a bit trickier when the distribution pays only a part of your student's qualified expenses. The treatment here is similar to that used for Section 529 plans (see Chapter 5) and for Coverdell Education Savings Accounts (see Chapter 8), with one major difference: While you're allowed to make a reasonable determination of how you want to assign your Coverdell and Section 529 distributions, you may use a distribution from a traditional IRA only to pay for qualified educational expenses left on the table after considering any of the following:

- ✔ Tax-free Coverdell and/or Section 529 withdrawals

- ✔ Tax-free scholarships

- ✔ Tax-free, employer-provided educational assistance

- ✔ Any other tax-free payment (other than a gift or bequest) that your student receives due to enrollment at a particular institution, such as veteran's benefits, AmeriCorps benefits, and the like

If your student receives payments or credits from these sources equal to or in excess of the total amount of their qualifying expenses, all of your traditional IRA distribution will be subject to the 10 percent penalty. If the IRA distribution partially exceeds the adjusted qualifying expenses, only that part that is in excess will be assessed the penalty.

For example, Julia's annual qualifying educational expenses at her university are currently $30,000 per year, and she expects that the total cost, including all nonqualifying expenses such as insurance and transportation, will be $35,000. This year, she's been extremely fortunate, and the university has given her a $5,000 scholarship. In addition, her mother's employer gives her a $1,000 scholarship. However, Julia's parents were late in starting a 529 plan for her benefit, so there is only $15,000 left in that account, and her parents distribute the full amount to cover part of her current expenses. Now, she has $21,000 towards the total $30,000 qualifying amount. To make up the funding gap, Julia's father has an old IRA account which doesn't play a huge role in his retirement planning, so he decides to cash it in to come up with the remaining $14,000 that Julia will need to pay her expenses, both qualifying and non, for the current year.

On the basis of these numbers, Julia's family will face the following tax consequences:

✔ Julia will pay no tax on the $15,000 Section 529 distribution, as the full amount of the distribution is used to pay for qualifying educational expenses, nor will she pay any tax on the $5,000 university scholarship or the $1,000 scholarship from her mother's employer.

✔ Julia's parents will pay income tax only on $9,000 of the total $14,000 IRA distribution, since that is the amount left on the table after all other tax-free sources of income were considered.

✔ Julia's parents will pay both income tax and a 10 percent penalty on the remaining $5,000 of the IRA distribution, since even though that money was used to pay Julia's expenses, those expenses were not qualified educational expenses.

Tapping into Your Roth IRA for College Savings

Among the more recent entries into the retirement savings field, the Roth IRA has been a valuable addition, especially for many middle-income people who couldn't make tax-free contributions into a traditional IRA. If you meet the income limitations and are permitted to make contributions, Roth IRA's allow you to save money by making after-tax contributions into a retirement account. Over time, your money grows as it earns interest, dividends, and capital gains. When you finally begin to take distributions, your withdrawals come back to you completely tax-free. There is no tax-deferral element here, either at the front end, when you make your contributions, or at the back end, when you take withdrawals. Instead, you pay the income tax upfront and take withdrawals tax-free.

Making distributions and avoiding penalties with a Roth IRA

Roth IRA's differ from traditional IRA's in many aspects, but especially regarding the distribution rules. There are certain requirements about who may take distributions and when they may take them. Failure to fulfill both of these requirements may result in a 10 percent penalty on the income portion of the distribution:

✔ **Your Roth IRA account must be open for a period of five years before you may take any distributions tax-free.** If you fail the five-year holding period test, the income portion will be taxed at your ordinary income tax rates, and you will, most likely, be charged a 10 percent penalty (although certain exceptions apply).

✔ **Your distribution must satisfy one of the following conditions:**

- It must be made on or after the date on which you attain the age of 59½.

- It must be made to your estate or your named beneficiary on or after your death.

- It must be attributable to your being disabled.

- Up to $10,000 may be used to pay for qualified first-time home-buyer expenses.

Clearly, if you're an older parent or grandparent (over age 59½) and you've had a Roth IRA sitting in the wings for at least five years, you're free to use it to pay whatever educational expenses you want. Because the distribution will be made to you and it's already designated as a tax-free distribution, you may choose to use that money for whatever purpose your heart desires.

If, on the other hand, you have a Roth IRA and you haven't yet reached that magic age, you're still allowed to take distributions from your Roth IRA to pay for qualified educational expenses. You should note, though, that the income portion of these distributions will be taxable to you, although no 10 percent penalty will be applied on money used to pay qualifying expenses. And here, the expenses that qualify are exactly the same as those for a traditional IRA. In essence, if you use your Roth IRA to pay for college and you're younger than 59½, the net result to you is almost identical as it would be if you used your traditional IRA — you pay the income tax, but you avoid the penalty.

Playing with Roth IRA's flexibility without getting burned

If you're eligible to make contributions to a Roth IRA, it's a terrific way to save for the future. And, if you're an older parent, it gives you a great deal of flexibility when you're trying to determine how much to save for college and how much for retirement. With a Roth, you can gain many of the same tax benefits of a Section 529 plan or Coverdell Education Savings Account without limiting the use of your savings to only future educational expenses.

If you're okay with the idea of gifting money to your teenage children, you may want to think about opening a Roth IRA in their name. You need to know, though, that for this strategy to work, your children must be earning some money in each year that you make a gift into their Roth IRA, since only earned income is eligible to be contributed to a Roth account. Creating these accounts when your kids are barely earning allows contributions to be made while paying little or no tax on them, and then the money is free to grow for a longer period of time. Down the road, if your children need to apply for financial aid, this account (and any other retirement accounts, life insurance policies, or prepaid tuition plans that they may own) won't be included in the FAFSA calculation of the *expected family contribution* (EFC) described in Chapter 17.

Making Early Distributions from Other Retirement Accounts

If you're like many people, you may not have a traditional IRA or a Roth IRA. Maybe you have some other form of retirement savings in some sort of retirement account. Not surprisingly, these accounts are intended to be there for you when you retire; however, many of them are available under limited circumstances to pay for other expenses, including qualified educational expenses.

The following list is by no means all-inclusive, but it does cover many of the major types of self-funded and employer-sponsored retirement plans and what the tax consequences are if you need to take a distribution to pay for college expenses:

- ✔ **401(k) plan:** This plan allows you to make pre-tax contributions to a retirement fund for your benefit. Your employer sets up and administers the plan and may match all or part of your contribution. If you take an early distribution (a so-called *hardship distribution*) from this plan to pay for educational expenses, be prepared to pay a lot of tax on the distribution. You'll pay income tax at your top tax bracket on the full amount (remember, you've never paid tax on any of it), plus a 10 percent penalty. If you absolutely must access money from this account, you're much better off taking a loan from your plan, if your employer allows it, and then making sure to pay it back within five years.

- ✔ **403(b) plan:** This is essentially the same as a 401(k) plan, but is offered to public sector and nonprofit organization employees. Once again, early distributions for educational expenses are fully taxable and subject to the penalty.

- ✔ **SEP IRA:** A *Simplified Employee Pension* (SEP) is administered in much the same way as a traditional IRA. The biggest difference is that your employer — not you — will make the contributions to this account for your benefit. Because it runs exactly like an IRA in all other respects, it follows the rules for traditional IRAs regarding early distributions to pay for qualified educational expenses. You'll pay the income tax, but there won't be any penalty.

✔ **SIMPLE retirement account:** A *Savings Incentive Match Plan for Employees* (SIMPLE) may be set up by your employer to follow either the 401(k) plan model or the traditional IRA model. It allows you to make contributions to your retirement fund that your employer matches. Your tax cost, should you take an early distribution to pay for qualified educational expenses, depends on what type of plan you belong to. Beware, though: If you put money in only to take it out within your first two years of participation in the plan, a 25 percent penalty may be tacked on to your tax bill for good measure.

Saving for college with retirement accounts: Good or bad idea?

So much of financial planning rests on the contents of your crystal ball, and any savings plan is only as focused as what you can see there. Which means that there is absolutely no clarity whatsoever when you're trying to decide where to save money and how much you need to put away.

Using retirement accounts to save for your retirement makes perfect sense. These accounts are designed to defer income you're earning now and pick it up later in your life. For most people, that means that you'll also be paying income tax on it at a time when your income will be more limited than it is now, thereby reducing overall the amount of income tax you'll pay on that money.

These accounts aren't intended to pay for college expenses, which doesn't mean that they can't be used for that purpose. It does mean, though, that you may lose many of the advantages that you might have were you to keep the money in the account until you hit retirement age.

As you look at all the assets you have available to pay for college expenses (including your retirement accounts), keep the following in mind:

✔ **Tax deferrals:** Should you take a distribution to pay for college expenses, you'll be picking up that income on your current year's tax returns. Many people are in their highest earning years when their children are in college, so you may find that you pay tax on these distributions at an even higher rate than you would have if you'd never put the money into the account.

✔ **Reduction in available retirement income:** You have no idea how long you'll live, or how much money you'll need to see you through the end of your life. Using retirement funds to pay for college expenses may compromise your future standard of living.

✔ **Great flexibility in uncertain family situations:** Face it: You don't know for certain whether your children will attend college, or where, or exactly how much it will cost. If you don't want to put too much into specific college savings accounts because of your uncertainties, adding a cushion to your retirement accounts may provide you with whatever extra you may need to meet all contingencies.

Rolling Over Retirement Accounts to Obtain Maximum Benefit

Clearly, when you're looking to raid your retirement accounts to pay for educational expenses, not all types of accounts are created equal. And, if you've spent your entire working life with one company, you have only the one retirement plan that company offers and may be out of luck. You aren't allowed to take money out of a retirement plan of the company you're currently working at and switch it to another sort of retirement plan.

On the other hand, if you're like most people, you probably have moved periodically from job to job over the course of your career as you looked for that perfect place to put down your working roots. And you may have accumulated one or more retirement accounts along the way. If so, you may be in luck.

A retirement account that you have with a company for whom you no longer work may legitimately be rolled over into a traditional or a Roth IRA account. For accounts with low value, the rollover may be mandatory after you leave that company. For accounts with greater value, you may choose to leave your retirement funds under that company's management for as long as you like; you may, however, roll over the funds at any time.

If you don't already have a traditional IRA or Roth IRA account, open the new account before you request the rollover, and then specify to your old company that you want a *trustee-to-trustee transfer*. When the money is transferred in this way, there is absolutely no tax consequence to you (unless you move the money into a Roth IRA, in which case you'll have to pay income tax on the transaction).

If you forget to make a trustee-to-trustee transfer, your original pension manager will withhold 20 percent of the value of the account for income tax, give you a check for 80 percent of the value of the account, and leave it up to you to deposit 100 percent of the old account value into the new account within 60 days after the withdrawal from the first account. You have to wait until you file your income tax returns the following year to recoup the 20 percent that was withheld.

Chapter 15

Selling or Refinancing Your Family's House

....

In This Chapter

▶ Using your house as a college savings plan

▶ Putting home equity to work

....

The college acceptance letters have all arrived, and you and your child have selected one lucky school. Then the first tuition bill arrives, and the theoretical amounts you've been looking at for the past 18 years become actual amounts, requiring payment. For many of you, the amount you've managed to stash away in your Section 529 plan (see Part II) or your Coverdell account (see Part III) by scrimping and saving will be painfully inadequate to tackle the size of this bill, and the ones that follow.

Welcome to the reality of paying, rather than saving, for college.

But wait! You may literally be sitting on a treasure that can be accessed to pay the (tuition) piper, money that you may be able to use without paying any additional tax. You may be reading this while sitting in that highly appreciated, mortgaged commodity called your home.

Although you may think that your house isn't something that you want to place on the table as a possible way to pay for a college education, in many instances, doing so may make a lot of sense. By doing a little research and taking careful stock of your own situation, you may uncover a previously untapped asset that you didn't think could provide your child with a loan-free education without unduly burdening you.

Saving for College in Your House

Many of you probably never thought about using your house as a piggy bank for your children's college tuition, but your house may be not only a place to lay your head at night but also a valuable asset to consider when saving for college tuition. Your house is similar to a college savings plan in the following ways:

- ✔ You put money into it each month.
- ✔ The money you put into it appreciates in value.
- ✔ You can cash in that value for your child's college education.

When you spend money at the grocery store or on clothes, what you purchase has a value that is quickly consumed. On the other hand, money that you spend on your house often creates value that you keep, the same as money that you put into a bank or college savings account. The following sections explain how the value contained in your house can increase, making your house an asset for your college savings.

Recognizing your house as an asset

If you're thinking of making your family house a player in the game of educational funding and saving, you first need to look at your house from the correct perspective so that you see it as an asset.

Distinguishing house from home

Your first step to gaining the correct perspective of your house is to recognize what is your *house* and what is your *home*. You own a *house,* not a *home.* The presence of four walls and a roof does not, by definition, create a home — you do. Your efforts turn a building into the warm and inviting nest that you use to shelter your family, especially your children. But your money turns that building into a house that you can cash in for a college education. So when you walk through the door, make sure that you can distinguish your home, a place full of memories, from your house, which you may choose to use as an alternative to other forms of college savings plans.

Discover the economics of house ownership. Whatever memories your home may hold, your house — those walls, floors, and ceilings — have specific monetary value. Your house is an asset that you own, which, over time, should appreciate significantly in value. Maintaining that value helps you to maintain an asset that may be cashed in, just like any other type of college savings plan.

Getting rid of housing debt

The easiest way to rid yourself of housing debt is by changing your perspective. Don't focus on the amount you owe on your *mortgage loan* (the amount of money you've borrowed against the value of your house). Instead, concentrate on the *net equity* in your house (the current market value less the balance remaining on your mortgage loan).

For example, if you have a $100,000 balance remaining on the mortgage loan you borrowed in order to buy your house, but your house is actually worth $250,000, you may choose to focus on your debt ($100,000) or on the amount of net equity you have ($150,000). That net equity represents more than enough savings to put at least one child through four years of college — don't ignore it.

Adding to your monthly savings

Whether or not you're able to adequately fund your specific college savings plans, if you own your own house and have one or more mortgages on it, you are adding an amount to your overall, nonspecific savings each and every month. While the payment plan for your mortgage loans may seem endless (and they often are), each monthly payment includes a small amount of *principal,* or a piece of the original face amount of the loan. The payment of this piece each month decreases the amount left owing on the loan, therefore increasing the net equity of your house. Remember, you now owe less; therefore, your equity is greater.

If you go back to the $100,000 30-year mortgage loan on a house worth $250,000 from the previous section (with a monthly payment amount of $600 per month), in the first year of that loan, you would pay off $1,228 of the principal balance (leaving a $98,772 balance yet to be paid), increasing your net equity in the house from $150,000 to $151,228. By the time you get to the fifteenth year of the mortgage (and assuming the value of the house has not increased at all), the amount of principal you will pay in one year on your mortgage loan will increase to $2,839, the total amount of principal you will have paid over the fifteen years will be $28,951, and your total net equity will have increased to $177,951.

Making home improvements

Whether you purchased an already existing house or built one from scratch, every time you add anything to it, you potentially increase that house's value. Over time, your construction/improvement program may substantially alter the value of what you initially bought, and add a significant amount to the total you feel you've saved. A new bathroom here, a rehabbed kitchen there, furnace or window upgrades, or a room addition — before you know it, you're talking about real money.

If you can pay cash for improvements, the net equity, or value, you have in your house increases accordingly and rapidly (although there's not a direct and absolute correlation between the cost of the improvement or repair and the increased value of the house). If, on the other hand, you need to take a second mortgage or home equity loan to pay for part or all of these changes and repairs, the net value of your house will increase more slowly and in the same way as it does with your first mortgage: Each monthly payment will contain a portion of principal that reduces the outstanding debt, thereby increasing the net value.

For example, you decide that you can no longer live with avocado appliances, rustic pine cabinets, and a no-wax floor that lost its shine two decades ago and has never found it since. And you discover that achieving the transformation you want will cost you $30,000. Now, despite the $30,000 price tag, your new kitchen adds only $20,000 to the value of your house.

Depending on whether you pay for the change out of current savings, or if you choose to finance the change with a home equity loan, a second mortgage or a complete refinance of your first mortgage loan, your net equity in your house will shift as shown in Table 15-1.

Table 15-1	Calculating Net Equity Changes from Home Updates	
	Paying with Cash	*Taking out a Loan*
Value of house before kitchen	$250,000	$250,000
Amount of outstanding loans before kitchen	$70,000	$70,000
Net equity in house before kitchen	$180,000	$180,000
Value of house after kitchen	$270,000	$270,000
Amount of outstanding loans after kitchen	$70,000	$100,000
Net equity in house after kitchen	$200,000	$170,000

If you finance the kitchen improvement, you'll need to factor the additional money you've borrowed into your monthly budget. How much more you'll have to pay each month will depend on a what type of loan you choose, current interest rates, and over how long you schedule your repayments.

No matter how you find yourself paying for this improvement program, over time, the net value of your house and your savings, will increase. As a result, when the day arrives that you need to tap into your house's equity, you may be pleased to find that the exorbitant cost of your new kitchen will also partially fund a college education.

Appreciating the appreciation

Finally, your home is increasing in value over time due to appreciation. Just like the stock market, real estate values can rise and fall on the basis of a number of factors, such as interest rates, employment rates, and availability of housing stock. If you own your house for a long period of time, chances are great that its value will increase without your doing anything at all to it. (If you do make improvements, however, its value will increase more than if you don't — a house with a 30-year-old kitchen is far less attractive to buyers than one whose kitchen is brand-new.) You need to be aware of trends in your area, though; real estate markets are, by definition, local, and what may be true in Boston may just not work in Boise.

Using Home Equity

If you've been saving money in your house (and I don't mean under your mattress or in the cellar floor — see the section "Saving for College in Your House" for more information), then you understand that your home increases in value as time passes (*appreciation*). Your house increases even more in value with all the money, such as mortgage payments or home improvements, that you put into it. And when you take that value and subtract from it the balance remaining on your mortgage, you have a rough estimate of the *equity* you have in your house. You can cash in that equity for college expenses, much like traditional college savings plans.

Check out the examples throughout this chapter of how you can cash in the equity of your house, but make sure that you review the warnings I include in the section "Being cautious when cashing in." Before you can realize the tax benefits (see the section "Considering the tax benefits," later in this chapter), be sure that using the equity in your house is a reasonable approach for you financially.

Being cautious when cashing in

Although the benefits of using home equity greatly outweigh the disadvantages (see the benefits in the section "Considering the tax benefits"), let me be very upfront and in your face about the downsides:

✔ If you sell your house to cash in your equity, then you need to find somewhere else to live, with its associated, although presumably lower, cost (new mortgage if you buy, otherwise rental expenses).

✔ If you choose to refinance your first mortgage or decide to take a second mortgage on your existing house to cash in your equity, you need to know that you'll be able to pay the increased monthly amount, if it increases. (Often, if the interest rate at the time you are refinancing is significantly lower than the one on your original loan, you may be able to take money out of your house without increasing your payment at all.)

If you can handle the costs associated with selling or refinancing your home, you may consider cashing in your home equity that you've saved to pay for college expenses.

Considering the tax benefits

No matter how you cash in the money you've saved in your house, as long as you can handle the warnings I discuss in the previous section, you can enjoy a tax benefit with each approach.

Figuring out which approach to cashing in the value of your house works best for you is the first decision you need to make. Consider the following circumstances to determine which approach works best for your situation:

✔ Selling your home makes sense under the following circumstances:

- You no longer need as big a house, and were thinking of downsizing anyway.

- Your current mortgage is either all paid, or substantially paid, so that your mortgage interest deduction is either all gone or shrinking away.

- You've been in your house a long time, and it's increased in value considerably over what you paid originally.

✔ Taking out a second mortgage may work better for you under the following circumstances:

- Interest rates are currently higher than they are on your first mortgage loan, and you want to limit the amount you will be paying back at a higher rate.

- You want the higher income tax deduction that comes with paying more mortgage interest.

✔ Refinancing your house may be the best approach under the following circumstances:

- Interest rates have dropped, and you may be able to borrow the amount of money you need and still make substantially the same payment as you currently are.

- You want the income tax deduction that comes with paying mortgage interest.

Whether you sell or refinance your house in order to access your equity, you have freed up savings that haven't come from a tax-deferred or tax-exempt source, such as a Section 529 or Coverdell plan. Therefore, you're probably not paying any income tax on these amounts when you withdraw them (just like distributions from these plans that are used to pay qualified education expenses). In addition, you're entitled to claim education tax credits (the Hope Credit and Lifetime Learning Credit) and/or the adjustment allowed for qualified tuition payments (all discussed in Chapter 16 and more thoroughly in *Taxes For Dummies,* written by Eric Tyson and David J. Silverman and published by Wiley) to the extent allowable. These credits are not insubstantial; at the time of this writing, they're $1,500 per year for the Hope Credit and $1,000 per year for the Lifetime Learning Credit and can be used to offset ordinary income taxes not associated with any sort of college savings scheme.

Because selling or refinancing your house is never something you undertake lightly (filling out mortgage applications is up there with having my teeth drilled as my favorite things to do), please be sure to go through this exercise only once. Take out as much equity as you think you'll need to complete your child's education the first time you either sell or refinance, so you don't have to do it again for that same purpose. After you have the cash in hand, safely stash any amounts you don't need to pay current education expenses in an investment account as outlined in Chapter 12.

Selling your home

When you sell your existing residence, you're selling an asset (your house) and may recognize a *capital gain* (the amount over and above your cost, or basis, in your house) on the sale. Federal tax law used to permit you to roll over that gain into the purchase of a new residence, but has now changed to allow you to exclude up to $250,000 (if you're single) or $500,000 (if you're married) from your total capital gain. For most people, this means that when you sell your house, you won't pay a penny of federal capital gains tax, provided you've lived in the house for at least two of the previous five years. Since the federal capital gains tax on $500,000 is a whopping $75,000, this exclusion represents a huge tax savings to you when you cash in a valuable asset (your house), and should provide enough cash (after you've arranged other housing) to see at least one or two students through college. If you no longer need the big family home as the youngest children head off to school, the proceeds from the sale of your house can be a bonanza that finances the education of multiple children.

For example, Charlie and Grace purchased their house in the suburbs 15 years ago for $100,000, and they have since redone their kitchen and one bathroom for $30,000, so their total *basis* (purchase price plus capital improvements) in their house is $130,000. Their last child is heading off to college in the fall, and they realize that they'd rather be living in a condominium in the city, closer to their jobs. They sell the house for $450,000. Their capital gain on the sale is $320,000 ($450,000 – $130,000), on which they'll pay no tax because they're married and have lived in the house for at least two of the previous five years, and, therefore, fall within the exclusion amount. (Remember, if they had to pay the federal capital gains tax on that amount, their tax bill would be $48,000.) From a tax standpoint, they have just earned $320,000 tax-free; from a cash position, even after they pay off their outstanding mortgage of $65,000, they will still have $385,000 with which to pay for their youngest child's education and buy a new residence.

Figure 15-1 shows how Charlie and Grace calculate the capital gain they realized when they sold their house.

Figure 15-1:
Calculating
capital
gains on the
sale of a
house.

Sales price of house		$450,000
SUBTRACT: Basis of house		
Purchase price of house	− $100,000	
Improvements (additions to basis)	− $30,000	
Total basis of house		−$130,000
Capital Gain		320,000
Amount of tax to be paid		NONE

Taking out an additional mortgage

Instead of selling your house, you may choose to take a second mortgage on your property. When you borrow money against the value of your house in the form of an additional mortgage, the amount of cash you receive from the loan isn't taxed in any way, and if you itemize your deductions on your income tax return, you can deduct some or all of the mortgage interest from your income, depending on the total size of your mortgage and your total income. When you add an additional mortgage loan to the one you already have, you undoubtedly raise the amount of your combined monthly payments; however, you haven't extended the life of your first mortgage loan, and over time (and depending on interest rates and whether you and your student are eligible for low-cost loans), borrowing money this way may be considerably cheaper than saddling yourself or your student with excessive student loans.

Here's how it works: Using the same set of circumstances as in the previous example (house valued at $450,000 with a current first mortgage value of $65,000), Charlie and Grace choose to add a second mortgage of $30,000 to their house rather than sell it. They choose this option for three reasons: the interest rates currently offered for second mortgages in their area are lower than the PLUS loans (see Chapter 17), which are all that they qualify for; the payback period is longer on the mortgage than it would be on the loan, lowering their monthly loan costs; and the interest for them is fully tax-deductible. Their current first mortgage loan payment is $734 per month (30 year note with 8 percent interest rate), and they manage to get a second mortgage for 15 years and a 5.75 percent interest rate. The payment on the second mortgage is $249, bringing their total monthly mortgage payment to $983.

Refinancing your house

You may decide that you want to stay in your current house but that completely *refinancing,* or borrowing enough to pay off your existing mortgage loan plus adding an additional amount to cover educational expenses, makes more sense than taking a second mortgage. You may benefit from a complete refinance if your current interest rate is higher than 1½ or 2 percent above interest rates currently being offered. Also, if you've already paid off a substantial amount of your first mortgage, refinancing may allow you to keep your monthly payment close to, or even less than, its current amount. You may even find it possible to move from a 30-year mortgage to a 15-year one while keeping your payment close to its current level and keeping the ending date of your new mortgage close to the ending date of your old one.

Sue and Leon purchased a house with a $250,000 30-year mortgage 15 years ago, with an interest rate of 9 percent. Today, their house is worth $350,000, they have a balance remaining of about $198,000 on their original mortgage, and their monthly payment is approximately $2,010. Now, their son is ready for college, and they anticipate a $50,000 shortfall between what they've managed to save and what they realistically think that sending him through four years of school will cost. They decide to explore the possibility of a complete refinance of their house, checking out what their payment would be if they refinance not only their house but also add to the new loan the additional money needed ($50,000) to complete their son's education.

When they actually fill out the necessary paperwork to apply for the new loan, Sue and Leon manage to obtain a much lower interest rate (5½ percent) than on their old mortgage, and they also choose a 15-year payback period instead of 30 years (they've already been paying on this house for 15 years, and they really want to finish on their original schedule). When the loan finally closes (the refinance process generally takes between four and eight weeks from start to finish), the face amount of the new loan is $250,000 ($198,000 balance on the first mortgage plus $50,000 for college expenses and $2,000 to take a vacation), and their new monthly mortgage payment is now $2,043. By refinancing, Sue and Leon will add only about $30 a month to their mortgage payment, and they'll still fully pay off the loan about the same time as they would have had they not refinanced.

Using the equity in a vacation home or rental property

A little place at the lake or in the mountains is the stuff dreams may be made of — but when it comes time to pay for college, if your college savings are shy of the full amount necessary, they may become the stuff of your children's education. Tapping into, or cashing out, the equity in a second or third residence or a piece of rental property may pay for a lot of tuition, but it may be a costly tax event. The following rules apply to any real estate that's not your primary residence:

✔ If you find that selling a piece of real estate makes the most sense for you, be aware that the $250,000 (single) or $500,000 (married) exemption amount for capital gains doesn't apply to the sale of anything except your principal residence.

✔ Mortgage interest paid on a second residence is subject to the same rules as mortgage interest paid on your primary residence, and most, if not all, is tax deductible (check with your tax advisor); if you have a third residence, you're out of luck.

✔ Mortgage interest (and all other expenses related to the care and feeding of a piece of rental real estate) is deductible on IRS Schedule E, Rental Real Estate, not Schedule A, Itemized Deductions. You may need to consult a tax professional to make sure that you take all the deductions you're entitled to but none of the ones that you aren't.

Chapter 16

Accessing Scholarships and Awards

*M*aybe you've been carefully saving for the day your child begins college, or perhaps you've worked on the assumption that Bruiser is going to be the starting nose tackle for a Division I school's football team and will receive a full athletic scholarship. No matter which category you fall into, as you move closer to that fateful day, you may find that your planning hasn't produced the desired results. Maybe the stock market didn't perform as well as you'd expected, or Bruiser is actually more comfortable ripping the guts out of a computer than a live opponent. As you look at that first tuition bill, you may realize that you don't have enough saved, and you can't possibly make up the full amount of the difference from your current earnings.

Now, you could panic — after all, you've told your child all along that you expect him to attend college and you'll somehow find a way to pay for it. A better option, however, is to take that same energy and begin researching what available free, and not-so-free, money is out there in the form of outright grants, scholarships, fellowships, and guaranteed payments for service, just waiting for your child to apply for it.

In this chapter, you discover the different groups and organizations that have money available to help you with those college expenses. You also find out what your student needs to do to qualify for that money. And you explore the differences between scholarships and low-cost loans in exchange for service commitments as opposed to outright grants that have no strings attached. Finally, you look at what tax consequences, if any, there are when your student receives scholarship aid.

You may also want to check out *Free $ For College For Dummies,* by David Rosen and Caryn Mladen (Wiley Publishing, Inc.), for more detailed tips and strategies on seeking out scholarships and grants.

Searching for Scholarships, Fellowships, and Grants

Fortunately, finding sources of free money isn't nearly as difficult as finding the lost ark or the sales receipt for the toaster that blew up the first time you used it. You just need to know the different places to look for the money.

Before you start your search, though, you should be aware that the words *scholarship, fellowship,* and *grant* are often used interchangeably by various organizations, but they essentially refer to the same thing: money that the organization provides to your student for higher education expenses without any expectation on the organization's part that they will be repaid. These terms do have some subtle differences, however. Generally speaking, a *scholarship* is paid to undergraduate students, a *fellowship* goes to graduate or postgraduate students (often with a research or teaching requirement attached), and *grants* are usually associated with need (but scholarships and fellowships may also be need-based). The basic theory is the same, however.

You may think that your child isn't smart enough, talented enough, or poor enough to warrant someone else picking up even a part of his tab at college, but you're probably wrong. Money is available from a wide variety of sources, and it runs the gamut from small stipends to full tuition grants. Many of these aren't based on either ability or need; they merely require that you apply for the funds. Do your research and check all available sources — you may be quite surprised to find out just how much money is out there. Use the info in this section as your guide for searching out the possibilities.

When conducting your search, keep track of all the different ways that your child may be able to access scholarship money. Scholarships are awarded not only on merit and need, but also on the basis of residency, ethnic or religious background, college choice, career path, and whether he is left-handed. Some scholarships are awarded only to incoming freshmen; others don't begin until a student's senior year. Don't assume that your child won't qualify; instead, work on the assumption that, if you dig hard enough, something out there has his name written on it. And, if you fail this year to snag some funding, don't give up — as any good Red Sox fan knows, just wait until next year.

Beware of scholarship scams, where for a small (or large) entry fee, your student is guaranteed a scholarship, or given access to scholarship information that is supposedly not available for free. Remember, all scholarship information is free for the asking, and you must apply to the scholarship directly (not through any middleman) for the grant. Anyone who asks for your credit card information or charges you a fee for any scholarship-related service is scamming you. Always keep in mind that scholarships are a classic case of receiving money on the basis of hard work, good looks, talent, or a combination of the three, and nothing else; there should be no need for you to pull out your wallet at any point in the application process.

Looking to your child's prospective college

Begin your scholarship search at your child's college, both in the admissions and the financial aid offices. Every college has a list of scholarships that are available if a student applies for them. Some of them are well known and very prestigious; others, though, are buried in obscurity, and you just have to be proactive enough to look for them and apply. Although the size and seeming abundance of the athletic scholarships have become the stuff of legend, your child may also qualify for academic scholarships.

Both athletic and academic scholarships are generally awarded before your student even begins his college career, and they need to be renewed for each subsequent year. Substandard performance may lead to a reduction in, or even total loss of, the scholarship.

Don't forget, though, that there are often smaller scholarships awarded to students who have already proven themselves at the college level. The annual history award may not carry much cachet outside the history department, but that's real money they're handing out with it.

Working with your employer

Two of the most worthwhile benefits an employer can offer are scholarship programs for the children of employees and tuition assistance programs for employees. These programs provide the company with valuable tax deductions and give huge boosts to the educational plans of their employees and their children.

Even if your employer doesn't directly offer either a scholarship program or some form of tuition assistance for employees, if you're a member of a union, the union may provide some aid. Assumptions that your union doesn't have anything like this in place will only hurt you — check with your union representative and find out.

Employer-sponsored scholarship programs

Company-sponsored scholarship programs generally aren't need based at all but are rather merit based. What company, after all, wants to admit that it doesn't pay its employees enough to enable them to easily send their children to college? The fact that these scholarships are merit based doesn't mean that your student needs to be a genius (she is, after all, competing only against other children of people employed by the same company). It does mean, however, that she must maintain reasonable grades in high school; she also may have to complete an application, take a test, or both.

Most of these programs don't provide full tuition assistance; instead, they usually give a more nominal amount. Still, any money that you receive will supplement what you've saved, and it may just bridge the gap between your savings and your student's potential costs.

The existence of a scholarship program may be buried deep inside your employee manual. Check with your human resources department to find if your company has such a program in place, what the requirements are, and what you and your child must do to apply.

If you're fortunate enough to work for a college, the most valuable benefit your employment contract contains may be that you, your spouse, and your children can attend that institution tuition-free and tax-free, or at least at a discounted rate. Unlike corporate and union scholarships, these tuition reductions aren't based on merit, but rather on your employment.

Help! We won too much money!

What if you've managed to save the necessary amount of money in either a Section 529 plan or a Coverdell Education Savings Account (ESA), and all of a sudden, a full scholarship lands in your student's lap? Well, first thank your lucky stars that you're one of the few who get to have this problem, and then consider your options for what to do with the unneeded savings account. You may choose any one of the following courses of action:

✔ **If your student has dreams of graduate school dancing in her head, keep it safely stashed for that day.** Remember, Section 529 or Coverdell plan funds can be used to pay for all postsecondary qualified educational expenses, not just undergraduate school expenses.

✔ **Distribute the money to your student or to yourself after graduation.** Remember, though, if money is left over in either your Section 529 plan or your student's Coverdell ESA after he's completed his education, distributions to either you or him will result in income tax owed on the earnings plus a 10 percent penalty.

✔ **Make distributions to your student in the years in which he receives his scholarship.** By making distributions in these years, he'll pay only the income tax, but no penalty.

✔ **Roll the account over to a new beneficiary.** By changing the designated beneficiary (see Chapters 5 and 8 for lists of who qualifies) and then using the money to pay qualified educational expenses for that student, you and your new beneficiary may escape paying any income tax at all on the distributions.

Employer-sponsored tuition assistance/reimbursement programs

Tuition assistance programs are one of the more highly touted benefits a company may offer, but they're often the most misunderstood. If you're contemplating returning to school to either hone your existing skills or to branch off in an entirely different direction, check with your supervisor and with your personnel or human resources office to see how much, if any, your company's program may cover. You may be pleasantly shocked to find that, even though you're taking a course that seems to be completely unrelated to your job, your company may feel that your new skills add value to the company, so it will cover at least a portion of your expenses.

Check out Chapter 3, which has a section on part-time and summer jobs, for ways your student can help out here.

Be prepared to pay the full cost of any course you take upfront, whether you pay cash or use a credit card. Most companies will reimburse you for your tuition expenses only after you successfully complete the course, not before. Also keep in mind that they usually expect a grade of a C or higher for reimbursement.

Scouting local civic groups

What do the Elks, the Moose, the Knights of Columbus, the Daughters of the American Revolution, and the Chamber of Commerce all have in common? They all provide prizes and awards to deserving high school seniors, who are nominated for the award either by their teachers or by members of the organization who are familiar with the students and their work.

Scholarships may be given for academic excellence, athletic prowess, or community service, depending on the organization. Some of these awards are in the form of books, but others are cash. The checks are generally made out directly to the student, not to the university that the student will be attending the following fall. These small scholarships may provide your student with necessary money to buy incidentals that often aren't covered by a university scholarship program but are necessary purchases nonetheless.

Competing for corporate-sponsored awards

You may be familiar with the Miss America and Miss U.S.A. pageants and know that these young women receive scholarships from these organizations to further their educations. What you may not realize is that other types of corporate competitions (that don't require parading around in a swimsuit in front of a national television audience), open to both genders, offer similar benefits to the winners. These competitions don't require that you work for a particular company or business in order for your child to compete; in fact, if you're an employee, your child may not be eligible (check the entry rules).

Corporate scholarships, such as those offered by Best Buy, Burger King, Coca-Cola, Calgon, and the Discover Card, among others, can be very lucrative if you manage to nab one. The first-place award often is more than enough to cover all the expenses for a single year, but even runner-up prizes can be worth thousands. Awards are usually made for only one year at a time. Some are renewable annually, provided your student kept up his grades. Others are good only for a single year; if students want further funding from that source, they'll have to apply for it each year they're eligible.

Corporate competitions are competitive — don't let foolish errors trip up your student's application. Read the entry requirements carefully, and follow them closely. If the application must be postmarked by October 31, don't mail it on November 1 and hope that officials won't notice — they will.

You may access lists of what corporations sponsor competitions, what the general requirements are for each, and how much money is at stake through a variety of Web sites. Plug *scholarship* into any search engine to access a list. Good places to start are at www.scholarships.com and www.fastweb.com, although new Web sites sprout almost daily in this very popular area. Libraries may also have books that give you this information, although the information in the books may not be as current as the Internet info.

Tracking down charitable foundations

The United States has thousands upon thousands of charitable foundations, and most of them are completely obscure. In fact, many of them, according to the terms of their establishing documents, can't give scholarship money directly to students. Instead, they must set up scholarships through another organization, such as a college or university. Check with your student's financial aid office to obtain a list of these charities.

Some charitable organizations, however, do provide scholarship and fellowship money directly to students to help defray the cost of education. Unfortunately, finding these organizations may be difficult (because many keep a very low profile). Still, you can locate them. Here are some suggestions:

✔ **Check with your state's attorney general.** The AG's office in each state usually keeps a list of all organized charities operating within the state. They're obligated to provide annual reports, and this information is available to the public.

✔ **Check with regional associations of grant makers.** Their lists may not be as complete as the one you get from the attorney general because charitable foundations don't have to register with them, but this may be the easiest way to access information from charitable foundations around the nation. Remember, if you can find a local foundation that's giving away money for schooling, your chances of snagging a scholarship from them may be greater than from a national charity because you're competing against a smaller pool of applicants.

✔ **Search the Internet.** Not every charitable foundation has a Web site; in fact, most don't. But you can often find the major charitable foundations that do provide scholarship assistance on the big scholarship search Web sites, such as www.scholarships.com and www.fastweb.com.

Snagging state and municipal scholarships

You may or may not want your tax money spent on scholarships, but most states and some cities and towns provide some scholarship aid to some of their neediest students. Even if you're not sure that your child will qualify, there's no harm in accessing the information and making sure.

If you're not sure how to begin searching for these taxpayer-funded scholarships, the Internet is always a good place to begin. You can plug in your state's (or town's) name and *scholarship* into any search engine and come up with a fairly extensive list of what's available to you from local sources. You should also check with your student's guidance counselor for any smaller grants that may not have Web sites. And, last but not least, check with your state and local departments of education to see if they have any pertinent information for you.

Generally, when you do receive assistance from the state, some strings are attached — for one, your student must attend a public institution in that state, whether it's a community college or a four-year college.

Acquiring College Funding in Exchange for Service

In these days of the all-volunteer military, you've probably seen recruitment ads on television that tout the benefits of the Montgomery GI Bill. Or, if you live in a major city, you'll surely have noticed the red jackets of AmeriCorps, those primarily college-aged nonstudents who give up a year of their time to community service in communities all over the country in exchange for limited tuition assistance.

While these are two of the more visible examples of college tuition assistance available in exchange for the completion of a public service commitment, they're not the only two. In all the examples in this section, either the federal or state government pays for all or a part of your education, while you give a period of service as a payback. Clearly, from the government's position, this is a winning strategy — it gives higher education to people who otherwise might do without and gets services in exchange. But for many people who enroll in these programs, it also helps to solve what otherwise might be an unsolvable problem: how to pay for the education they need in order to begin the career they want.

You and your child should ponder a few points before embarking on this road toward financing your student's education:

- ✓ **Your student may have very little control over what type of service he does and where he does it.** While the military, the Public Health Service, and AmeriCorps try very hard to put people where they want to be, not everyone can play in the Marine Corps Band, fly fighter jets, or be in the Army Corps of Engineers.

- ✓ **Once your student actually begins to receive money, his window to back out of the deal closes quickly.** Although the various branches of the service allow a freshman ROTC scholarship student to cancel his scholarship, once you move beyond that first year, your child has pretty much committed to fulfilling his military service obligation. The same holds true for loans with service obligations from the Public Health Service; although you can buy out of your service period, the cost far exceeds the actual amount you received.

- ✓ **The amount of money your student receives may not be enough to pay for the education he wants.** Benefits from the Montgomery GI Bill generally pay for a four-year education at a public college or university, but you'll come up short if your child's greatest desire is to attend a private four-year college. Even with additional benefits available, you still won't have enough, and you'll have to make up the difference, either through savings, current earnings, or loans.

If you're still game even after the warning, read on and find out more about your options.

Marching in the military

The military provides one of the best bargains around in educational funding. This is true whether your child enlists in a branch of the military or any state National Guard right out of high school, enrolls in the *Reserve Officer Training Corps* (ROTC) at her college, or is fortunate enough to obtain a nomination to a military service academy (West Point, U.S. Naval Academy, U.S. Coast Guard Academy, U.S. Air Force Academy, or the U.S. Merchant Marine Academy). In exchange for either active or reserve service in one of the four branches of the military or the merchant marine, your child will receive enough funding from the government to provide at least a bare-bones postsecondary education. In many cases, the educations provided by the military are some of the finest available.

Programs for active duty, reserves, and veterans

Several programs are available to military personnel who have completed a period of active duty and/or reserve duty, and other programs are open to veterans or their families. Among these are the following:

- ✔ **The Montgomery GI Bill:** This bill provides a cash education incentive to either active duty personnel (after they've served one tour of active duty) or veterans for up to 36 months of postsecondary education, including, but not limited to, two- and four-year colleges, vocational and technical training, correspondence courses, apprenticeships/job training, and flight training. The amount your student receives is pegged to the length of his service and whether that service was active duty or reserve/National Guard duty. In addition, amounts he or she is eligible to receive are adjusted annually for increases in the cost of living.

- ✔ **Tuition assistance:** Enlisted servicemen and servicewomen may use this aid to pay for secondary and postsecondary courses during the time that they're on active duty (including reserve and National Guard duty). These benefits have an annual limit, but they may be supplemented by amounts from the Montgomery GI Bill.

- ✔ **Army/Navy/Marine Corps College Funds:** This program is supplemental to the Montgomery GI Bill and may increase the amount of money the military will contribute to your child's education. Awards aren't automatic, and they're not available to everyone; they're made based on academic merit.

- ✔ **Community College of the Air Force:** Open only to active-duty members of the Air Force, it offers primarily technical and scientific courses leading to an associate's degree. The Air Force pays up to 75 percent of the cost of the courses.

- ✔ **Survivors' and Dependents' Educational Assistance Program:** This program provides up to 45 months of educational assistance and/or vocational training to the eligible children and spouse of a veteran who has died or become permanently and totally disabled from a service-related incident, or who died after becoming permanently disabled, or who was either a prisoner of war or is currently missing in action. Benefits are provided to veterans' children only between the ages of 18 and 26, and to the veteran's spouse for a ten-year period from the date that spouse becomes eligible or from the date the veteran dies. If you think you, or your children, may qualify for this, you should contact your local Veteran's Administration Office for all the details.

ROTC and service academy scholarships

These scholarships are available to college students who attend one of the five service academies or a college with an ROTC program. Upon graduation from either the service academy or the ROTC program, your student is immediately commissioned as an officer in one branch of the military, and he or she is committed to serving for a specific period of time, depending on the size and duration of the scholarship. A graduate from West Point, for example, is committed to at least five years of active duty and three additional years of reserve and/or National Guard duty. Because ROTC programs vary between schools, you should check with the ROTC recruiter at your student's school about the after-graduation commitment for this program.

- ✓ **ROTC scholarships:** These scholarships may vary in length from two to four years, and in amounts up to 100 percent of the tuition, fees, and expenses of a particular institution. These scholarships are intensely competitive; don't assume that, because your student signs up for ROTC as a freshman, he or she will automatically receive one of these scholarships. You can find out about the general outlines of the ROTC scholarship programs at www.armyrotc.com or www.military.com. For more specific information about a specific program, you should contact the ROTC recruiter at the particular college your student is interested in.

- ✓ **Service academy appointments:** These appointments provide a wonderful education and the assurance of a job at the other end. For that reason, they're few and far between, and they require far more legwork on your, and your student's, part to make it happen (not to mention the nomination of your U.S. representative or senator). In fact, all the service academies recommend that your student begin the application process in the spring of his or her junior year of high school. If your student is so fortunate as to get one of these appointments, he or she will receive the cost of full tuition plus a living stipend for the four years it takes to complete that undergraduate degree.

Helping others (and yourself) with AmeriCorps

A part of the Corporation for National & Community Service, AmeriCorps encompasses a network of national service programs and projects in a variety of areas, including health, education, environment, disaster relief, youth mentoring, elder care, and affordable housing. In fact, the list of programs under the umbrella is massive, and chances are good that whatever your, or your student's, interest, you'll probably find something there to suit it.

AmeriCorps can provide services in all these areas by tapping into the better nature of its volunteers. In exchange for an approximate one-year commitment (either full- or part-time), AmeriCorps may provide a volunteer with a modest living allowance plus health insurance, training, and a student loan deferment during that year if that volunteer has existing student loans. Volunteers who successfully complete their commitment become entitled to a modest education award that may be used toward college or graduate school or to pay back existing student loans.

AmeriCorps is open to U.S. citizens, nationals, and lawful residents. Provided the volunteer is over age 17, the program doesn't have any age or education restrictions; you, or your student, may choose to serve at any time.

The services that AmeriCorps volunteers provide are, without a doubt, priceless in terms of providing needed services at very low cost. But that fact hasn't prevented AmeriCorps from being caught in the crosshairs of annual budget fights between Congress and the President, who all agree that this is a wonderful program and then proceed to slash its funding. Because it does require appropriations from Congress to fund the programs and pay the volunteer stipends and education awards, you may not want to count on a huge number of available openings in AmeriCorps in the future. Still, if your student is determined to do something worthwhile with a year of her life and pick up some assistance for college, no matter how large or small, she could do a lot worse than spend a year here.

Getting paid by the Public Health Service

The U.S. Public Health Service provides various sorts of educational assistance, from loans to outright grants, to students who are pursuing careers in health-related fields. These programs are designed to provide access to these professions for underprivileged individuals and to entice students into health-related professions that are currently experiencing shortages.

Programs that are offered may change to respond to changing needs. Among the scholarships and low-cost loan programs currently available are the following:

- ✔ **Scholarships for Disadvantaged Students Program:** Scholarships are available for financially needy full-time students enrolled in health professions and nursing programs who come from disadvantaged backgrounds. Scholarship recipients are selected by their schools and awarded full tuition costs plus a reasonable amount for education and living expenses.

- ✔ **Loans for Disadvantaged Students Program:** This program provides low-cost, long-term loans to financially needy full-time students pursuing a degree in allopathic (Western) medicine or osteopathic (specializing in musculoskeletal therapy) medicine, dentistry, optometry, podiatry, pharmacy, or veterinary medicine. Loans may cover not only tuition but also reasonable expenses, as determined by the school.

- ✔ **Health Professions Student Loan Program:** Similar to the Loans for Disadvantaged Students Program, this program provides long-term, low-cost loans to full-time, financially needy students in dentistry, optometry, pharmacy, podiatry, or veterinary medicine only. Loans may not exceed the cost of tuition and a reasonable amount for education and living expenses, and they're awarded by the participating school.

✔ **Primary Care Loan Program:** This program offers long-term, low-interest rate loans to full-time, financially needy medical students pursuing a degree in allopathic medicine or osteopathic medicine. Students receiving loans through this program must agree to enter and complete residency training in one of the primary care specialties within four years of graduation. They also must practice in primary care medicine for the life of the loan. Participating schools award these loans, which are not to exceed the cost of tuition plus reasonable educational and living expenses.

✔ **Nursing Student Loan Program:** Long-term, low-interest loans are provided to full- and part-time nursing students pursuing any nursing degree, from diploma through graduate levels. Participating schools select loan recipients and the amount of each individual's loan amounts, not to exceed the cost of tuition plus reasonable educational and living expenses.

Many of these scholarship and loan programs may be used for undergraduate degrees, but others may be used only for graduate programs. For more information regarding these programs, call your school's financial aid office.

Looking at Tax Issues Regarding Scholarships, Fellowships, and Grants

Whenever your student receives any money in the form of a scholarship, a fellowship, or an outright grant, you need to determine whether some, or all, of that money is subject to income tax, payable by the student. If the money that the student receives is in the form of a loan, there are no tax consequences upfront, although as the loan is being repaid, some of the interest may be tax-deductible.

Financial aid officers are generally a pretty savvy group of people who have a great knowledge of tax issues surrounding students, but they may not have much idea of your personal circumstances. If your student receives a financial aid award that creates tax problems for you or for your student, don't hesitate to contact the financial aid office and try to reformulate the terms of the award to either minimize or totally eliminate the tax implications. Although it's best to make any changes before any money changes hands, you may still be able to change the terms of the award as long as payments remain to be made.

Figuring out what's taxable and what's not

According to the IRS, the following requirements must be met in order for the scholarship money not to be taxed:

✔ **The student must be a degree candidate at an educational institution that maintains a regular faculty and curriculum and has a regularly enrolled student body in a place where it carries on its activities.** In other words, your student may attend a primary, secondary, or post-secondary school, and whether or not she ever receives her degree, she has to be working towards one. Scholarships for continuing education courses that don't lead to a degree won't qualify here; neither will fees that you pay to audit a course.

✔ **The scholarship or fellowship payment may not be considered as payment for services performed.** Money received for a research or teaching assistantship generally is taxable, but money received as tuition reduction is not.

✔ **The money has to go toward tuition and/or required fees and expenses.** The student has to pay tax on all other funds that are used to pay for room and board and other living expenses. The fact that the organization granting the scholarship may not make this breakdown for you doesn't mean that you don't have to — you do. It's your responsibility to keep track of both your expenses and the resources used to pay for them.

Table 16-1, based on IRS Publication 520, shows how the IRS breaks down what's taxable and what isn't:

Table 16-1   Tax Treatment of Scholarship and Fellowship Payments

Payment for	Degree Candidate	Non-degree Candidate
Tuition	Tax free	Taxable
Fees	Tax free	Taxable
Books	Tax free	Taxable
Supplies	Tax free	Taxable
Equipment	Tax free	Taxable
Room	Taxable	Taxable
Board	Taxable	Taxable
Travel	Taxable	Taxable
Teaching	Taxable	Taxable
Research services	Taxable	Taxable
Other services	Taxable	Taxable

Amounts received to cover tuition, fees, books, supplies, and equipment are nontaxable only if those expenses are required of all students in that course. For example, suppose that your student chooses to buy a computer that isn't required but that makes his life easier and allows him to achieve better results than he would have without the computer. Even if your student receives an A when he might otherwise have received a B, he still has to declare the funds used to buy the computer on his income tax returns, and pay any tax due.

As you know, all rules have exceptions. Most scholarships and fellowships can be broken down into their taxable and nontaxable components fairly easily by using Table 16-1, but here are some special situations:

- Veterans' benefits, including any money that you receive through laws administered by the Department of Veterans Affairs, whether or not that money is used to pay for required tuition and fees or for living expenses, is tax-free.

- All amounts received under the National Health Service Corps Scholarship Program and the Armed Forces Health Professions Scholarship and Financial Assistance Program are tax-free even if you use a portion of that money to pay living expenses.

- Qualified tuition reduction programs for graduate students that are provided in exchange for teaching or research are tax-free if the value of the fellowship is used to offset tuition charges. In other words, the student here is teaching or doing research in exchange for tuition, not in exchange for a living-expense stipend.

Dealing with self-employment income from fellowships

Even if your student needs to report a portion of his scholarship or fellowship to the IRS, chances are good that any income tax liability on that money will be minimal; after all, students are not famous for being high-bracket taxpayers.

Unfortunately, if your student receives a fellowship or stipend in the form of payment in exchange for research or teaching in excess of $400 (as opposed to tuition reduction), and if that student is not treated as an employee of the organization paying the money, she's also subject to self-employment tax, the tax that any individual pays for Social Security and Medicare *plus* the matching amount that an employer would be required to contribute if you were employed by someone else.

And this tax really hurts — it's a flat 15.3 percent (the 7.65 percent you always pay for Social Security and Medicare taxes *plus* the matching 7.65 percent your employer would normally pay) of 92.35 percent (your full self-employment income less the 7.65 percent employer match that you now have to pay) of your self-employment income. No itemized deductions or exemptions are allowed (although valid expenses incurred in the process of earning this money can be deducted). The self-employment tax isn't graduated to be kinder to lower-income individuals, and you aren't allowed to apply any credits against it. So a graduate student who receives a $500 stipend in exchange for creating the index for a professor's book may well not pay any income tax on that money, but would have to cough up $70.65 to the IRS in self-employment tax. Your starving student will, no doubt, appreciate the fact that, 45 years down the road, she'll be entitled to receive Social Security and Medicare because she's made this payment now.

Claiming the Hope Credit, Lifetime Learning Credits, and tuition and fees deductions

If your student has to pay some tax on a scholarship, fellowship, or grant, he may also be eligible to take advantage of the Hope Credit, the Lifetime Learning Credit, or the tuition and fees deduction on his income tax return.

The precise rules of who may, or may not, use these credits and deductions, and to offset what expenses, are somewhat complex. The general point of all of them, however, is to give some tax relief to parents and/or students (depending on who is actually paying the education expenses) for the taxable income they're using to pay tuition and required fees at a qualified college. You aren't allowed to use expenses for room, board, books, supplies, and living expenses in order to qualify for the credit, and income limitations exist for all three — if the person trying to claim the relief is making too much money, the credit or deduction will be limited or eliminated altogether.

The basic outlines of these credits and deductions are as follows:

- **Hope Credit:** This is a $1,500 credit (100 percent of the first $1,000, and 50 percent of the second $1,000) against qualified tuition paid per student in the first two years of postsecondary education leading to a degree. You may claim this credit for only two years for each student, and you may not also claim a Lifetime Learning Credit for the same student in a year in which you claim the Hope Credit.

- **Lifetime Learning Credit:** This is a credit of up to $1,000 against the cost of qualified tuition payments at a rate of 20 percent (you need $5,000 worth of tuition expenses to claim the full credit). You may claim this for as many years as you have qualified expenses, but the credit is per tax return, not per student.

- **Tuition and fees deduction:** Up to $3,000 of qualified tuition and fees paid to a qualified postsecondary educational institution may be deducted from gross income if you used taxable funds to pay for those expenses and if you don't use those same taxable funds to claim either the Hope Credit or the Lifetime Learning Credit. You may claim this deduction for as many years as you like, the courses for which you're paying tuition don't have to lead to a degree, and tuition for all members of your family for whom you claim a dependency exemption qualify.

Just as you do with almost every other tax provision, be careful not to double dip and use the same expenses to try to qualify for both a Hope or Lifetime Learning Credit and the tuition and fees deduction. On the other hand, many people pay tuition expenses far in excess of what is covered by any one of these credits or deductions. If you have enough qualified tuition expenses for enough people in your family, you could be eligible for both credits and the tuition and fees deduction in a single year.

If you think that your educational expenses qualify for these credits or deductions, check out the latest edition of *Taxes For Dummies,* by Eric Tyson and David J. Silverman (Wiley Publishing, Inc.), for the precise details and what you need to do to claim these amounts.

Chapter 17

Turning On the Financial Aid Faucet

*I*n bygone times, if you didn't have the cash upfront to pay for your child's education, your child did without or waited until you did have enough. And, once the flow of money slowed down to a trickle, so did that kid's educational opportunities. It was a pay-as-you-go world, and those who could pay went to college; those who couldn't didn't. Today, however, federal and private programs are available to help you out, so even though college may be a financial burden, it doesn't have to be an impossible dream.

In this chapter, I let you know what sorts of grants, loans, and other programs are available to help you finance your child's education; what you need to do to apply for them; and to whom you have to apply. I also discuss how money you've saved can impact your financial aid eligibility and what you can do to maximize the amount of aid flowing out to you.

This chapter contains the bare essentials of financial aid, which is certainly enough to get you on your way. But if you want in-depth info on how to get that much-needed financial aid money flowing in, check out *Free $ For College For Dummies,* by David Rosen and Caryn Mladen (Wiley Publishing, Inc.).

Financial Aid 101

People tend to use the term *financial aid* to refer to any sort of outside money that your student may receive to help pay for his education. However, as I discuss in Chapter 16, aid may come to your student based on merit, as in the case of many scholarships, or because he and you lack sufficient resources to pay the full amount at the time the payment is due.

And it is this second category, the need-based one, that best fits the definition of true financial aid, or assistance that you and your child receive to help pay for higher education costs. If you're fortunate, some or all of that assistance may come to you in the form of outright grants, or money that carries only the string of satisfactory academic achievement from your student, rather than any work obligation or repayment plan. The vast majority of money, though, is not given outright, but rather through work-study and student loan programs.

Knowing where the money comes from

Loans, work-study money, and need-based grants are available from a variety of sources. Among these are the following:

- **United States government:** Uncle Sam provides outright grant money (through Pell Grants and Federal Supplemental Educational Opportunity Grants), low-rate interest loans (through the Perkins Loan program), and federal work-study funds. It also offers access to and guarantees for other types of loans, such as Stafford and PLUS loans.

- **State governments:** Depending on the state where you live, tuition grants may be available for your in-state student and, occasionally, for a state resident attending an out-of-state school.

- **Colleges and other postsecondary educational institutions:** Very often, schools have money available to help offset the costs for their students. These funds are typically awarded based on need, merit, or some combination of the two. The funds available and the basis for awarding the funds vary significantly among colleges.

- **Private lenders, such as commercial banks, savings and loan associations, and credit unions:** These institutions lend money directly to you or to your student through a variety of loan programs, some of which the federal government guarantees.

Finding out what's available

You can choose from a wide variety of financial aid programs, but be aware that they come with an even broader expanse of qualifying rules and regulations. Although I can't possibly cover every program and every requirement, the following subsections highlight the most common forms of financial aid available.

Grants

A grant is free money (it doesn't have to be paid back), and it is often one of the component parts of a financial aid award. This money may come from the federal government in the form of Pell Grants or Federal Supplemental Educational Opportunity Grants (FSEOGs), which are awarded solely on need. Grant money may also come from the schools themselves (see Chapter 16), which may choose to award money based on need, merit, or a combination of the two.

- ✔ **Pell Grants:** These need-based outright grants — given by the federal government — currently are available in amounts up to $4,050 per academic year (adjusted annually as a result of federal appropriations — and not always upward). They're generally only for undergraduate students who haven't yet received a bachelor's or professional degree. If your child qualifies for a Pell Grant in any year, he will receive it. These grants aren't subject to any work requirements or loan repayments, and they may be used to pay for any portion of the college's established cost of attendance, including room and board, books, transportation, and so on.

- ✔ **Federal Supplemental Educational Opportunity Grant (FSEOG):** The federal government awards this grant to undergraduate students with exceptional financial need (the need requirements here are even stricter than for Pell Grants). These grants, which presently range from $100 to $4,000, don't need to be paid back, nor is there any work requirement.

  Generally, students who qualify for a FSEOG also receive a Pell Grant; however, even if your student qualifies for a FSEOG, he or she may not receive any money from this program. Funds are extremely limited and are awarded to the schools themselves, which then determine which students will receive the available money and in what amounts.

Loans

As college costs soar and grant amounts remain fairly constant, loans have become the meat-and-potatoes measure that parents and students use to plug funding gaps. Some of these loans come directly from the federal government. Others come from private sources but carry federal guarantees so that, if the borrower doesn't pay the amount due, the lender isn't left holding the bag. Still others come from private sources and carry no guarantees (for which you'll pay a higher rate of interest) but may provide you with some added flexibility.

If you need to borrow some money to pay for college costs, here are a few types of loans you should be familiar with before you begin:

- ✔ **Federal Perkins Loans:** These low-interest loans are available to both graduate and undergraduate students with significant financial need. Your student's school is the lender (albeit with government funds), and you or your student must repay these loans to the school.

  A student may borrow a maximum of $4,000 a year as an undergraduate and $6,000 a year as a graduate student; individual schools determine actual amounts lent based on the funding they receive from the government and the number of students who can demonstrate need. Interest on this loan is paid by the federal government while a student is attending school and for nine months after that student leaves school. Loan repayments are made over ten years, are the responsibility of the student, and don't begin until after your student has left school or drops below half-time status.

✔ **Subsidized Stafford Loans and Unsubsidized Stafford Loans:** Need is one of the criteria for subsidized Stafford Loans, as is filing a FAFSA, discussed in the section "Applying for Aid (Yes, the Dreaded FAFSA)" later in this chapter. But all students may borrow under the Stafford Loan program. These relatively low-cost loans are available for both undergraduate and graduate education. Yearly and lifetime loan ceilings vary, depending on whether a student is a graduate student or an undergraduate student and whether he is financially independent of his parents.

Interest accrues on the loan amounts over the life of the loan. Loan payments may be made while a student is in school, but you're not required to do so; the unpaid interest, however, continues to accrue and add to the amount of principal that's been borrowed.

The major difference between a subsidized and an unsubsidized Stafford Loan is that the federal government pays the interest on a subsidized loan while a student is still enrolled in school and for a short deferral period after graduation. Stafford Loans are provided through two sources:

• **The Federal Family Education Loan Program (FFELP):** This program uses private lenders while providing federal loan guarantees. If the student defaults, the government will pay back the lender for the unpaid amount.

• **The Federal Direct Student Loan Program (FDSLP):** The government lends the amount to students, not parents (typically making payments directly to their universities), and is the student's responsibility to repay.

✔ **Federal Parent Loan for Undergraduate Students (PLUS):** You may choose to use these loans to plug the gaps between what you have saved, your student's actual financial aid award, and the real dollar cost of attending a particular school. These loans carry with them a higher interest rate than either the Perkins or Stafford loans, repayment begins 60 days after the loan proceeds are disbursed, and the repayment term is 10 years. Unlike Perkins or Stafford loans, these loans are the parents', not the student's, responsibility. Loan amounts may be as great as the full cost of attendance at a particular school, and the loans may be obtained either through the FFELP (private lenders) or directly (from the government).

✔ **Private loans:** These loans are available to parents from private lenders based on the lender's own criteria. Because these loans have no federal guarantees, they generally carry higher interest rates (similar to those on car loans or other sorts of consumer debt). They may be used to pay for any expenses that you haven't already covered through other forms of funding, whether savings, student loans, or PLUS loans. Because these loans aren't part of any federal program, repayment terms may be more liberal than for the federal loan programs, including the ability to defer payments until after your student has graduated, although interest begins to accrue on the amount borrowed as soon as you receive the money.

Work-study

If your student is able to juggle his schoolwork with employment and has demonstrated financial need, the federal Work-Study Program may be the answer to your prayers. This program provides part-time employment for eligible undergraduate and graduate students through their university or in public service work in the community. These jobs generally pay at least the minimum wage, and earnings are subject to federal and state income taxes; however, Social Security and Medicare taxes (FICA) are not withheld. Although the federal government provides the funds for this program, they're allocated directly by the individual schools based on the need of a particular student and the number of students who can demonstrate need.

Applying for Aid (Yes, the Dreaded FAFSA)

In the world of financial aid, equitable allocation of available resources is the name of the game. This allocation can be made only when comparing apples to apples, assets to assets, and income to income. The financial aid powers that be make this comparison by using financial aid applications. You and your student have to apply for financial aid every year that your student needs assistance. And your child's need is determined based on the information that you provide regarding the year just past — otherwise known as the *base year.* In other words, if your student is beginning college in the fall of 2004 for the academic 2004-2005 year, you need to fill out a financial aid application using base year information for 2003. On this application, you must provide information not only about your child's income and assets but also your own (unless your child is an independent student, in which case she'll be completing her own application without any parental information). Every academic year your child is in school will have its own base year; a four-year college course will have four corresponding base years and four sets of financial aid forms.

Depending on where your child intends to attend school, you may have to complete more than one financial aid application. Although individual schools and many states have their own forms that they require you to complete, here are the two most common and the information you must provide:

✔ **Free Application for Federal Student Aid (FAFSA):** As long and as seemingly complicated as the FAFSA is, everyone needs to fill one of these out each academic year, if you need or want aid from any of the federal grant or loan programs. These applications are free (as the name suggests). You may complete the form online or use the more-traditional paper form after January 1 of the year in which you need the aid, using base year income figures and current asset information for both you and your student. You can take most of the required information directly from your, and your student's, base year income tax returns; the rest comes from current bank and investment account statements and your business's balance sheet (if you own part or all of a business). The amount of debt that you have, including mortgages, car loans, and credit card debt, isn't included on the FAFSA.

You can get detailed info on the FAFSA and complete the online form of the application by visiting `www.fafsa.ed.gov`.

✔ **CSS PROFILE:** Administered by the College Scholarship Service, this form is required by many private colleges and universities in place of or, in most cases, in addition to the FAFSA. The CSS PROFILE contains much of the same data you put on your FAFSA; however, the information it requests is far more detailed and includes the amount of your net home equity (the value of your primary residence less any outstanding mortgage loans). You may complete the CSS PROFILE in the fall of the base year (unlike the FAFSA, which may be submitted only after January 1 of the following year). Also unlike the FAFSA, this isn't a free service; you pay a nominal application fee, plus an additional fee for every school you request your application be forwarded to.

For more info, go online to `http://profileonline.collegeboard.com`.

The purpose of these and other financial aid applications is to help the federal government and your student's school determine your family's need for outside sources of funding and your ability to repay loans. Federal financial aid eligibility is determined by a strict formula known as the Federal Methodology based on FAFSA information. Although CSS PROFILE information is far more specific, it impacts only institutional aid (not federal grants, loans, and work-study). Individual financial aid officers are allowed to exercise great latitude in determining need based not only on the CSS PROFILE but also on any other information you may provide. If you believe your financial circumstances are not accurately reflected in the information provided on these forms, talk with the financial aid officer at your prospective colleges about your circumstances and the possibility of a "professional judgment," which allows the financial aid officer to make an aid award based on all the factors you present, not just the ones contained on your financial aid applications.

Don't lie on a financial aid application or even try to bend the truth a little. Although copies of your income tax returns and bank statements are not required attachments, you may be asked to provide them at a later date for verification purposes. Any intentional misrepresentation on your FAFSA may result in your having to repay any grant or loan money your child receives. In addition, you're also liable for fines up to $10,000, a prison sentence, or both.

Squeezing Out Every Drop of Available Money

After you begin to suspect that your savings and amounts available from current earnings will fall short of your child's anticipated educational costs, some forward planning may well increase the amount of outright grants and very low-cost loans your student may qualify for.

Hoping to hit the lottery or hiding your head in the sand are both very common responses to savings shortfalls. They won't help you, though, when you're trying to sort out how to make that dream education happen for your son or daughter. Be alert, be proactive, and plan ahead. All is not lost if you fail to save enough, but failing to recognize early in the process that you won't have enough may cost you more in the long run. By not planning for this eventuality earlier, you may be forced to take more loans with higher interest rates, than you would have done otherwise.

If you apply for financial aid, you join a group of other parents whose savings are also falling short. Funds are limited, and they're supposed to be distributed as equitably as possible. The following strategies aren't intended to somehow skew the system in your favor, but rather to make sure that your child receives a fair and reasonable award. Be honest in your assessment of what you can afford; don't make yourself out to be more destitute than you really are.

Timing the receipt of taxable and tax-exempt income

Many a financial aid application has been turned down because the applicant sold something in a base year that produced a large *capital gain* (the amount of money you receive on a sale in excess of what that particular piece of property cost you), received a large year-end bonus, exercised some stock options, took an unplanned distribution from a pension plan, or rolled over a traditional IRA to a Roth IRA.

If you know when your child is due to begin college, do your best to schedule large infusions of income and cash two years or more before she is due to start; the financial aid folks won't care about what's on your income tax return in any years other than your base years. So, if you need to sell an investment, do it sooner rather than later. If you're going to receive a year-end bonus, try to defer it to a non-base year, if possible.

If you can't avoid large amounts of extra income in one of your base years, try to take that income earlier in the year, rather than later, to give yourself the best part of a year to find ways to offset at least some of it. For example, you may want to give more to charity, take capital losses, or make extra mortgage payments, all of which should reduce the amount of income you show on your return as well as the amount of cash you have in your account on the day you complete your FAFSA application. And, if you need to access money from a pension plan, try to borrow the money rather than take a distribution; although the borrowed funds may show up as cash in your account, they won't show up on any tax return, but the full amount of any distribution will.

If you absolutely must raise cash in one of your base years, try to raise it in a way that increases your cash flow, but not your taxable or tax-exempt income. For example, if you must sell stocks, try to offset any capital gains with capital losses. This gives you the opportunity to realize some of the appreciation in your great stock picks while also getting rid of some dogs.

Paying down debt

You know, of course, that debt is bad, but in the case of financial aid, it's horrible! Not only do you have those debt payments to make each and every month, but you don't even get any credit for them on your financial aid application. All the application is concerned with is how much you have in income and assets, not how much you owe.

To minimize the value of assets you show on your aid application, get rid of your debt. Sell some assets, if necessary, to pay off your car loan, make extra mortgage payments, and bring your credit card balances to zero. Complete all these transactions before you fill in your aid applications; the FAFSA folks are concerned only with the value of your assets on the day that you complete the application — not the day before and not the day after. Your good intentions will be worth less than nothing if you raise the cash but fail to pay off your debt before filing your application.

Making sure assets are not in your child's name

The financial aid people realize that you may have something other than college to spend at least some of your money on, but they assume that anything your child owns is fair game when they try to assess how much your family can afford to contribute toward the cost of a college education. Accordingly, they include at most 5.6 percent of parents' includable assets in their calculation of *expected family contribution* (EFC), the amount that the U.S. Department of Education figures you should be able to cough up for one child's educational costs in any given year. They expect your child to kick in a whopping 35 percent of her assets as a part of the same EFC for one year.

If you want to minimize the amount of your EFC, keep assets in your name alone, joint with your spouse, or in the name of another relative outside the household. If your child has accumulated assets since birth — for example, in a Coverdell Education Savings Account (Chapter 8) or Uniform Gifts to Minors Act/Uniform Transfers to Minors (UGMA/UTMA) account (Chapter 12) — spend down these assets first. You may not qualify at all for financial aid in the first year or so of college while you're depleting these accounts, but you'll be better off down the road, once only you have assets to be counted, and not your child. Of course, spending down your assets may not work for some families; if your income is too high, it won't make any difference what the value of your assets are. The EFC calculation will still place your family outside of the need-based range, depending on what college your child will be attending.

Beware of using your dependent child's money to buy items that you are expected, as his parent, to provide for him. Your money must be used to supply food, clothing, and shelter, but your child's funds may legitimately purchase computers, trips, a car, life insurance, or anything else extra that you feel may benefit him but isn't essential to his health and well-being.

Anticipating your expenses

No one is suggesting that you run out and buy that new Mercedes or sink your money into a new boat, but most people have large expenses that they tend to defer, such as replacing a car or a roof. The natural tendency, when facing these expenses at the same time as the first college tuition bill, is to postpone these expenditures as long as possible, hopefully until your student completes college.

A certain amount of self-deprivation is normal for parents, but indulging yourself a little may actually help your student's overall financial aid picture. Replace that old rust bucket that's been held together with duct tape for the last three years (but remember, pay cash — don't finance it unless you absolutely must), and repair the roof. Paying for these items will deplete your cash and asset balances, which you must, of course, report accurately on the FAFSA. Because the value of the new car and the house repairs isn't included on your aid application, you can successfully convert reportable assets into nonreportable assets and also take care of some necessary expenses in the process.

Spreading your available assets across multiple students

You may have more than one child who dreams of attending college. If your children are relatively close in age, your dreams may more closely resemble nightmares, thinking of how you're going to pay for their education.

You may be surprised to find out that, while each of your children will have to file his or her own FAFSA application, your EFC will not be the same for each student. The portion of the EFC that is calculated based on your income will be divided by the number of students you currently have in college. The student's portion (based on his income and assets) will then be added on each application, arriving at the EFC for each student. The more members of your family who are attending a postsecondary school at any given time, the greater the potential financial aid award for each student. Although the total that you'll be expected to pay will likely be greater for multiple students than it would be if you just had one in school, the per-student cost should be less (unless your income and/or asset value is very large).

Your family consists of your children *and* you and your spouse. If either you or your spouse has any plans to return to school, the best time to do it may be when your children are also in school. That all-important EFC also applies to educational expenses that you and your spouse incur.

Postponing gifts

You may be fortunate enough to have other family members or friends who want to contribute money toward your child's education. If those additional funds still aren't enough to pay the full amount, even with your own contribution, you may want to encourage them to postpone making gifts in any base year and instead wait until after your child finishes school.

Any money that is gifted directly to your child into a Coverdell ESA or a UGMA/UTMA account or paid directly to your child's college as tuition is included in the EFC at a rate of 35 percent. Your child's benefactor may be working from the most noble of intentions, but the effect of that gift during those all-important base years may be harmful to your attempts at receiving outright grants and low-cost loans.

Financial food for thought

Face it: Without the existence of federal financial aid programs, state aid, corporate sponsorship, and university support, many people who have attended postsecondary schools would not have been able to. The fact that money is available to anyone who wants to attend has leveled the playing field, making college now accessible to anyone who wants to go. And given the opportunity, who wouldn't want to go? From a statistical standpoint, the earnings potential of someone with any postsecondary education is far superior to someone who stopped school after high school, and the more education you have, the more your income should increase. As investments go, college is one of the best.

But there has to be a price, and it's constantly growing. With tuition costs rising much faster than the rate of inflation, you may find that you have to borrow a substantial portion, or even all, of the money to purchase your child's education. As a result, you may saddle yourself and your child with huge debt just as she begins her first, lowest-paying job and as you head into retirement. As scenarios go, this one isn't great, yet without adequate savings upfront, far too many people face this situation.

Still, if you feel that student loans are an inevitable part of your and your child's future, you may want to think about a few points:

✔ **Knowing upfront that he's going to have to pay a large bill at the other end may vest your child more fully in his education and may help him select a college that works financially for the family.** Value of anything is much easier to ascertain when someone places a price tag on it — when your student knows just how much it's going to cost him down the road, he may study harder to make sure that he's getting value for his money.

✔ **The high cost of borrowing money may limit your student's options.** An expensive education may not be better than a less-pricey option. By borrowing the money to pay for an education, you may actually be encouraging your student to be more efficient in her use of resources in order to limit the amount of the future payback. Borrowing money may, however, also discourage your child from pursuing dreams that are costlier to fulfill — graduate or professional schools may appear out of reach for a student who already has hefty amounts of college loans to pay back.

✔ **When facing large monthly payments because of large student loans, you can consolidate the debt and extend payment schedules.** Depending on the total amount of federal loans you and/or your student take, repayment schedules may extend to as many as 30 years by consolidating multiple loan balances into one promissory note. Doing so will increase the total amount of interest you'll pay on your loans, but your monthly payment should drop considerably, giving your too-tight monthly budget some relief. Remember, though, current rules only allow you to do this once, so make sure to do it when interest rates are low, and after you're reasonably certain you've completed your education.

Part V
The Part of Tens

The 5th Wave   By Rich Tennant

"and here's our returning champion, spinning
for her 3rd & 4th year college tuition..."

In this part . . .

What's a book without a Part of Tens? A good book? Possibly. A *For Dummies* book? Not on your life. Consider this part to be the frosting on your cake. The ivy covering on your halls of academia. The . . . well, you get the point.

Understanding the theory isn't enough if you're going to be successful at this savings gig. So in this part, I give you an easily accessible list of savings strategies and techniques. I also throw in a top-ten list that covers tax tips, hints, and heads ups. Remember, saving money is good; investing that money and earning a good rate of return is better; but limiting the size of the tax man's bite on those earnings is the best.

Chapter 18

Ten Musts for Successful Savings

This book is entirely about saving money, albeit about a certain type of saving with a specific purpose and end in mind. But saving money is, at its very heart, only saving money. Without good strategies, techniques, and know-how in place, any savings plan is only as good as the mattress you stash the money under.

No savings plan is foolproof; there are way too many variables, some of which rest on your side of the table (such as how much, when, and where you save), and others over which you have absolutely no control (for example, federal monetary policy, which generally defies any sort of reasonable explanation). What you do manage, however, is how you respond to these variables; after all, you know (or hopefully have some idea of) how much you need to have saved by a specific date.

No matter how little you understand about why interest rates are so low and mutual fund fees are so high, you ultimately bear the responsibility for the success or the failure of your savings program. This chapter highlights some main strategies that may enable you to save enough to see one or more children through college without resorting to loans.

Paying Into Your Savings Plans First and Regularly

Putting money into your savings before you pay anything else and doing so on a regular schedule may seem like obvious advice. Every financial advisor will tell you to do this, but it's not as easy as it sounds. Your savings programs stand the best chance of succeeding if you provide them with more, rather than less, raw material: money.

To successfully save any money anywhere, you really have to impose some discipline on yourself and on your budget. There's just no getting around that fact. If you find that you're unable to put money away on a regular basis (once a year probably won't cut it here, unless you know your Christmas bonus is going to be really huge), now is the time to accept some help in making sure that you really save money.

If you're already having deductions made from your paycheck for a retirement plan, you know how easy it is not to spend money that you never receive. And you probably also get some real satisfaction from seeing the size of that account grow. See whether you can make the same sort of paycheck deduction into either a Section 529 plan or into U.S. Series EE or Series I savings bonds. Although both of these deductions are made using after-tax dollars (unlike your retirement account contributions), the paycheck you receive will already have these amounts taken out, and you'll know that whatever money you receive will be yours to spend on your monthly bills.

If your payroll office can't (or won't) make these deductions for you, talk to your bank. Set up automatic monthly withdrawals from your account into your Section 529 or Coverdell accounts. Just make sure that you subtract the money from your balance before you pay your monthly bills so that you aren't in any danger of bouncing checks.

Be as generous as you can in funding your savings accounts. You'll soon find that you adjust your spending accordingly once you know that a certain amount of money is leaving your account every month for this new savings venture.

Understanding Your Investments

Don't ever let yourself be talked into putting money into an investment that you just don't understand. If you read a *prospectus* (the document any company must provide investors and prospective investors that explain what the investment is and how it works) and you just don't get it or you think it's not for you, trust your instincts and stay away. If, on the other hand, you can see how the wheels in a certain investment turn and they seem reasonably well oiled and connected, by all means consider that particular investment on its merits.

Don't ever be afraid to ask advice, but know that accepting advice doesn't absolve you of responsibility. Pick the brain of someone who knows and understands an investment to help *you* understand the investment. Don't simply accept an outright recommendation to either buy, or not buy, a particular issue.

If something looks fishy, sounds fishy, and smells fishy, chances are good you're not buying a plum.

Changing Investments When Necessary

Everyone miscalculates, and so will you. Don't assume that, because an investment's value is dropping, it will recover and go on to achieve fame and fortune. That type of wooly thinking is what keeps lotteries profitable and casinos in business.

When you keep current with what's happening in your accounts, you have the opportunity to get rid of investments that aren't performing up to your expectations (remembering to keep your expectations realistic at all times). The value of your investment is only one indicator, but it is an important warning sign. If it begins to fall for no reason, it may mean that bad news is looming that you aren't yet privy to. Likewise, unwarranted and rapid gains may be a sign that the stock is becoming speculative, and you may want to get out now. Do your research first, and make your decision only after you're sure that you're acting from a position of knowledge rather than fear.

Keep careful track of any mutual funds you own as compared to other, similar mutual funds (check out Morningstar's mutual fund lists for lists of comparable funds at www.morningstar.com). If your fund is performing well below comparable funds, change to one of the other funds. Not every fund manager is equal, and you want your money to be invested by someone who clearly understands the current market, not last year's.

Waiting for a failing investment to recover is a fool's game. So is waiting until you're sure that an investment has peaked. Keep your expectations reasonable and your losses to a minimum, and know that changing underperforming assets is a key component to successful investing.

Staying Current on Tax Law Changes

You may think that ongoing changes to the tax code don't really affect your tax-deferred or tax-exempt college savings accounts. You're wrong. Even though you may not begin tapping into these accounts for many years, the current changes may well impact how you choose to save.

For example, the decrease in tax rates on long-term capital gains and corporate dividends may make you decide to put your non-tax-deferred or exempt savings into either individual stocks or stock-based mutual funds instead of keeping them in savings accounts, bonds, or real estate. Of course, when Congress finally wakes up and realizes the actual cost of this particular tax reduction and reinstates higher rates on these forms of income, you'll also want to be ready to readjust how, and where, your money is invested so that you obtain maximum benefit from your savings and from any tax deferrals or exemptions you may be entitled to.

Being Realistic about Investment Returns

You may have earned 20 percent, 30 percent, or even 100 percent per year on your investments in the late 1990s, and that probably felt pretty good. With those rates of returns, you had to save only relatively small amounts out of your current earnings to achieve Harvard for each of your 16 kids and a fully-paid retirement in Monte Carlo.

Reality is a bit different, and the stock and bond markets have retreated from fantasyland to a place where more reasonable average rates of return of between 4 percent and 8 percent reside. Your savings will earn real money with those rates of return, but you won't get rich on them without some serious infusions of cash out of your pocket. If Harvard and Monte Carlo are your goals, you need to do more than wait for the stock markets to expand exponentially if you're realistically going to achieve them.

Not Counting on Great-Aunt Sadie's Inheritance

Reality dictates that, while Great-Aunt Sadie can't take it with her, she's probably going to spend most of it before she goes, and no matter what she's told you, whatever's left may well be going to help save the North Atlantic salmon.

Funding Your Account Now — Not Later

Yes, you may win the lottery and suddenly have the money you need to see your children through college. And your salary may suddenly triple, so you'll have what you need when you need it. And all of this may well happen on a Wednesday in August, just before the first tuition bill comes due.

It's far more likely that none of these things will happen, all except that the first tuition bill will surely roll in on schedule, and probably for far more money than you currently expect.

You need to be saving now, when your future need for the money is still in the future, and you need to be saving as much as you possibly can, all the way along the road. Statistically, you're far more likely to encounter periods of less income, rather than more, along the way. You'll also probably face times when you'll have to reduce the amounts you're able to save. Take full advantage of every opportunity to save for college now, while you can, to have enough when you need it.

Feeding Your Retirement Plan

With the future of Social Security uncertain and company pension plans biting the dust right and left, you may be just a bit shortsighted if you fund your children's college savings plans without also saving, just as actively, for your own retirement. Especially for parents who began their families in their 30s, retirement is going to come hard on the heels of your children's college years, and you're not going to have a lot of time to make up deficiencies in your retirement savings.

You can borrow for college, but you can't borrow for retirement. As you save for college, always keep sight of your future retirement needs, and make sure that you don't shortchange yourself.

Asking Questions of the Experts

No one can possibly know and understand every type of investment and every effect of every tax code provision on your savings. That's okay. No one expects you to be an expert in every area of your life.

What's not okay is to pretend understanding when you just don't get it. Find someone reliable — a professional, a family member, or friend — who does get it, and pick that person's brain. Stop the person when the answers get too technical. Make the person back up and go over the information again and again, until you do understand it. Don't accept the assumption that you should know what someone else is talking about, and don't ever feel like you're an idiot because you just don't get it.

Whoever said that ignorance was bliss was mistaken. Ignorance in any of your finances may well lead to disaster.

Learning from Your Mistakes

Making mistakes is what makes people human, and you're no exception. You will screw up in your savings programs, especially at the beginning, and you can't escape that reality. And that's all right — don't apologize to yourself or to anyone else.

At the same time, don't make the same mistake twice. If you lose money on an investment and might have limited the losses by selling sooner, learn from that. If you're failing to save as regularly or as much as you should, change your ways. If you miss the timing on a tax code change and so pay more tax than you would have had you been more attentive, that's okay. Once. Any of these errors can happen to anyone, but the success of your savings program depends on your making them only once and then doing better the next time.

Crying over lost opportunities and lost money only creates an ocean of tears; fixing what went wrong may help repair the damage.

Chapter 19

Ten Ways to Dodge the Tax Code Minefield

• •

In This Chapter

▶ Keeping tabs on contributions and qualified expenses

▶ Making sure you don't overfund your account

▶ Understanding how the tax laws apply to you

▶ Turning to experts for answers to your questions

• •

Almost everything in life carries with it some tax consequences. Some are unavoidable, such as paying a sales tax every time you purchase a roll of toilet tissue. Others you may voluntarily choose, such as contributing more tax to the total pot when you begin earning a higher salary. The government tries to discourage certain behaviors by highly taxing products related to those behaviors (such as tobacco and alcohol). Not every consequence makes sense, though: Married couples pay a higher tax for the privilege of being married. Frankly, if you try to make sense of the social policies that are entwined with taxes, you may go nuts. Suffice it to say that tax policies touch your life in a myriad of ways.

And, for the most part, because taxes are such a part of your life, you live your life without paying much attention to the number of ways in which you're taxed. If you're like most people, you tend to focus only on newsworthy items, which are generally the ones that affect you the least: things like the drop in the capital gains and dividends tax, the estate tax, and so on. Although you may realize a small amount of tax relief from these reductions, you'd really be far better off if the government magically halved the gasoline tax, which is a tax that really hits you in your pocket.

So it will come as no surprise to you that tax implications figure hugely in any discussion about savings and that you may positively impact your savings program by focusing on the various rules and regulations surrounding college savings accounts. This chapter points out several areas where you may want to pay careful attention so that you can maximize your savings and minimize the amount that you hand over to the government.

Knowing Who's Giving and How Much

Anonymous benefactors belong in fiction, not in your life. If someone other than you is making gifts to your children in Coverdell Education Savings Accounts (ESAs) or in any other type of account, you need to know about it. The regulations are especially strict in Coverdell (no more than a total of $2,000 may be given per child per year without triggering excess contribution rules and penalties), but anything that is gifted to your child needs to be on your financial radar. You need to know about any assets your child is accumulating that may impact financial need down the road. In addition, should some well-meaning but potentially misguided person be making contributions into an Uniform Gifts to Minors Act or Uniform Transfers to Minors Act (UGMA/UTMA) account, you need to crank up the level of money management skills your child will have by the time he reaches majority (age 18 or 21, depending on what state your child lives in). On that date, she's going to be in charge of a reasonably large sum of money, and she needs to know how to use it wisely.

Being Aware of Your Income and Phaseout Amounts

If you're using a Coverdell ESA or U.S. Series EE or Series I savings bonds to save for your child's education, you need to know how much your annual income is and how that number slots into the phaseout rules for these savings schemes. Unfortunately, claiming ignorance won't help you here, and a certain amount of both short- and long-term crystal ball reading is required.

Coverdell accounts limit and/or prohibit the amount higher-income taxpayers are allowed to contribute, but the phaseout amounts are always subject to change, as is your income. If you are trying to fund a Coverdell account and feel that your income may begin touching the limitation amounts, you may want to wait until after the end of the year before making your contribution; you have until your tax filing deadline to make a contribution for a prior year. Remember, contributions from taxpayers who fail to meet the income requirements are considered excess contributions and are subject to an excise tax until the excess amount (including all income earned on it) is removed from the account and paid to the beneficiary.

If, on the other hand, you're buying Series EE or Series I savings bonds now with the intention of using them later, tax-free, to pay for your child's educational expenses, you don't need to be concerned with your income at the time you purchase the bonds. If your income increases up to and beyond the phaseout range in the years that you need to redeem the bonds, however, you may end up paying income tax on the interest you've earned in the interim period.

Keeping Track of Your Contributions

The current rules regarding the tax-exempt status of qualified distributions from Coverdell ESAs and Section 529 plans are only temporary. Your guess is as good as mine as to whether they'll become permanent. Only qualified distributions currently receive tax-exempt treatment, and many accounts will have at least one nonqualified distribution to close out the account at the end of your child's education. For those reasons, you need to know how much money you contributed to the account and how much income was earned on that money in order to accurately calculate any tax and penalties due.

You've already paid federal income tax on your contributions, and you don't want to have to pay tax again on that money simply because you've kept poor records. Keep an ongoing tally of what you give, and make sure that your plan manager, custodian, or trustee agrees with your number. If they don't, investigate and fix the problem. When the time comes to make distributions, the IRS relies on the records of the financial institution, not yours, to determine any taxable amounts.

Avoiding the Penalties from Overfunding an Account

True, you don't know how much sending your child to college will cost, and that makes it really difficult to calculate just how much you should save in a Section 529 plan or a Coverdell account. Still, given the penalties that you'll pay if you save more than you need in either type of account, you're probably better off saving slightly less than you think you'll need rather than more.

Savings shortfalls in these accounts may be made up from other, nonexempt savings accounts that you have or even from current earnings. Overfunding accounts, on the other hand, will cost you in the long run.

Knowing Your Effective Tax Rate

If you read articles about college savings plans, you're probably convinced that there are only two tax brackets: the highest one (which is yours, of course) and the lowest one (your child's). When you're using these extremes, the examples in these articles always show how beneficial it is to push income to your child, who pays taxes at a lower rate.

The reality is that the gap between your tax bracket and your child's is usually not as great as the illustrations show. The vast majority of taxpayers pay tax at one of the two lowest levels, so the benefit of paying tax at the student's level rather than at the parents' level is generally not all that great.

When looking at the best way for you to save, look at your situation, not someone else's. You may be surprised to find that something that is highly touted as providing huge tax savings to you may really offer you only very limited tax benefits. Of course, that same financial product may provide you with other advantages that are equally valuable.

Staying Aware of Tax Laws in Your State

Although federal tax regulations for college savings plans are the same for everyone, state laws vary, and no two states are exactly alike. Be sure that you understand how your college savings plans are taxed in your state before you begin funding any plan. Before you open any account, check carefully into available income tax deductions for current contributions, the tax-exempt status of qualified distributions, and how other states' plans are treated in your state if you're considering a 529 plan.

Of course, knowing what the laws are when you create a plan is one thing; keeping track of any changes is something else altogether. If you move, don't assume that you must change your plan — you may not need to. Likewise, don't think that current state laws are set in stone — college savings plans represent a huge amount of currently untapped tax revenues for many states, and currently advantageous laws are always subject to change, particularly in tough economic times.

Keeping Track of Your Qualified Education Expenses

The tax-exempt nature of qualified distributions from Coverdell accounts and Section 529 plans and tax-exempt redemptions from Series EE and Series I savings bonds are powerful incentives for you to save in these vehicles. Keep in mind, though, that anything that is so attractive is also something that is ripe for abuse, and the IRS may be very vigilant in policing these tax-exempt distributions and redemptions.

Keep copies of paid tuition bills and other qualified educational expenses together with your tax returns, and destroy them only after you're certain that you're well past the date for audit from the IRS or your state tax department. If one of these agencies calls you for proof of your expenses, your honest face and forthright manner won't hold much water, but receipted bills will.

Staying Informed about Changes in Current Laws

As a tax professional, I love to see Congress change tax law on a frequent basis — that's what keeps me in demand. As a taxpayer, however, I find that trying to keep track of the current law seems to be an exercise in futility — as soon as I think I've got it, Congress changes it.

And this is especially true of Congress's tinkering with any sort of tax-deferred or tax-exempt savings plan, including Section 529 plans and Coverdell accounts. Almost yearly since their inception, Congress has made changes in the rules and regulations governing these accounts, from who may participate to how much may be contributed to what expenses you may pay for using distributions from these accounts. Both Coverdell accounts and Section 529 plans will continue to evolve, especially because many of the current provisions are set to expire after 2010, unless Congress renews them.

Being Honest about Your Child's College Plans

When you look at your newborn for the first time, you've no doubt that this child is headed for an Ivy League school. With that vision in mind, you open a college savings account. As the years go by, however, that same child, who isn't exactly thriving in school, begins to live inside the engine of your car and comes up for air only long enough to raid your refrigerator.

The lesson here is to be honest with yourself about what your dreams and aspirations are — and what his are. Funding a college savings account only for the sake of keeping *your* dreams alive is expensive in the long run. If you're not sure how much money, if any, your child will use for postsecondary qualified expenses, save money in ways that allow you more latitude, such as in personal investment accounts or in a trust for that child's benefit. The tax savings may not be as great while you're actually putting money away in these types of accounts because there are no tax deferrals and you annually pay the income tax that's due on that year's earnings. Still, if your child ends up not needing your savings for college expenses, your overall results may be as good as, or even better than, saving the same amount of money entirely in a Section 529 plan or a Coverdell account. Unlike nonqualified distributions from Section 529 or Coverdell accounts, any distribution that your child takes from a personal investment or trust account is only taxed to the extent that he receives current, untaxed income as part of that distribution. Any amounts previously taxed won't be taxed again to him, and a nonqualified distribution penalty is never imposed.

Getting Answers by Asking Questions

Some tax considerations are complicated, new and different tax provisions crop up frequently, and old provisions are reinterpreted. Consequently, you may find yourself in the position of not being exactly sure what you should do in a given situation. If so, join the crowd. Although college savings accounts are actively marketed as do-it-yourself vehicles, they're do-it-yourself in the same way that bicycle construction instructions are so simple that a 4-year-old could build it.

When you find yourself wavering between two or more options and unsure of where the true benefit to yourself and your family lies, don't hesitate to ask for advice. Don't rely solely on what you read or on what "everyone else" seems to be doing. Take your particulars to a person you trust, such as your accountant or your attorney, ask your questions, and listen carefully to the answers. There is no one-size-fits-all answer here — your situation will dictate the best choice for you. And don't ever make your decisions based only on tax consequences; by doing so, you may do your family a disservice.

Appendix

Section 529 Plans, State by State

Go ahead. Pick a state, any state. What you see before you is a brief outline of the Section 529 plans offered by each state. I've stuck a bunch of letters in the first column, so you'll need a handy navigation guide. A word of warning, though: States can change the rules, regulations, and who's running the show of any plan at any time. Check out the particular plan you're interested in before you invest. With that in mind, here it is:

- **A:** Plan Name
- **B:** What Is Covered
- **C:** Plan Manager
- **D:** Types of Investments
- **E:** Investment Return
- **F:** Participating Colleges
- **G:** Enrollment Period
- **H:** Taxability of Investments
- **I:** Who May Invest

Alabama

	Savings Plan	Prepaid Plan
A	**Higher Education Fund** (invest directly with state or through financial adviser)	**Prepaid Affordable Tuition Plan (PACT)** (invest directly with state)
B	Qualified educational expenses for postsecondary education	Tuition and mandatory fees only for postsecondary education
C	Van Kampen Asset Management, Inc.	Alabama State Treasurer's Office (PACT Trust Fund)
D	Choice of age-based and static professionally managed investment funds	Combination of equities and fixed-income securities and money market funds

(continued)

Alabama (continued)

	Savings Plan	Prepaid Plan
E	Variable — depends on market conditions and chosen funds	Contracts purchased now guaranteed to pay full tuition and fees at Alabama public school. Benefits for out-of-state and private schools not to exceed the weighted average tuition and fees at Alabama public schools.
F	Any U.S. 2 and 4 year college and university, postsecondary trade and vocational school, and graduate and professional school that is eligible for federal financial aid	Any U.S. 2 and 4 year college and university, postsecondary trade and vocational school, and graduate and professional schools that is eligible for federal financial aid
G	Open enrollment; join at any time	September of each year
H	Distributions used for qualifying educational expenses are state and federally tax-exempt, subject to 2010 sunset provision	Distributions used for qualifying educational expenses are state and federally tax-exempt, subject to 2010 sunset provision
I	May only invest directly if account owner or designated beneficiary is an Alabama resident	Both residents and nonresidents. Beneficiary age restrictions apply.

Alaska

	Savings Plan
A	**University of Alaska College Savings Plan** (invest directly with state) **Manulife College Savings** (invest through financial advisers only) **T. Rowe Price College Savings** (invest directly with state)
B	Qualified educational expenses for postsecondary education
C	T. Rowe Price Associates, Inc.
D	Choice of age-based and static professionally managed investment funds
E	Variable — depends on market conditions and funds chosen (University of Alaska College Savings Plan guaranteed to keep pace with tuition costs at University of Alaska)
F	Any U.S. 2 and 4 year college and university, postsecondary trade and vocational school, and graduate and professional school that is eligible for federal financial aid

	Savings Plan
G	Open enrollment; join at any time
H	Distributions used for qualifying educational expenses are federally tax-exempt, subject to 2010 sunset provision. Alaska has no state income tax.
I	Both residents and nonresidents

Arizona

	Savings Plan
A	**Arizona Family College Savings Program** (College Savings Bank) (invest directly with state) **Waddell & Reed InvestEd Plan** (invest through Waddell & Reed or Legend financial advisers only) **Arizona Family College Savings Program (SM&R)** (invest directly with state or with financial advisers) **Pacific Funds 529 College Savings Plan (AZ)** (invest directly with state or with financial advisers)
B	Qualified educational expenses for postsecondary education
C	Arizona Family College Savings Program: College Savings Bank; Waddell & Reed InvestEd Plan: Waddell & Reed; Arizona Family College Savings Program (SM&R): Securities Research & Management; Pacific Funds 529 College Savings Plan: Pacific Life
D	Arizona Family College Savings Program offers the CollegeSure Certificate of Deposit only. Arizona Family College Savings Program and Pacific Funds 529 College Savings Plan only offer static professionally managed investment funds. Waddell & Reed InvestEd Plan offers a choice of age-based and static professionally managed investment funds.
E	Variable — depends on market conditions and funds chosen
F	Any U.S. 2 and 4 year college and university, postsecondary trade and vocational schools, and graduate and professional school that is eligible for federal financial aid
G	Open enrollment; join at any time
H	Distributions used for qualifying educational expenses are state and federally tax-exempt, subject to 2010 sunset provision.
I	Both residents and nonresidents; however, nonresidents may only invest in Pacific Funds 529 College Savings Plan through a financial adviser.

Arkansas

	Savings Plan
A	**GIFT College Investing Plan** (invest directly with state or with financial advisers)
B	Qualified educational expenses for postsecondary education
C	Mercury Advisors
D	Choice of age-based and static professionally managed investment funds
E	Variable — depends on market conditions and funds chosen
F	Any U.S. 2 and 4 year college and university, postsecondary trade and vocational schools, and graduate and professional school that is eligible for federal financial aid
G	Open enrollment; join at any time
H	Distributions used for qualifying educational expenses are state and federally tax-exempt, subject to 2010 sunset provision
I	Both residents and nonresidents; however, nonresidents may only invest through a financial adviser.

California

	Savings Plan
A	**Golden State ScholarShare College Savings Trust** (invest directly with state)
B	Qualified educational expenses for postsecondary education
C	TIAA-CREF Tuition Financing, Inc.
D	Choice of age-based and static professionally managed investment funds
E	Variable — depends on market conditions and funds chosen
F	Any U.S. 2 and 4 year college and university, postsecondary trade and vocational school, and graduate and professional school that is eligible for federal financial aid
G	Open enrollment; join at any time
H	Distributions used for qualifying educational expenses are state and federally tax-exempt, subject to 2010 sunset provision. 2.5% California penalty assessed to earnings from non-qualified distributions.
I	Both residents and nonresidents

Colorado

	Savings Plan	Prepaid Plan
A	**CollegeInvest — Scholars Choice College Savings Program** (invest directly with state or with financial advisers) **CollegeInvest — Stable Value Plus College Savings Program** (invest directly with state)	**CollegeInvest — Prepaid Tuition Fund** (not currently enrolling new participants or taking new contributions for existing plans)
B	Qualified educational expenses for postsecondary education	Qualified educational expenses for postsecondary education
C	CollegeInvest — Scholars Choice College Savings Program: Citigroup Asset Management; CollegeInvest — Stable Value Plus College Savings Program: Travelers Insurance Company	Colorado Student Obligation Bond Authority (CSOBA) and State Treasurer
D	CollegeInvest — Scholars Choice College Savings Program offers a choice of age-based and static professionally managed investment funds. CollegeInvest — Stable Value Plus College Savings Program offers a guaranteed return on your investment as determined (and guaranteed) by The Travelers Insurance Company.	Fixed investment plan as determined by plan manager and professional investment advisers
E	Variable — depends on market conditions, funds chosen, and current interest rates.	Guaranteed 4% annual return, due to be revised by Colorado legislature
F	Any U.S. 2 and 4 year college and university, postsecondary trade and vocational school, and graduate and professional school that is eligible for federal financial aid	Any U.S. 2 and 4 year college and university, postsecondary trade and vocational school, and graduate and professional school that is eligible for federal financial aid
G	Open enrollment; join at any time	Not currently open for enrollment or contribution

(continued)

Colorado (continued)

	Savings Plan	Prepaid Plan
H	Distributions used for qualifying educational expenses are state and federally tax-exempt, subject to 2010 sunset provision. Contributions (other than rollovers) are deductible from Colorado resident income tax returns.	Distributions used for qualifying educational expenses are state and federally tax-exempt, subject to 2010 sunset provision. Contributions (other than rollovers) are deductible from Colorado resident income tax returns.
I	Both residents and nonresidents	Both residents and nonresidents. Beneficiary age restrictions apply.

Connecticut

	Savings Plan
A	**Connecticut Higher Education Trust (CHET)** (invest directly with state)
B	Qualified educational expenses for postsecondary education
C	TIAA-CREF Tuition Financing Inc.
D	Choice of age-based and static professionally managed investment funds
E	Variable — depends on market conditions and funds chosen
F	Any U.S. 2 and 4 year college and university, postsecondary trade and vocational school, and graduate and professional school that is eligible for federal financial aid
G	Open enrollment; join at any time
H	Distributions used for qualifying educational expenses are state and federally tax-exempt, subject to 2010 sunset provision.
I	Both residents and nonresidents

Delaware

	Savings Plan
A	**Delaware College Investment Plan** (invest directly with state)
B	Qualified educational expenses for postsecondary education
C	Fidelity Investments

	Savings Plan
D	Choice of age-based and static professionally managed investment funds
E	Variable — depends on market conditions and funds chosen
F	Any U.S. 2 and 4 year college and university, postsecondary trade and vocational school, and graduate and professional school that is eligible for federal financial aid
G	Open enrollment; join at any time
H	Distributions used for qualifying educational expenses are state and federally tax-exempt, subject to 2010 sunset provision.
I	Both residents and nonresidents

District of Columbia

	Savings Plan
A	**DC 529 College Savings Program** (invest directly with state or with financial adviser)
B	Qualified educational expenses for postsecondary education
C	Calvert Asset Management Co., Inc.
D	Choice of age-based and static professionally managed investment funds
E	Variable — depends on market conditions and funds chosen
F	Any U.S. 2 and 4 year college and university, postsecondary trade and vocational school, and graduate and professional school that is eligible for federal financial aid
G	Open enrollment; join at any time
H	Distributions used for qualifying educational expenses are state and federally tax-exempt, subject to 2010 sunset provision. Annual contributions up to $3,000 ($6,000 for married filing joint returns) may be deducted from D.C. resident income tax returns. Excess contributions may be carried over, and deducted, for up to five years.
I	Both residents and nonresidents; however, nonresidents may only invest through a financial adviser.

Florida

	Savings Plan	Prepaid Plan
A	**Florida College Investment Plan** (invest directly with state)	**Florida Prepaid College Program** (invest directly with state)
B	Qualified educational expenses for postsecondary education	Depending on type of contract purchased, will cover tuition and mandatory fees, but also may include dormitory fees.
C	Florida Prepaid College Board	Florida Prepaid College Board
D	Choice of age-based and static professionally managed investment funds	Fixed investment plan as determined by Florida Prepaid College Board
E	Variable — depends on market conditions and funds chosen	Guaranteed to equal increase in rate of tuition, mandatory fees and, where applicable, dormitory housing, based on costs at Florida public community colleges, colleges, and universities.
F	Any U.S. 2 and 4 year college and university, postsecondary trade and vocational school, and graduate and professional school that is eligible for federal financial aid	Any U.S. 2 and 4 year college and university, postsecondary trade and vocational school, and graduate and professional school that is eligible for federal financial aid
G	Open enrollment; join at any time	October, 2003 to January, 2004. Check with plan manager for future enrollment periods.
H	Distributions used for qualifying educational expenses are federally tax-exempt, subject to 2010 sunset provision. Florida has no state income tax, and account isn't subject to Florida intangibles tax.	Distributions used for qualifying educational expenses are federally tax-exempt, subject to 2010 sunset provision. Florida has no state income tax, and account isn't subject to Florida intangibles tax.
I	Both residents and nonresidents	Only available to Florida resident beneficiaries. Beneficiary age restrictions apply.

Georgia

	Savings Plan
A	**Georgia Higher Education Savings Plan** (invest directly with state)
B	Qualified educational expenses for postsecondary education
C	TIAA-CREF Tuition Financing, Inc.
D	Choice of age-based and static professionally managed investment funds
E	Variable — depends on market conditions and funds chosen
F	Any U.S. 2 and 4 year college and university, postsecondary trade and vocational school, and graduate and professional school that is eligible for federal financial aid
G	Open enrollment; join at any time
H	Distributions used for qualifying educational expenses are state and federally tax-exempt, subject to 2010 sunset provision. Contributions up to $2,000 are deductible from Georgia resident income tax returns for taxpayers who itemize and who have adjusted gross income of less than $50,000 if single, or $100,000 if married and filing jointly.
I	Both residents and nonresidents

Hawaii

	Savings Plan
A	**TuitionEDGE** (invest directly with state or with financial adviser)
B	Qualified educational expenses for postsecondary education
C	Delaware Investments
D	Choice of age-based and static professionally managed investment funds
E	Variable — depends on market conditions and funds chosen
F	Any U.S. 2 and 4 year college and university, postsecondary trade and vocational school, and graduate and professional school that is eligible for federal financial aid
G	Open enrollment; join at any time
H	Distributions used for qualifying educational expenses are state and federally tax-exempt, subject to 2010 sunset provision.
I	Both residents and nonresidents; however, nonresidents may only invest through a financial adviser.

Idaho

	Savings Plan
A	**Idaho College Savings Program (IDeal)** (invest directly with state)
B	Qualified educational expenses for postsecondary education
C	TIAA-CREF Tuition Financing, Inc.
D	Choice of age-based and static professionally managed investment funds
E	Variable — depends on market conditions and funds chosen
F	Any U.S. 2 and 4 year college and university, postsecondary trade and vocational school, and graduate and professional school that is eligible for federal financial aid
G	Open enrollment; join at any time
H	Distributions used for qualifying educational expenses are state and federally tax-exempt, subject to 2010 sunset provision. Up to $4,000 of contributions ($8,000 if married filing jointly) may be deducted annually from Idaho resident income tax returns; however, Idaho taxpayers must include 100% of non-qualifying distributions on income tax return, whether or not they deducted their contribution.
I	Both residents and nonresidents

Illinois

	Savings Plan	Prepaid Plan
A	**Bright Start College Savings Program** (invest directly with state or with participating Illinois banks)	**College Illinois!** (invest directly with state)
B	Qualified educational expenses for postsecondary education	Tuition and mandatory fees only for postsecondary education, based on fees charge by Illinois public institutions
C	Citigroup Asset Management	Illinois Student Assistance Commission
D	Choice of age-based and static professionally managed investment funds	Fixed investment plan as determined by plan manager and professional investment advisers

	Savings Plan	*Prepaid Plan*
E	Variable — depends on market conditions and funds chosen	Guaranteed to provide number of prepaid semesters at Illinois public community colleges and universities; will provide average mean-weighted credit hour value of public in-state costs at private and out-of-state schools.
F	Any U.S. 2 and 4 year college and university, postsecondary trade and vocational school, and graduate and professional school that is eligible for federal financial aid	Any U.S. 2 and 4 year college and university, postsecondary trade and vocational school, and graduate and professional school that is eligible for federal financial aid
G	Open enrollment; join at any time	October 29, 2003 to March 31, 2004. Check with plan manager for future enrollment periods.
H	Distributions used for qualifying educational expenses are state and federally tax-exempt, subject to 2010 sunset provision. Contributions (other than rollovers) are deductible from Illinois resident income tax returns.	Distributions used for qualifying educational expenses are state and federally tax-exempt, subject to 2010 sunset provision. Contributions to this plan aren't income tax deductible.
I	Both residents and nonresidents	Account owner or designated beneficiary must be an Illinois resident for at least one year prior to enrollment. Beneficiary age restrictions apply.

Indiana

	Savings Plan
A	**CollegeChoice 529 Plan** (invest directly and with financial advisers; direct purchases are subject to adviser distribution charges)
B	Qualified educational expenses for postsecondary education
C	One Group Investments
D	Choice of age-based and static professionally managed investment funds
E	Variable — depends on market conditions and funds chosen

(continued)

Indiana (continued)

	Savings Plan
F	Any U.S. 2 and 4 year college and university, postsecondary trade and vocational school, and graduate and professional school that is eligible for federal financial aid
G	Open enrollment; join at any time
H	Distributions used for qualifying educational expenses are state and federally tax-exempt, subject to 2010 sunset provision.
I	Both residents and nonresidents, but only through financial adviser.

Iowa

	Savings Plan
A	**College Savings Iowa** (invest directly with state)
B	Qualified educational expenses for postsecondary education
C	State Treasurer; Vanguard
D	Choice of age-based professionally managed investment funds.
E	Variable — depends on market conditions and funds chosen
F	Any U.S. 2 and 4 year college and university, postsecondary trade and vocational school, and graduate and professional school that is eligible for federal financial aid
G	Open enrollment; join at any time
H	Distributions used for qualifying educational expenses are state and federally tax-exempt, subject to 2010 sunset provision. Contributions of up to $2,230 (in 2003) are deductible from Iowa resident income tax returns.
I	Both residents and nonresidents. Beneficiary age restrictions apply.

Kansas

	Savings Plan
A	**Kansas Learning Quest Education Savings Program** (invest directly with state or with financial adviser)
B	Qualified educational expenses for postsecondary education
C	American Century Investment Management Inc.
D	Choice of age-based professionally managed investment funds
E	Variable — depends on market conditions and funds chosen

	Savings Plan
F	Any U.S. 2 and 4 year college and university, postsecondary trade and vocational school, and graduate and professional school that is eligible for federal financial aid
G	Open enrollment; join at any time
H	Distributions used for qualifying educational expenses are state and federally tax-exempt, subject to 2010 sunset provision. Up to $2,000 of contributions ($4,000 if married filing jointly) may be deducted annually from Kansas resident income tax returns.
I	Both residents and nonresidents

Kentucky

	Savings Plan	*Prepaid Plan*
A	**Kentucky Education Savings Plan Trust (KESPT)** (invest directly with state)	**Kentucky Affordable Prepaid Tuition (KAPT)** (invest directly with state)
B	Qualified educational expenses for postsecondary education	Tuition and mandatory fees only for postsecondary education
C	TIAA-CREF Tuition Financing, Inc.	KAPT Board of Directors and Office of the State Treasurer
D	Choice of age-based and static professionally managed investment funds	Fixed investment plan as determined by plan manager and professional investment advisers
E	Variable — depends on market conditions and funds chosen	Depending on type of tuition plan purchased, full tuition and mandatory fees at participating community and technical colleges and Kentucky public universities. Amount available to pay tuition and fees paid to all other institutions will increase at rate as tuition and mandatory fees at the most expensive Kentucky public university.
F	Any U.S. 2 and 4 year college and university, postsecondary trade and vocational school, and graduate and professional school that is eligible for federal financial aid	Tuition plans can be used at community and technical colleges, Kentucky public universities, and all other postsecondary educational institutions eligible for federal financial aid.

(continued)

Kentucky (continued)

	Savings Plan	Prepaid Plan
G	Open enrollment; join at any time	New enrollments and contributions to existing accounts currently suspended. May resume after June 30, 2004.
H	Distributions used for qualifying educational expenses are state and federally tax-exempt, subject to 2010 sunset provision.	Distributions used for qualifying educational expenses are state and federally tax-exempt, subject to 2010 sunset provision.
I	Both residents and nonresidents	Plans may be purchased (when available) only for beneficiaries who either are Kentucky residents, or who plan to attend a Kentucky postsecondary educational institution. Beneficiary age restrictions apply.

Louisiana

	Savings Plan
A	**START Saving Program** (invest directly with state)
B	Qualified educational expenses for postsecondary education
C	Louisiana State Treasurer
D	Choice of age-based (beginning late in 2003) and static professionally managed investment funds
E	Variable — depends on market conditions and funds chosen
F	Any U.S. 2 and 4 year college and university, postsecondary trade and vocational school, and graduate and professional school that is eligible for federal financial aid
G	Open enrollment; join at any time
H	Distributions used for qualifying educational expenses are state and federally tax-exempt, subject to 2010 sunset provision. Up to $2,400 of contributions may be deducted annually from Louisiana resident income tax returns; contributions in excess of $2,400 per year may be carried forward to, and deducted from income, in subsequent tax years.
I	Account owner or account beneficiary must be a Louisiana resident

Maine

	Savings Plan
A	**NextGen College Investing Plan — Client Direct Series** (invest directly with state) **NextGen College Investing Plan — Client Advisor Series** (invest with Merrill Lynch financial adviser, or with certain Maine distribution agents)
B	Qualified educational expenses for postsecondary education
C	Merrill Lynch
D	Choice of age-based and static professionally managed investment funds
E	Variable — depends on market conditions and funds chosen
F	Any U.S. 2 and 4 year college and university, postsecondary trade and vocational school, and graduate and professional school that is eligible for federal financial aid
G	Open enrollment; join at any time
H	Distributions used for qualifying educational expenses are state and federally tax-exempt, subject to 2010 sunset provision.
I	Both residents and nonresidents

Maryland

	Savings Plan	Prepaid Plan
A	**College Savings Plans of Maryland — College Investment Plan** (invest directly with state)	**College Savings Plans of Maryland — Prepaid College Trust** (invest directly with state)
B	Qualified educational expenses for postsecondary education	Tuition and mandatory fees only for postsecondary education
C	T. Rowe Price Associates, Inc. Investment Board	Maryland Higher Education
D	Choice of age-based and static professionally managed investment funds	Assets invested in a group of predetermined no-load mutual funds.

(continued)

Maryland (continued)

	Savings Plan	Prepaid Plan
E	Variable — depends on market conditions and funds chosen	Guaranteed to pay full in-state tuition and mandatory fees at public Maryland institutions. Will pay an amount equal to the weighted average tuition and mandatory fees of Maryland public institutions for any private post-secondary educational institution.
F	Any U.S. 2 and 4 year college and university, postsecondary trade and vocational school, and graduate and professional school that is eligible for federal financial aid	Any U.S. 2 and 4 year college and university, postsecondary trade and vocational school, and graduate and professional school that is eligible for federal financial aid
G	Open enrollment; join at any time	November to March of each year
H	Distributions used for qualifying educational expenses are state and federally tax-exempt, subject to 2010 sunset provision. Up to $2,500 of contributions may be deducted annually from Maryland resident income tax returns; contributions in excess of $2,500 per year may be carried forward to, and deducted from income, for up to 10 subsequent tax years.	Distributions used for qualifying educational expenses are state and federally tax-exempt, subject to 2010 sunset provision. Up to $2,500 of contributions may be deducted annually from Maryland resident income tax returns; con-tributions in excess of $2,500 per year may be carried forward to, and deducted from income, for up to 10 subsequent tax years.
I	Both residents and nonresidents	Plan owner or beneficiary must be a resident of either Maryland or the District of Columbia. Beneficiary age restrictions apply.

Massachusetts

	Savings Plan	Prepaid Plan
A	**U.Fund** (invest directly with state)	**U.Plan** (not under Section 529) (invest directly with state)
B	Qualified educational expenses for postsecondary education	Tuition and mandatory fees only for postsecondary education
C	Fidelity Investments	Massachusetts Educational Financing Authority (MEFA)

	Savings Plan	Prepaid Plan
D	Choice of age-based and static professionally managed investment funds	Special Massachusetts Bonds
E	Variable — depends on market conditions and funds chosen	Guaranteed to equal increase in rate of tuition and mandatory fees at participating colleges in Massachusetts. For non-participating schools, interest on investment will compound annually at rate of the Consumer Price Index.
F	Any U.S. 2 and 4 year college and university, postsecondary trade and vocational school, and graduate and professional school that is eligible for federal financial aid	Currently more than 80 participating Massachusetts 2 and 4 year colleges and universities
G	Open enrollment; join at any time	May 1 to June 15 of each year.
H	Distributions used for qualifying educational expenses are state and federally tax-exempt, subject to 2010 sunset provision.	Federally and Massachusetts tax-exempt. Not subject to sunset provision after 2010.
I	Both residents and nonresidents	Both residents and nonresidents. Account owner must be related to designated beneficiary.

Michigan

	Savings Plan	Prepaid Plan
A	**Michigan Education Savings Program** (invest directly with state)	**Michigan Education Trust (MET)** (invest directly with state)
B	Qualified educational expenses for postsecondary education	Tuition and mandatory fees only for postsecondary education
C	TIAA-CREF Tuition Financing, Inc.	Michigan Education Trust Board of Directors and Department of Treasury
D	Choice of age-based and static professionally managed investment funds	Fixed investment plan as determined by plan manager and professional investment advisers

(continued)

Michigan (continued)

	Savings Plan	Prepaid Plan
E	Variable — depends on market conditions and funds chosen	Depending on type of program purchased, return is guaranteed to equal increase in rate of in-state tuition and mandatory fees at Michigan public community coleges, colleges, and universities.
F	Any U.S. 2 and 4 year college and university, postsecondary trade and vocational school, and graduate and professional school that is eligible for federal financial aid	May only be used at Michigan public community colleges, colleges, and universities
G	Open enrollment; join at any time	Check with plan manager for future enrollment periods.
H	Distributions used for qualifying educational expenses are state and federally tax-exempt, subject to 2010 sunset provision. Annual contributions of up to $5,000 ($10,000 for married filing joint returns) are deductible from Michigan resident income tax returns.	Distributions used for qualifying educational expenses are state and federally tax-exempt, subject to 2010 sunset provision. All contributions are deductible from Michigan income tax returns.
I	Both residents and nonresidents	Beneficiary must be a Michigan resident. Beneficiary age restrictions apply.

Minnesota

	Savings Plan
A	**Minnesota College Savings Plan** (invest directly with state)
B	Qualified educational expenses for postsecondary education
C	TIAA-CREF Tuition Financing, Inc.
D	Choice of age-based and static professionally managed investment funds
E	Variable — depends on market conditions and funds chosen
F	Any U.S. 2 and 4 year college and university, postsecondary trade and vocational school, and graduate and professional school that is eligible for federal financial aid

	Savings Plan
G	Open enrollment; join at any time
H	Distributions used for qualifying educational expenses are state and federally tax-exempt, subject to 2010 sunset provision.
I	Both residents and nonresidents

Mississippi

	Savings Plan	Prepaid Plan
A	**Mississippi Affordable College Savings (MACS) Program** (invest directly with state) **Mississippi Affordable College Savings (MACS) 529 Advisor Program** (invest with financial advisers only)	**Mississippi Prepaid Affordable College Tuition (MPACT) Program** (invest directly with state)
B	Qualified educational expenses for postsecondary education	Tuition and mandatory fees only for postsecondary education
C	TIAA-CREF Tuition Financing, Inc.	Mississippi Treasury Department
D	Choice of age-based and static professionally managed investment funds in direct-sold program; only static investment options carrying a variety of risk levels are available in the adviser-sold program.	Invested in a managed, balanced investment portfolio identical to that of the Mississippi State Public Employees Retirement System
E	Variable — depends on market conditions and funds chosen	Return is guaranteed to equal increase in rate of in-state tuition and mandatory fees at Mississippi public community colleges, colleges, and universities.
F	Any U.S. 2 and 4 year college and university, postsecondary trade and vocational school, and graduate and professional school that is eligible for federal financial aid	Any U.S. 2 and 4 year college and university, postsecondary trade and vocational school, and graduate and professional school that is eligible for federal financial aid
G	Open enrollment; join at any time	September 1 to November 30 of each year.

(continued)

Mississippi (continued)

	Savings Plan	Prepaid Plan
H	Distributions used for qualifying educational expenses are state and federally tax-exempt, subject to 2010 sunset provision. Up to $10,000 ($20,000 for married filing joint returns) is deductible from Mississippi resident income tax returns.	Distributions used for qualifying educational expenses are state and federally tax-exempt, subject to 2010 sunset provision. All contributions are deductible from Mississippi resident income tax returns.
I	Both residents and nonresidents	Account owner or designated beneficiary must be a Mississippi resident. Beneficiary age restrictions apply.

Missouri

	Savings Plan
A	**Missouri Saving for Tuition (MO$T) Program** (invest directly with state or with financial adviser)
B	Qualified educational expenses for postsecondary education
C	TIAA-CREF Tuition Financing, Inc.
D	Choice of age-based and static professionally managed investment funds in direct-sold program; only static investment options carrying a variety of risk levels are available in the adviser-sold program.
E	Variable — depends on market conditions and funds chosen
F	Any U.S. 2 and 4 year college and university, postsecondary trade and vocational school, and graduate and professional school that is eligible for federal financial aid
G	Open enrollment; join at any time
H	Distributions used for qualifying educational expenses are state and federally tax-exempt, subject to 2010 sunset provision. Annual contributions up to $8,000 are deductible from Missouri resident income tax returns.
I	Both residents and nonresidents

Montana

	Savings Plan
A	**Montana Family Education Savings Program** (College Savings Bank) **Pacific Funds 529 College Savings Plan (MT)** (invest directly with state or with financial adviser)
B	Qualified educational expenses for postsecondary education
C	College Savings Bank
D	CollegeSure CD offered by Montana Family Education Savings Program; choice of static professionally managed investment funds available through Pacific Funds 529 College Savings Plan.
E	Variable — depends on market conditions, funds chosen, and current interest rates.
F	Any U.S. 2 and 4 year college and university, postsecondary trade and vocational school, and graduate and professional school that is eligible for federal financial aid
G	Open enrollment; join at any time
H	Distributions used for qualifying educational expenses are state and federally tax-exempt, subject to 2010 sunset provision. Annual contributions of up to $3,000 ($6,000 for married filing joint returns) are deductible from Montana resident income tax returns.
I	Both residents and nonresidents may invest in the Montana Family Education Savings Program and the adviser-sold Pacific Funds 529 College Savings Plan. Only residents may invest in the direct-sold Pacific Funds 529 College Savings Plan.

Nebraska

	Savings Plan
A	**College Savings Plan of Nebraska** (invest directly with state or with financial adviser) **A I M College Savings Plan** (invest with financial adviser only) **State Farm College Savings Plan** (sold by State Farm VP Management Corp. registered representative only) **TD Waterhouse 529 College Savings Plan** (invest with TD Waterhouse brokerage only)
B	Qualified educational expenses for postsecondary education
C	Union Bank & Trust Company (A I M College Savings Plan and State Farm College Savings Plan are managed by Union Bank & Trust Company and A I M Capital Management, Inc.)

(continued)

Nebraska (continued)

	Savings Plan
D	Choice of age-based and static professionally managed investment funds
E	Variable — depends on market conditions and funds chosen
F	Any U.S. 2 and 4 year college and university, postsecondary trade and vocational school, and graduate and professional school that is eligible for federal financial aid
G	Open enrollment; join at any time
H	Distributions used for qualifying educational expenses are state and federally tax-exempt, subject to 2010 sunset provision. Annual contributions of up to $1,000 ($500 for married filing separate returns) are deductible from Nebraska resident income tax returns.
I	Both residents and nonresidents

Nevada

	Savings Plan	**Prepaid Plan**
A	**American Skandia College Savings Program** (invest through financial advisers only) **The Strong 529 Plan** (invest directly with state) **The Upromise College Fund** (invest directly with state) **USAA College Savings Plan** (limited to USAA members) **The Vanguard 529 Savings Plan** (invest directly with state) **Columbia 529 Plan** (invest through financial advisers only)	**Nevada Prepaid Tuition Program**
B	Qualified educational expenses for postsecondary education	Tuition and mandatory fees only for postsecondary education

	Savings Plan	*Prepaid Plan*
C	American Skandia College Savings Program: Strong Capital Management, Inc.; The Strong 529 Plan: Strong Capital Management, Inc.; The Upromise College Fund: Upromise Investments, Inc.; USAA College Savings Plan: Strong Capital Management, Inc.; The Vanguard 529 Savings Plan: Upromise Investments, Inc.; Columbia 529 Plan: Columbia Management Group	Nevada State Treasurer's Office
D	Choice of age-based and static professionally managed investment funds	Fixed investment plan as determined by the Board of Trustees of the Nevada Higher Education Tuition Trust Fund and professional investment advisers
E	Variable — depends on market conditions and funds chosen	Plan purchased will provide 100% of 2 or 4 years of in-state tuition and mandatory fees at public community colleges, universities, or a combination of the two. Value of contract may also be used at public out-of-state, and private postsecondary educational institutions.
F	Any U.S. 2 and 4 year college and university, postsecondary trade and vocational school, and graduate and professional school that is eligible for federal financial aid	Any U.S. 2 and 4 year college and university, postsecondary trade and vocational school, and graduate and professional school that is eligible for federal financial aid
G	Open enrollment; join at any time	Check with plan manager for future enrollment periods.
H	Distributions used for qualifying educational expenses are federally tax-exempt, subject to 2010 sunset provision. Nevada has no state income tax.	Distributions used for qualifying educational expenses are federally tax-exempt, subject to 2010 sunset provision. Nevada has no state income tax.
I	Both residents and nonresidents	Account owner or account-designated beneficiary must be a Nevada resident at time contract is purchased. Beneficiary age restrictions apply.

New Hampshire

	Savings Plan
A	**Fidelity Advisor 529 Plan** (invest with financial advisers only) **UNIQUE College Investing Plan** (invest directly with state)
B	Qualified educational expenses for postsecondary education
C	Fidelity Investments
D	Choice of age-based and static professionally managed investment funds
E	Variable — depends on market conditions and funds chosen
F	Any U.S. 2 and 4 year college and university, postsecondary trade and vocational school, and graduate and professional school that is eligible for federal financial aid
G	Open enrollment; join at any time
H	Distributions used for qualifying educational expenses are federally income tax-exempt, subject to 2010 sunset provision, and qualify for exemption from New Hampshire dividends and interest tax. (New Hampshire doesn't have an income tax.)
I	Both residents and nonresidents

New Jersey

	Savings Plan
A	**NJBEST 529 College Savings Plan** (invest directly with state) **Franklin Templeton 529 College Savings Plan** (invest with financial adviser)
B	Qualified educational expenses for postsecondary education
C	Franklin Templeton Distributors, Inc.
D	Choice of age-based and static professionally managed investment funds
E	Variable — depends on market conditions and funds chosen
F	Any U.S. 2 and 4 year college and university, postsecondary trade and vocational school, and graduate and professional school that is eligible for federal financial aid
G	Open enrollment; join at any time

	Savings Plan
H	Distributions used for qualifying educational expenses are state and federally tax-exempt, subject to 2010 sunset provision.
I	Both residents and nonresidents may invest in the Franklin Templeton 529 College Savings Plan; the NJBEST 529 College Savings Plan may only be purchased by a New Jersey resident account owner, or on behalf of a New Jersey resident designated beneficiary.

New Mexico

	Savings Plan	Prepaid Plan
A	**The Education Plan's College Savings Program** (invest directly with state or with financial adviser) **Scholar'sEdge** (invest through financial advisers only) **CollegeSense 529 Higher Education Savings Plan** (invest through financial advisers only) **Arrive Education Savings Plan** (invest through financial advisers only)	**The Education Plan's Prepaid Tuition Program** (invest directly with state)
B	Qualified educational expenses for postsecondary education	Tuition and mandatory fees only for postsecondary education
C	Schoolhouse Capital, LLC (Scholar'sEdge is managed by Schoolhouse Capital, LLC, and by OppenheimerFunds Distributor, Inc.; CollegeSense 529 Higher Education Savings Plan is managed by Schoolhouse Capital, LLC, and by New York Life Investment Management.)	Schoolhouse Capital, LLC
D	Choice of age-based and static professionally managed investment funds	Fixed investment plan as determined by plan manager and professional investment advisers

(continued)

New Mexico (continued)

	Savings Plan	Prepaid Plan
E	Variable — depends on market conditions and funds chosen	Each contract purchased will provide up to 100% of in-state tuition and mandatory fees at public branch universities, community colleges, comprehensive universities, and research universities. Value of contract may also be used at public out-of-state and private postsecondary educational institutions.
F	Any U.S. 2 and 4 year college and university, postsecondary trade and vocational school, and graduate and professional school that is eligible for federal financial aid	Any U.S. 2 and 4 year college and university, postsecondary trade and vocational school, and graduate and professional school that is eligible for federal financial aid
G	Open enrollment; join at any time	September 1 to December 31 of each year
H	Distributions used for qualifying educational expenses are state and federally tax-exempt, subject to 2010 sunset provision. All contributions to plan are deductible from New Mexico resident income tax returns.	Distributions used for qualifying educational expenses are state and federally tax-exempt, subject to 2010 sunset provision. All contributions to plan are deductible from New Mexico resident income tax returns.
I	Both residents and nonresidents	Account owner or account-designated beneficiary must be a New Mexico resident. Plan must be purchased a minimum of 5 years before it is used.

New York

	Savings Plan
A	**New York's College Savings Program** (invest directly with state or with financial adviser)
B	Qualified educational expenses for postsecondary education
D	Choice of age-based and static professionally managed investment funds
E	Variable — depends on market conditions and funds chosen

	Savings Plan
F	Any U.S. 2 and 4 year college and university, postsecondary trade and vocational school, and graduate and professional school that is eligible for federal financial aid
G	Open enrollment; join at any time
H	Distributions used for qualifying educational expenses are state and federally tax-exempt, subject to 2010 sunset provision. Annual contributions of up to $5,000 ($10,000 for married filing joint returns) are deductible from New York State (including New York City) resident income tax returns.
I	Both residents and nonresidents

North Carolina

	Savings Plan
A	**National College Savings Program** (invest directly with state or with financial adviser)
B	Qualified educational expenses for postsecondary education
C	College Foundation, Inc.
D	Choice of age-based and static professionally managed investment funds
E	Variable — depends on market conditions and funds chosen
F	Any U.S. 2 and 4 year college and university, postsecondary trade and vocational school, and graduate and professional school that is eligible for federal financial aid
G	Open enrollment; join at any time
H	Distributions used for qualifying educational expenses are state and federally tax-exempt, subject to 2010 sunset provision.
I	Both residents (including North Carolina workers) and nonresidents; however, nonresidents may only invest through a financial adviser.

North Dakota

	Savings Plan
A	**College SAVE** (invest directly with state or with financial adviser)
B	Qualified educational expenses for postsecondary education

(continued)

North Dakota *(continued)*

	Savings Plan
C	Morgan Stanley
D	Choice of age-based and static professionally managed investment funds
E	Variable — depends on market conditions and funds chosen
F	Any U.S. 2 and 4 year college and university, postsecondary trade and vocational school, and graduate and professional school that is eligible for federal financial aid
G	Open enrollment; join at any time
H	Distributions used for qualifying educational expenses are state and federally tax-exempt, subject to 2010 sunset provision.
I	Both residents and nonresidents

Ohio

	Savings Plan
A	**Ohio CollegeAdvantage Savings Plan — Variable Investment Option** (invest directly with state or with financial adviser) **Putnam CollegeAdvantage Savings Plan** (invest through financial advisers only) **Ohio CollegeAdvantage — Guaranteed Option** (invest directly with state)
B	Qualified educational expenses for postsecondary education
C	Putnam Investments
D	Ohio CollegeAdvantage — Variable Investment Option and Putnam CollegeAdvantage Savings Plan offer a choice of age-based and static professionally managed investment funds. Ohio CollegeAdvantage — Guaranteed Option has a fixed investment plan as determined by professional managers.
E	Returns for Ohio CollegeAdvantage — Variable Investment Option and Putnam CollegeAdvantage Savings Plan Variable will depend on market conditions and funds chosen. Return for Ohio CollegeAdvantage — Guaranteed Option will be guaranteed, so that each 100 units purchased will pay one year of the weighted average tuition and mandatory fees at the 13 Ohio public schools.
F	Any U.S. 2 and 4 year college and university, postsecondary trade and vocational school, and graduate and professional school that is eligible for federal financial aid

	Savings Plan
G	Open enrollment; join at any time
H	Distributions used for qualifying educational expenses are state and federally tax-exempt, subject to 2010 sunset provision. Nonqualifying distributions made on account of death, disability, or scholarship receipt are exempt from Ohio income tax. Up to $2,000 of contributions may be deducted annually from Ohio resident income tax returns; contributions in excess of $2,000 per year may be carried forward indefinitely, until completely used.
I	May only invest in Ohio CollegeAdvantage — Guaranteed Option and directly in Ohio CollegeAdvantage Savings Plan — Variable Investment Option if either account owner or designated beneficiary is an Ohio resident. Both residents and nonresidents may invest through a financial adviser in Ohio CollegeAdvantage Savings Plan — Variable Investment Option and Putnam CollegeAdvantage Savings Plan.

Oklahoma

	Savings Plan
A	**Oklahoma College Savings Plan** (invest directly with state)
B	Qualified educational expenses for postsecondary education
C	TIAA-CREF Tuition Financing, Inc.
D	Choice of age-based and static professionally managed investment funds
E	Variable — depends on market conditions and funds chosen
F	Any U.S. 2 and 4 year college and university, postsecondary trade and vocational school, and graduate and professional school that is eligible for federal financial aid
G	Open enrollment; join at any time
H	Distributions used for qualifying educational expenses are state and federally tax-exempt, subject to 2010 sunset provision. Annual contributions of up to $2,500 may be deducted annually from Oklahoma resident income tax returns.
I	Both residents and nonresidents

Oregon

	Savings Plan
A	**Oregon College Savings Plan/FACTS 529 Plan** (invest directly with state or with financial adviser) **MFS 529 Savings Plan** (invest through financial advisers only) **USA CollegeConnect** (invest through financial advisers only)
B	Qualified educational expenses for postsecondary education
C	Oregon College Savings Plan/Facts 529 Plan: Strong Capital Management, Inc.; MFS 529 Savings Plan: MFS Investment Management; USA CollegeConnect: Schoolhouse Capital
D	Choice of age-based and static professionally managed investment funds
E	Variable — depends on market conditions and funds chosen
F	Any U.S. 2 and 4 year college and university, postsecondary trade and vocational school, and graduate and professional school that is eligible for federal financial aid
G	Open enrollment; join at any time
H	Distributions used for qualifying educational expenses are state and federally tax-exempt, subject to 2010 sunset provision. Annual contributions up to $2,000 ($1,000 for married filing separate returns) may be deducted from Oregon resident income tax returns
I	Both residents and nonresidents

Pennsylvania

	Savings Plan	Prepaid Unit/Guaranteed Savings Plan
A	**TAP 529 Investment Plan** (invest directly with state or with financial adviser)	**TAP 529 Guaranteed Savings Plan** (invest directly with state)
B	Qualified educational expenses for postsecondary education	Qualified educational expenses for postsecondary education
C	Delaware Investments	Delaware Investments
D	Choice of age-based and static professionally managed investment funds	Fixed investment plan as determined by professional managers.

	Savings Plan	Prepaid Unit/Guaranteed Savings Plan
E	Variable — depends on market conditions and funds chosen	Depending on amount invested and level of tuition credits purchased, guaranteed to equal increase in rate of tuition and mandatory fees in each class (Pennsylvania system of higher education, Pennsylvania-related universities, private 4-year schools, Ivy League schools, or community colleges) of postsecondary school.
F	Any U.S. 2 and 4 year college and university, postsecondary trade and vocational school, and graduate and professional school that is eligible for federal financial aid	Any U.S. 2 and 4 year college and university, postsecondary trade and vocational school, and graduate and professional school that is eligible for federal financial aid
G	Open enrollment; join at any time	Open enrollment; join at any time
H	Distributions used for qualifying educational expenses are state and federally tax-exempt, subject to 2010 sunset provision.	Distributions used for qualifying educational expenses are state and federally tax-exempt, subject to 2010 sunset provision.
I	Accounts with nonresident owners or designated beneficiaries may only be opened through a financial adviser.	Account owner or designated beneficiary must be a Pennsylvania resident.

Rhode Island

	Savings Plan
A	**CollegeBoundfund** (invest directly with state or with financial adviser) **JP Morgan Higher Education Plan**
B	Qualified educational expenses for postsecondary education
C	Alliance Capital; JP Morgan Higher Education Plan is also managed by JP Morgan Investment Management.
D	Choice of age-based and static professionally managed investment funds
E	Variable — depends on market conditions and funds chosen

(continued)

Rhode Island *(continued)*

	Savings Plan
F	Any U.S. 2 and 4 year college and university, postsecondary trade and vocational school, and graduate and professional school that is eligible for federal financial aid
G	Open enrollment; join at any time
H	Distributions used for qualifying educational expenses are state and federally tax-exempt, subject to 2010 sunset provision. Annual contributions of up to $500 ($1,000 for married filing joint returns) may be deducted from Rhode Island resident income tax returns; excess contributions may be carried forward indefinitely, until completely used.
I	May only invest directly in CollegeBoundfund if Rhode Island resident, employee of a Rhode Island company, maintain a principal place of business in Rhode Island, or if the named designated beneficiary is a Rhode Island resident. Both residents and nonresidents may invest in either CollegeBoundfund or JP Morgan Higher Education Plan through a financial adviser.

South Carolina

	Savings Plan	Prepaid Plan
A	**Future Scholar 529 College Savings Plan** (invest directly with state or with financial adviser)	**South Carolina Tuition Prepayment Program** (invest directly with state)
B	Qualified educational expenses for postsecondary education	Tuition and mandatory fees only for postsecondary education
C	Bank of America Advisors, LLC	Office of the State Treasurer
D	Choice of age-based and static professionally managed investment funds	Fixed investment plan as determined by professional managers
E	Variable — depends on market conditions and funds chosen	Guaranteed to equal increase in rate of tuition and mandatory fees at South Carolina public schools. Value of contract may also be used at public out-of-state, and private postsecondary educational institutions.

	Savings Plan	Prepaid Plan
F	Any U.S. 2 and 4 year college and university, postsecondary trade and vocational school, and graduate and professional school that is eligible for federal financial aid	Any U.S. 2 and 4 year college and university, postsecondary trade and vocational school, and graduate and professional school that is eligible for federal financial aid
G	Open enrollment; join at any time	October 1 to January 31 of each year
H	Distributions used for qualifying educational expenses are state and federally tax-exempt, subject to 2010 sunset provision. All contributions into plan are deductible from South Carolina resident income tax returns.	Distributions used for qualifying educational expenses are state and federally tax-exempt, subject to 2010 sunset provision. All contributions into plan are deductible from South Carolina resident income tax returns.
I	May only invest directly if account owner or designated beneficiary is a South Carolina resident or state employee, or an employee of Bank of America.	Designated beneficiary must be a South Carolina resident for at least one year prior to enrollment. Beneficiary age restrictions apply.

South Dakota

	Savings Plan
A	**CollegeAccess 529** (invest directly with state or with financial adviser) **Legg Mason Core4College 529 Plan** (invest with Legg Mason financial adviser or account representative for full access to all investment options within fund)
B	Qualified educational expenses for postsecondary education
C	PIMCO Advisors Distributors
D	Choice of age-based and static professionally managed investment funds
E	Variable — depends on market conditions and funds chosen
F	Any U.S. 2 and 4 year college and university, postsecondary trade and vocational school, and graduate and professional school that is eligible for federal financial aid
G	Open enrollment; join at any time

(continued)

South Dakota (continued)

	Savings Plan
H	Distributions used for qualifying educational expenses are federally tax-exempt, subject to 2010 sunset provision. South Dakota has no state income tax.
I	May only invest directly in CollegeAccess 529 if account owner or designated beneficiary is a South Dakota resident. Legg Mason Core4College 529 Plan is open to residents and nonresidents alike.

Tennessee

	Savings Plan	Prepaid Tuition/Guaranteed Savings Plan
A	**Tennessee's BEST Savings Plan** (invest directly with state)	**Tennessee's BEST Prepaid College Tuition Plan** (invest directly with state)
B	Qualified educational expenses for postsecondary education	Qualified educational expenses for postsecondary education
C	TIAA-CREF Tuition Financing, Inc.	Tennessee State Treasurer and Treasury Department
D	Choice of age-based and static professionally managed investment funds	Fixed investment plan as determined by professional managers
E	Variable — depends on market conditions and funds chosen	Each 100 units purchased is guaranteed to pay one year of the weighted average tuition and mandatory fees at the Tennessee public universities.
F	Any U.S. 2 and 4 year college and university, postsecondary trade and vocational school, and graduate and professional school that is eligible for federal financial aid	Any U.S. 2 and 4 year college and university, postsecondary trade and vocational school, and graduate and professional school that is eligible for federal financial aid
G	Open enrollment; join at any time	Open enrollment; join at any time

	Savings Plan	Prepaid Tuition/Guaranteed Savings Plan
H	Distributions used for qualifying educational expenses are state and federally tax-exempt, subject to 2010 sunset provision. All contributions into plan are deductible from Tennessee resident income tax returns.	Distributions used for qualifying educational expenses are state and federally tax-exempt, subject to 2010 sunset provision. All contributions into plan are deductible from Tennessee resident income tax returns.
I	Both residents and nonresidents	Account owner or beneficiary must be a Tennessee resident.

Texas

	Savings Plan	Prepaid Plan
A	**Tomorrow's College Investment Plan** (invest directly with state or with financial advisor)	**Texas Guaranteed Tuition Plan** (new enrollments suspended until further notice)
B	Qualified educational expenses for postsecondary education	Tuition and mandatory fees only for postsecondary education
C	Enterprise Capital Management, Inc.	Enterprise Capital Management, Inc.
D	Choice of age-based and static professionally managed investment funds	Fixed investment plan as determined by professional managers and the Treasury Division of the State Comptroller's Office.
E	Variable — depends on market conditions and funds chosen	Guaranteed to pay full in-state tuition and required fees at any public university or junior college in Texas. Value of contract may also be used at public out-of-state, and private postsecondary educational institutions.
F	Any U.S. 2 and 4 year college and university, postsecondary trade and vocational school, and graduate and professional school that is eligible for federal financial aid	Any U.S. 2 and 4 year college and university, postsecondary trade and vocational school, and graduate and professional school that is eligible for federal financial aid

(continued)

Texas (continued)

	Savings Plan	Prepaid Plan
G	Open enrollment; join at any time	Enrollments for new participants have been suspended until further notice.
H	Distributions used for qualifying educational expenses are federally tax-exempt, subject to 2010 sunset provision. Texas has no state income tax.	Distributions used for qualifying educational expenses are federally tax-exempt, subject to 2010 sunset provision. Texas has no state income tax.
I	Both residents and nonresidents. Only residents may invest in the direct-sold savings plan.	Account owner or beneficiary must be a Texas resident for a minimum of one year before enrolling. Beneficiary age restrictions apply.

Utah

	Savings Plan
A	**Utah Educational Savings Plan (UESP) Trust** (invest directly with state)
B	Qualified educational expenses for postsecondary education
C	Utah State Board of Regents
D	Choice of age-based and static professionally managed investment funds
E	Variable — depends on market conditions and funds chosen
F	Any U.S. 2 and 4 year college and university, postsecondary trade and vocational school, and graduate and professional school that is eligible for federal financial aid
G	Open enrollment; join at any time
H	Distributions used for qualifying educational expenses are state and federally tax-exempt, subject to 2010 sunset provision. Annual contributions of up to $1,435 in 2003 per beneficiary (provided account was opened prior to beneficiary's 18th birthday) are deductible from Utah resident income tax returns.
I	Both residents and nonresidents

Vermont

	Savings Plan
A	**Vermont Higher Education Investment Plan** (invest directly with state)
B	Qualified educational expenses for postsecondary education
C	TIAA-CREF Tuition Financing, Inc.
D	Choice of age-based and static professionally managed investment funds
E	Variable — depends on market conditions and funds chosen
F	Any U.S. 2 and 4 year college and university, postsecondary trade and vocational school, and graduate and professional school that is eligible for federal financial aid
G	Open enrollment; join at any time
H	Distributions used for qualifying educational expenses are state and federally tax-exempt, subject to 2010 sunset provision. Beginning in 2004, Vermont resident taxpayers may claim a non-refundable tax credit of up to $100 per beneficiary.
I	Both residents and nonresidents

Virginia

	Savings Plan	Prepaid Plan
A	**Virginia Education Savings Trust (VEST)** (invest directly with state) **CollegeAmerica** (invest through financial advisers only)	**Virginia Prepaid Education Program (VPEP)** (invest directly with state)
B	Qualified educational expenses for postsecondary education	Tuition and mandatory fees only for postsecondary education
C	Virginia College Savings Plan (for both plans) and American Funds (for CollegeAmerica only)	Virginia College Savings Plan
D	Choice of age-based and static professionally managed investment funds for VEST; a variety of static investment funds offered by American Funds for CollegeAmerica.	Fixed investment plan as determined by professional managers

(continued)

Virginia (continued)

	Savings Plan	Prepaid Plan
E	Variable — depends on market conditions and funds chosen	For a fully funded contract used at a Virginia public school — full tuition and mandatory fees. For a fully funded contract used at a Virginia private school, the lesser of (1) contributions plus actual rate of return or (2) the current highest cost of in-state tuition and mandatory fees at a Virginia public school, For a fully funded contract used at an out-of-state school, the lesser of (1) contributions plus actual rate of return or (2) the current average cost of in-state tuition and mandatory fees at a Virginia public school.
F	Any U.S. 2 and 4 year college and university, postsecondary trade and vocational school, and graduate and professional school that is eligible for federal financial aid	Any U.S. 2 and 4 year college and university, postsecondary trade and vocational school, and graduate and professional school that is eligible for federal financial aid
G	Open enrollment; join at any time	Check with plan manager for future enrollment periods.
H	Distributions used for qualifying educational expenses are state and federally tax-exempt, subject to 2010 sunset provision. Non-qualifying distributions made on account of death, disability, or scholarship receipt are exempt from Virginia income tax. Up to $2,000 of contributions may be deducted annually from Virginia resident income tax returns; contributions in excess of $2,000 per year may be carried forward indefinitely, until completely used.	Distributions used for qualifying educational expenses are state and federally tax-exempt, subject to 2010 sunset provision. Non-qualifying distributions made on account of death, disability, or scholarship receipt are exempt from Virginia income tax. Up to $2,000 of contributions may be deducted annually from Virginia resident income tax returns; contributions in excess of $2,000 per year may be carried forward indefinitely, until completely used.
I	Both residents and nonresidents	Account owner, designated beneficiary, or parent of designated beneficiary must be a Virginia resident. Beneficiary age restrictions apply.

Washington

	Prepaid Tuition/Guaranteed Savings Plan
A	**Guaranteed Education Tuition (GET)** (invest directly with state)
B	Tuition and mandatory fees for postsecondary education; to the extent a program has been funded with excess units, the excess units may be used to pay for other qualified postsecondary educational expenses.
C	Washington State Higher Education Coordinating Board
D	Fixed investment plan as determined by Washington State Investment Board
E	Each 100 units purchased is guaranteed to pay one year of tuition and mandatory fees at the highest cost Washington State public university. Return is guaranteed by Washington State.
F	Any U.S. 2 and 4 year college and university, postsecondary trade and vocational school, and graduate and professional school that is eligible for federal financial aid
G	September 15 to March 31 of each year.
H	Distributions used for qualifying educational expenses are federally tax-exempt, subject to 2010 sunset provision. Washington State has no state income tax.
I	Designated beneficiary of plan must be a resident of Washington State.

West Virginia

	Savings Plan	Prepaid Plan
A	**SMART529 College Savings Option** (invest directly with state or with financial adviser) **Leaders SMART529** (invest through financial advisers only)	**SMART529 Prepaid Tuition Plan** (not currently enrolling new participants or taking new contributions for existing plans)
B	Qualified educational expenses for postsecondary education	Tuition and mandatory fees only for postsecondary education
C	Hartford Life Insurance Company	Hartford Life Insurance Company
D	Choice of age-based and static professionally managed investment funds	Fixed investment plan as determined by plan manager and professional investment advisers

(continued)

West Virginia *(continued)*

		Savings Plan	Prepaid Plan
	E	Variable — depends on market conditions and funds chosen	Each semester unit purchased will provide up to 100% of one semester of in-state tuition and mandatory fees at 4-year West Virginia state universities. Value of contract may also be used at public out-of-state, and private postsecondary educational institutions.
	F	Any U.S. 2 and 4 year college and university, postsecondary trade and vocational school, and graduate and professional school that is eligible for federal financial aid	Any U.S. 2 and 4 year college and university, postsecondary trade and vocational school, and graduate and professional school that is eligible for federal financial aid
	G	Open enrollment; join at any time	Enrollment for new participants and contributions into existing plans has been suspended until further notice.
	H	Distributions used for qualifying educational expenses are state and federally tax-exempt, subject to 2010 sunset provision. All contributions into plan are deductible from West Virginia resident income tax returns.	Distributions used for qualifying educational expenses are state and federally tax-exempt, subject to 2010 sunset provision. All contributions into plan are deductible from West Virginia resident income tax returns.
	I	May only invest directly if account owner or designated beneficiary is a West Virginia resident.	Account owner, designated beneficiary, or parent of designated beneficiary must be a West Virginia resident. Beneficiary age restrictions apply.

Wisconsin

		Savings Plan
	A	**EdVest** (invest directly with state or with financial adviser) **tomorrow's scholar** (invest only through American Express financial advisers)
	B	Qualified educational expenses for postsecondary education
	C	Strong Capital Management, Inc.

	Savings Plan
D	Choice of age-based and static professionally managed investment funds
E	Variable — depends on market conditions and funds chosen
F	Any U.S. 2 and 4 year college and university, postsecondary trade and vocational school, and graduate and professional school that is eligible for federal financial aid
G	Open enrollment; join at any time
H	Distributions used for qualifying educational expenses are state and federally tax-exempt, subject to 2010 sunset provision. Annual contributions of up to $3,000 per beneficiary are deductible from Wisconsin resident income tax returns.
I	Both residents and nonresidents

Wyoming

	Savings Plan
A	**College Achievement Plan** (invest directly with state or with a financial adviser)
B	Qualified educational expenses for postsecondary education
C	Mercury Advisors
D	Choice of age-based and static professionally managed investment funds
E	Variable — depends on market conditions and funds chosen
F	Any U.S. 2 and 4 year college and university, postsecondary trade and vocational school, and graduate and professional school that is eligible for federal financial aid
G	Open enrollment; join at any time
H	Distributions used for qualifying educational expenses are federally tax-exempt, subject to 2010 sunset provision. Wyoming has no state income tax.
I	Both residents and nonresidents

Index

• K •

• J •

• L •

FOR DUMMIES®

The easy way to get more done and have more fun

PERSONAL FINANCE & BUSINESS

Investing FOR DUMMIES
A Reference for the Rest of Us!
Eric Tyson, MBA

0-7645-2431-3

Home Buying FOR DUMMIES
2nd Edition
Eric Tyson, MBA
A Reference for the Rest of Us!

0-7645-5331-3

Grant Writing FOR DUMMIES
Bev Browning
A Reference for the Rest of Us!

0-7645-5307-0

Also available:

Accounting For Dummies
(0-7645-5314-3)

Business Plans Kit For
Dummies
(0-7645-5365-8)

Managing For Dummies
(1-5688-4858-7)

Mutual Funds For Dummies
(0-7645-5329-1)

QuickBooks All-in-One Desk
Reference For Dummies
(0-7645-1963-8)

Resumes For Dummies
(0-7645-5471-9)

Small Business Kit For
Dummies
(0-7645-5093-4)

Starting an eBay Business
For Dummies
(0-7645-1547-0)

Taxes For Dummies 2003
(0-7645-5475-1)

HOME, GARDEN, FOOD & WINE

Feng Shui FOR DUMMIES
David Daniel Kennedy
A Reference for the Rest of Us!

0-7645-5295-3

Gardening FOR DUMMIES
2nd Edition
Michael MacCaskey
Bill Marken
The Editors of the National
Gardening Association
A Reference for the Rest of Us!

0-7645-5130-2

Cooking FOR DUMMIES
2nd Edition
A Reference for the Rest of Us!

0-7645-5250-3

Also available:

Bartending For Dummies
(0-7645-5051-9)

Christmas Cooking For
Dummies
(0-7645-5407-7)

Cookies For Dummies
(0-7645-5390-9)

Diabetes Cookbook For
Dummies
(0-7645-5230-9)

Grilling For Dummies
(0-7645-5076-4)

Home Maintenance For
Dummies
(0-7645-5215-5)

Slow Cookers For Dummies
(0-7645-5240-6)

Wine For Dummies
(0-7645-5114-0)

FITNESS, SPORTS, HOBBIES & PETS

Fitness FOR DUMMIES
2nd Edition
Suzanne Schlosberg
Liz Neporent, M.A.
A Reference for the Rest of Us!

0-7645-5167-1

Golf FOR DUMMIES
2nd Edition
Gary McCord
A Reference for the Rest of Us!

0-7645-5146-9

Guitar FOR DUMMIES
Jon Chappell
A Reference for the Rest of Us!

0-7645-5106-X

Also available:

Cats For Dummies
(0-7645-5275-9)

Chess For Dummies
(0-7645-5003-9)

Dog Training For Dummies
(0-7645-5286-4)

Labrador Retrievers For
Dummies
(0-7645-5281-3)

Martial Arts For Dummies
(0-7645-5358-5)

Piano For Dummies
(0-7645-5105-1)

Pilates For Dummies
(0-7645-5397-6)

Power Yoga For Dummies
(0-7645-5342-9)

Puppies For Dummies
(0-7645-5255-4)

Quilting For Dummies
(0-7645-5118-3)

Rock Guitar For Dummies
(0-7645-5356-9)

Weight Training For Dummies
(0-7645-5168-X)

Available wherever books are sold.
Go to www.dummies.com or call 1-877-762-2974 to order direct

 **WILEY**

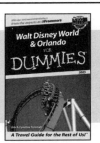